Effectiveness of Sales Promotion in Influencing the Consumer Behaviour

Dr.V. Vijayaganesh

Dr.M. Gomatheeswaran

Published by

BONFRING®
Intellectual Integrity

Copyright © 2017 by Bonfring

ISBN 978-93-86638-35-9

Authors

Dr.V. Vijayaganesh
Dr.M. Gomatheeswaran

Bonfring

309, 2nd Floor, 5th Street Extension, Gandhipuram,
Coimbatore-641 012.
Tamilnadu, India.
E-mail: info@bonfring.org | Website: www.bonfring.org
Phone: 0422 4213231

CHAPTER I

INTRODUCTION AND DESIGN OF THE STUDY

1.1.   Preamble

There is nobody in the world that is left out of the class of consumers. The consumer hood Continues till one's last breath in the world. It was during the 1950s, that marketing concept developed and thus the need to study the behaviour of consumers was recognised. Consumer behaviour is a complex, dynamic, multidimensional process and all marketing decisions are based on assumptions about consumer behaviour. When everything revolves around the consumer, then the study of consumer behaviour becomes a necessity. It starts with the buying of goods. Goods can be bought individually, or in groups. Goods can be bought for comfort and luxury in small quantities or in bulk. For all this, exchange is required. This exchange is usually between the seller and the buyer. The buyer who buys for consumption is known as consumer. The consumer is a person who consumes, especially one that acquires goods or services for direct use or ownership rather than for re-sale or use in production and manufacturing.

Consumer behaviour is the study of when, why, how and where people do or do not buy a product. It blends elements from psychology, sociology, social anthropology and economics.

It attempts to understand the buyer decision making process, both individually and in groups. It studies characteristics of individual consumers such as demographics and behavioural variables in an attempt to understand people's needs. It also tries to assess influences on the consumer from groups such as family, friends, reference groups, and society in general. The following definition will help us to understand the meaning of consumer behaviour.

"Consumer behaviour signifies the totality of consumer decisions with respect to the acquisition, consumption and disposition of goods, services, time and ideas by human decision making units.

The consumer purchases a variety of goods and services to satisfy his needs and he is always influenced in his purchasing activities by some consideration which leads him to select a particular commodity. So, consumer buying is more complex. Consumer purchases are likely to be influenced by physiological, psychological and sociological factors. The commodities and services are brought by the consumer to satisfy his basic needs, for comfort, pleasure, recreation and happiness. Every individual has physiological need such as hunger, shelter, thirst, etc., which have to be satisfied for survival. The psychological factors like status, prestige and social factors like friends, neighbours, colleagues and relatives influence their purchasing activities.

Knowledge of consumer behaviour directly affects marketing strategy. This is because of the marketing concept, i.e., the idea that firms exist to satisfy customer needs.

A customer (sometimes known as client, buyer or purchaser) is the recipient of a good, service, product or idea, obtained from a particular seller for a monetary or valuable consideration. Customers are generally categorized in to two types. They are Intermediate customer and ultimate customer. An intermediate customer or trade customer is a dealer that purchases goods for resale. An ultimate customer who does not in turn resell the things bought but either passes them to the consumer or actually is the consumer.

A customer may or may not also be a consumer, but the two notions are distinct, even though the terms are commonly confused. A customer purchases goods; a consumer uses them. An ultimate customer may be a consumer as well, but just as equally may have purchased items for someone else to consume. An intermediate customer is not a customer at all.

Customer behaviour study is based on consumer buying behaviour, with the customer playing the three distinct roles of user, payer and buyer. Relationship marketing is an influential asset for customer behaviour analysis as it has a keen interest in the re-discovery of the true meaning of marketing through the re-affirmation of the importance of the customer or buyer. A greater importance is also placed on consumer retention, customer relationship management, personalisation, customisation and one-to-one marketing. Social functions can be categorized into social choice and welfare functions.

Firms can satisfy those needs only to the extent that they understand their customers. For this reason, marketing strategies must incorporate knowledge of consumer behaviour into every facet of a strategic marketing plan.

1.2. History of Sales Promotion

Promotions refer to the entire set of activities, which communicate the product, brand or service to the user. There are several types of promotions. Above the line promotions include advertising, press releases, consumer promotion (schemes, discounts, contests), while below the line include trade discounts, freebies, incentive trips, awards and so on. Sales promotion is a part of the overall promotion effort.

Sales promotion has a very rich and interesting history. Marketers have developed and used a variety of techniques over the past century to give consumers an extra incentive to make their products and services sought after. Quite few of the sale premium offers is its promotion offers that motivates consumers have been in vogue for nearly a century and more. The earliest and quite effective sales promotion tool is the cent-off coupon. Coupons have been around since 1895 when the C.W.Post.co first began using the penny-off coupon to help sell its grape nuts cereal. Procter and Gamble began using the coupons in 1920 and its first ones were in the form of metal coins that were good for discounts or buy-one and get-one free deals. These were soon replaced by cheaper and more convenient paper versions that are around even today. Another classical promotional tool is the premium offer which dates back to 1895 when Cracker Jack began offering "a piece in every box." Pepsi is another company that took its promotional programs to the streets with its launch of the famous "Pepsi challenge" in 1975. It was one of the most successful promotion techniques ever used to attract habitual users of a competing brand. Pepsi took on its arch rival and leading industry Coca-Cola in a hard hitting promotion campaign that challenged consumers to taste the two brands in blind taste tests. Pepsi ran the challenge promotion for nearly a decade and re-launched it again in the year 2000.

1.3. Meaning of Sales Promotion

Sales promotion as a technique of promotion has been developed to supplement and coordinate advertising and personal selling efforts of a firm. It is any short-term incentive used by a firm to increase the sales of its product. It consists of all those promotional activities that help in enhancing sales through non-repetitive and one time communication. It aimed at stimulating market demand and consumer purchasing. It focuses the selling efforts on a selected small group of people.

Sales promotion is one of the seven aspects of the promotional mix. The other six parts of the promotional mix are advertising, personal selling, direct marketing, publicity or public relations, corporate image and exhibitions. Sales promotions can be directed either at the customer, sales staff or distribution channel members (such as retailers). Sales promotions targeted at the consumer are called consumer sales promotions. Sales promotions targeted at retailers and wholesaler are called trade sales promotions. Some sale promotions, particularly ones with unusual methods, are considered gimmicks by many. Sales promotion includes several communication activities that attempt to provide added value or incentives to consumers, wholesalers, retailers or other organizational customers to stimulate immediate sales. These efforts can attempt to stimulate product interest, trial or purchase. Examples of devices used in sales promotion include coupons, samples, premiums, point-of-purchase (POP) displays, contests, rebates and sweepstakes.

1.4. History of Vegetable and Edible Oils Used for Cooking in India

In India oils are used for cooking for about four thousand years. Such oil has been part of human culture for millennia. A vegetable oil is a triglyceride extracted from a plant. The term "vegetable oil" can be narrowly defined as referring only to substances that are liquid at room temperature or broadly defined without regard to a substance's state of matter at a given temperature. The vegetable oil industry in India is likely to set two records in the year 2010-11. First, the consumption is estimated to hit a record high, at 15.7 million tonnes during oil year 2010-11 (November-October); it was 14.8 mt in the previous year.

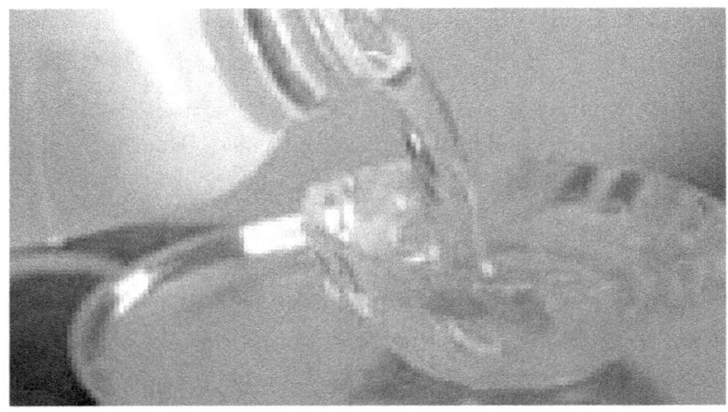

With an estimated rise in per capita consumption to 12.75 kg in 2010-11 as against 12.2 kg this year, total consumption of vegetable oil is forecast to increase 4.4 per cent this year as against four per cent in the previous year. "Consumption will be supported by changing food behaviour, with more and more people opting to eat outside, especially in a hotel, motel and small eateries, where oil is abundantly used. Since average income is rising due to overall growth, the change in behaviour looks sustainable and therefore, we can safely estimate India's vegetable oil consumption will meet the targeted consumption of 15.7 mt next year," said Dorab Mistry, director of Godrej International.

According to a forecast by GG Patel & Nikhil Research Company, availability from domestic seed crushing is also likely to increase this year by 600,000 tonnes, as a bumper Kharif crop will raise seed output, resulting in higher crushing. Total oilseed output is forecast to rise to 14.08 mt during the 2010-11 kharif seasons as against 12.3 mt in the previous year.

Favourable climatic condition will help output this year, said Patel. And, bumper soyabean production this year will result in higher availability of bean for crushing. As a consequence, soymeal exports which slipped to 2.38 mt last year will see a record rise this year, he added. Mistry hoped India's vegetable oil imports will surpass nine mt this year on rising retail consumption. They rose by 64 per cent to 10,65,641 tonnes in August 2010-11 as compared to 6,50,603 tonnes in the corresponding month of the previous year. In the first 10 months of the oil year (November 2009 on), however, vegetable oil imports recorded only a marginal rise of five per cent, to 74,47,955 tonnes as compared to 70,70,491 tonnes in the corresponding period of the previous year. Oilseeds' minimum support price (MSP) is too low. That for soybean translates to a price of $8.40 per bushel, about 25 per cent below the current world price. The central government raised the MSP of yellow soybean to Rs 1,440 a quintal for the 2010-11 seasons, from Rs 1,390 a quintal fixed last year.

1.5.   World Consumption of Vegetable Oils

Vegetable oils are composed of triglycerides, as contrasted with waxes which lack glycerin in their structure. Although many plant parts may yield oil, in commercial practice, oil is extracted primarily from seeds. The following triglyceride vegetable oils account for almost all worldwide production, by volume. All are used as both cooking oils and as SVO or to make biodiesel. According to the USDA, the total world consumption of major vegetable oils in 2007/08 was.

The majority of European rapeseed oil production is used to produce biodiesel or used directly as fuel in diesel cars which may require modification to heat the oil to reduce its higher viscosity. The suitability of the fuel should come as little surprise, as Rudolf Diesel originally designed his engine to run on peanut oil.

Other significant triglyceride oils include:

- Corn oil is one of the most common cooking oils. As of 2006 the US produced about 1.09 million metric tons of corn oil, which is used for cooking oil, salad dressing, margarine, mayonnaise, prepared goods like spaghetti sauce and baking mixes and to fry prepared foods like potato chips and French fries.[14]
- Grape seed oil was used in cooking and cosmetics.
- Hazelnut and other nut oils
- Linseed oil, from flax seeds
- Safflower oil, flavourless and colourless cooking oil

Table 1.1: Oil Source and World Consumption

Oil source	World consumption (million metric tons)	Notes
Palm	41.31	The most widely produced tropical oil, also used to make biofuel.
Soya bean	41.28	Accounts for about half of worldwide edible oil production.
Rapeseed	18.24	One of the most widely used cooking oils, canola is a variety (cultivar) of rapeseed
Sunflower seed	9.91	A common cooking oil, also used to make biodiesel
Peanut	4.82	Mild-flavored cooking oil
Cottonseed	4.99	A major food oil, often used in industrial food processing
Palm kernel	4.85	From the seed of the African palm tree
Coconut	3.48	Used in soaps and cooking
Olive	2.84	Used in cooking, cosmetics, soaps and as a fuel for traditional oil lamps
Sesame oil	3.20	Used as a cooking oil, and as a massage oil, particularly in India. It is produced from sesame seeds.
Rice bran oil	1.81	Produced from rice grains and used as a cooking oil

World Vegetable oil importers market has been divided into two parts, first, the markets of American continent including Argentina and Brazil and secondly the markets of South-East Asian countries including Malaysia and Indonesia. Now India has entered this cut-throat competitive market by the import contract of groundnut oil.

Cooking oil is plant, animal or synthetic fat used in frying, baking and other types of cooking. It is also used in food preparation and flavouring that doesn't involve heat, such as salad dressings and bread dips and in this sense might be more accurately termed edible oil.

Cooking oil is typically a liquid, although some oils that contain saturated fat, such as coconut oil, palm oil and palm kernel oil, are solid at room temperature. Types of cooking oil include: olive oil, palm oil, soybean oil, canola oil (rapeseed oil), pumpkin seed oil, corn oil, sunflower oil, safflower oil, peanut or ground nut oil, grape seed oil, sesame oil, argan oil, rice bran oil and other vegetable oils. Oil can be flavoured with aromatic foodstuffs such as herbs, chillies or garlic.

1.6. Importance of Edible Oils

Edible oils, as an important item of consumption, have rightly acquired considerable importance all these days. Being an essential food item for general population, its importance can be gauged from the fact that it is used all over the world, as a major source of nutrition for the human beings. Oils are used in the form of raw oils, refined and vanaspathi constituting 15 to 20 per cent of the consumer's monthly budget. In this context the productivity of edible oil has assumed vital relevance to the economy of the world in general and the country's economy like India in particular. Besides, oil industry has become a major organised sector with over 100 units in operation all over the country providing direct or indirect employment to over a million people.

1.7. Indian Economy

India's annual economic growth in the January-March quarter 2012 declined to a nine-year low of 5.3% as the manufacturing sector contracted and the rupee declined to a record low. GDP growth of 6.5% in 2011-12 was the lowest since 4% in 2002-03 and a sharp slowdown from the previous year's 8.4%. The impact of the euro zone debt crisis, a slowdown in economic reforms and high interest rates staggered India's growth, affecting the agriculture, manufacturing, mining and construction sectors.

1.8. Indian Edible Oil Industry

The Indian edible oil sector is the world's fourth-largest after the US, China and Brazil and is the world's fifth largest oil-seed producing nation with a wide range of oil seed crops comprising groundnut, mustard, rapeseed, sesame, safflower, linseed and niger seed, among others. India is also a leading player in edible oils, being the world's largest importer (ahead of the EU and China) and the world's third-largest consumer (after China and the EU). India consumes over 18 million tonnes of edible oil every year. Growing population and increasing consumption and per capita income is accelerating edible oil demand in India. The country currently contributes 6-7% of the global oil seed production. The domestic edible oil market is estimated at USD 15 billion and is set to grow at 5-6% over the next five years. There are 15,000 oil mills, 711 solvent extraction units, 600 vegetable oil refineries and 250 vanaspathi units in India employing more than a million people. But the domestic turnover of the vegetable oil industry is pegged at over Rs. 100,000 cr, import-export turnover is estimated at about Rs.50,000 cr. a year. Oilseeds in India are grown mainly on marginal and sub-marginal lands under low input usage. Only 25% of crop is irrigated, leaving the sector exposed to weather-related yield risks. Over decades, this phenomenon has been forcing the country to continuously depend on imports. India's yields at 1,000 kg a hectare, is less than the global average.

Table 1.2: Domestic Demand Supply Dynamics

Year	2008 -09	2009 -10	2010 -11	2011-12	2012-2013 (F)
Population	1.2	1.2	1.3	1.3	1.4
Total demand(MT)	14.5	15.3	16.3	17.1	18
Domestic supply of edible oils (MT)	5.7	6.2	7.7	8	8.2
Import of edible oils (MT)	8.8	9.1	8.6	9.1	9.8
Import as share of demand (%)	60.6	59.3	52.8	53.4	54.4

1.8.1. Production of Edible Oil in India

Total edible oil production in 2012-13 is likely to increase to 7.3 million tonnes, 3% above the previous year. Most of the increase is likely to be in rapeseed-mustard oil. Edible oil production for the current year is estimated at 7.1 million tonnes, which includes 2.3 million tonnes of rapeseed oil, 1.7 million tonnes of soybean oil, 1.3 million tonnes of peanut oil, 1.2 million tonnes of cottonseed oil and 600,000 tonnes of coconut, palm and sunflower oils.

1.8.2. Consumption of Edible Oil in India

India's per capita edible oil consumption is increasing (estimated at 14.1 kg for 2011-12). However, this remains below the estimated world average of 21.6 kg. Growing population, rising income levels and improved supply conditions are likely to increase edible oil consumption in 2012-13 to 17.1 million tonnes, up 693,000 tonnes over the previous year.

Palm oil will continue to be the largest consumed edible oil. Considering its versatility in blending with other edible oils, relatively lower prices and increased usage across the vanaspathi (partially hydrogenated vegetable oil) confectionary and margarine industries, in 2012-13 food use consumption is expected to increase to 7.4 million tonnes.

Soyabean is the third largest oilseed crop in India next to Groundnut & Mustard accounts for 25% of the total oilseeds produced in the country in a year. Soya oil contributes about 10% of total vegetable oils produced in the country. Groundnut is the most widely consumed and traded edible oil determining edible oil economics. India is the world's second largest producer of groundnut, next only to China. But groundnut being primarily a Kharif (monsoon) crop is vulnerable to vagaries of monsoon and also speculative activities. After palm oil, soy, rapeseed and peanut oils are the largest edible oil segments in the Indian market, estimated at 2.8 million tonnes, 2.4 million tonnes and 1.5 million tonnes respectively.

1.8.3. Consumption Factors in India

The Per capita consumption of edible oil is low (14 kg) but rising gradually. The country's top-10% of the population consumes 20 kg per capita and the bottom 30%, less than 5 kg per capita. There is strong regional preference for `first press` oils with natural flavour-mustard, groundnut and coconut oils. Inadequate quality control and quality assurance mechanism in India has lead to adulteration. Food laws are antiquated and its implementation is poor. There is low depth liquidity in future market. There is no self-reliance in edible oils and dependence on imports is rising, which currently constitute 53% of the aggregate consumption.

1.8.4. Imports of Edible Oil in India

Considering the widening gap between domestic consumption and production, vegetable oil imports is expected to increase 2%, from 9.5 mt to 9.7 mt in 2012-13. The import forecast includes 7.6 million tonnes of palm oil, 1.1million tonnes of soy oil, 1 million tonnes of sunflower oil and 10,000 tonnes of other edible oils. Total edible oil imports during the first five months of 2011-12 were up 14% at 3.4 million tonnes. With the tariff remaining unchanged since September 2006, strong international prices of edible oils have not reduced demand for imported oils, particularly refined edible oils. While the import duty remains officially at 7.5% advalorem, the current zero tariff on crude edible oils is encouraging traders to continue building stocks. Based on current trends, total imports in 2011-12 are likely to grow 15% from 8.21 million tonnes to 9.5 million tonnes.

1.8.4.1 Palm Oil

Being the cheapest, palm oil constitutes the largest proportion (about 44% of the total edible oil consumption) of the overall oil consumed. However, the growth rate depends on the price difference it enjoys with respect to soybean oil and other substitutes.

Historically, whenever, palm oil was 20% or more cheap than other oils (soybean and rapeseed/mustard), palm oil demand was higher compared with soybean and rapeseed/ mustard oil. On the other hand, when this discount narrowed during 2010-2011, demand for soybean oil and other oil (rapeseed/mustard/sunflower) grew at a much higher rate. Currently, palm oil is over 20% cheaper than other oils suggesting stronger growth rate in its demand in comparison with other edible oils (except sunflower oil, which shows consistently high growth). India is a large importer of palm oil with a major proportion being imported from Indonesia.

1.8.4.2 Outlook of Oil Seed Production in India

Rising oilseed production is expected to increase edible oil production to 7.3 million tonnes in 2012-13, up 3% over the previous year. Growing population, rising income levels and improved supply conditions will likely to raise edible oil consumption in 2012-13 to 17.1 million tonnes. Given the widening gap between domestic consumption and production of vegetable oils, edible oil imports in 2012-13 is expected to increase to 9.7 million tonnes. While India`s per capita edible oil consumption is increasing (estimated at 14.1 kg for 2011-12), it is still far below the estimated world average per capita consumption of 21.6 kg (Source: GAIN report, USFDA). However, demand for edible oils is projected to rise between 22.8-29.4 million tonnes in the near future in tandem with the average per capita income growing at 4-6%.

Table 1.3: Domestic Demand/Supply Dynamics of Edible Oil in India

Year	A	B	C	D	E	F	G
2009	1.19	12.37	14.75	12.73	15.18	13.10	15.61
2010	1.21	12.87	15.61	13.37	16.22	13.89	16.85
2011	1.24	13.38	16.53	14.04	17.34	14.72	18.18
2012	1.26	13.92	17.50	14.74	18.53	15.60	19.62
2013	1.28	14.48	18.53	15.48	19.81	16.54	21.17
2014	1.30	15.05	19.62	16.25	21.18	17.53	22.84
2015	1.33	15.66	20.77	17.06	22.63	18.58	24.65

A = Population @1.8% growth in billion

B = Consumption @ 4% growth - Per capita (kg)

C = Consumption @ 4% growth - Million tonnes

D = Consumption @ 5% growth - Per capita (kg)

E = Consumption @ 5% growth - Million tonnes

F = Consumption @ 6% growth - Per capita (kg)

G = Consumption @ 6% growth - Million tones

1.8.4.3 Growth Drivers for Consumption of Edible Oils in India

With a population of 1.1 billion, India represents one of the largest consumer markets in the world. Additionally, the country enjoys one of the largest and most balanced demographics in terms of age, as the country has more than 50% of its population below the age of 25 and more than 65% is below the age of 35. Currently, 63.38% of the population is between 15-59 years. The tremendous growth in the population of young individuals is likely to bring about an increase in food demand in India. This provides an impetus for growth of the edible oil industry.

1.8.4.4 Per Capita Consumption in India

India is the fourth-largest edible oil economy in the world. With annual consumption of 17 MT, the per capita consumption at 14 kg per annum is low compared with the world average of 21 kg. By 2015, Indian per capita consumption is expected to rise to between 17-18 kg per annum. Further, there is a supply mismatch in the edible oil segment with domestic supply being approximately 7.72 million tonnes against demand of 12 million tonnes. The shortfall is made up by imports, the second largest import bill item for India. This highlights the opportunity available for domestic edible oil manufacturers to grow and expand their business.

1.8.4.5 Position of Indian Edible Oil Sector

The Indian edible oil sector (especially mustard oil market) is largely fragmented and unorganised (85% market share), which is shifting to the organised (15% market share) sector owing to tax reforms (VAT) and on account of preference for packaged and branded products. Increase in awareness regarding adulteration and health consciousness (mustard oil is one of the healthiest oils as it contains the least amount of saturated fat) has further aided organised sector growth. Also, it is used in various ayurvedic applications for skin treatments and building immunity, among others.

1.9. Nutritional and Health Concerns about Edible Oils

All oils are made from three main types of fatty acids: saturated, monounsaturated and polyunsaturated. For the most part, the human body is able to manufacture all the different types of fat it needs from the fat and other nutrients in the diet. The only fatty acids which need to be eaten are the so-called essential fatty acids or EFAs-linoleic and linolenic-(also known as Omega-3 and Omega-6 fatty acids). The overwhelming conclusion of current dietary research is that while the intake of saturated fats is both unhealthy and unnecessary, a minimum of 3% of calorie intake should be in the form of EFAs. There is an increasing body of opinion, based, for example, on the evidence of diets high in olive oil that the monounsaturated fats may be either neutral or benign.

- But there are a number of other important considerations to be borne in mind when looking at the nutritional or health implications of using a particular oil or fat:

- During subjection to high temperatures, and especially if this is prolonged-as in many cooking or frying processes- poly unsaturated fats are converted to saturates.

- Saturated fats are much more stable under heat than poly unsaturated. With care; saturated fats may last twice as long as polyunsaturated types.

- During refining, many liquid oils are subjected to the process of hydrogenation, whereby hydrogen is bubbled through the oil at a controlled temperature. This is a completely harmless process and is widely used, (for example in the manufacture of margarine or extended-life oils from Soya or Sunflower oils), both to make the oil more stable, thereby increasing its useful life and to harden it to a desired consistency at specific temperatures. Hydrogenation changes the chemical structure of the oil and increases the saturated fats content. The effect of this might be that semi-solid cooking oil made from base oil high in polyunsaturated, such as sunflower, could actually have a higher level of saturated fats than non-hydrogenated oil such as rapeseed.

1.10. Need and Importance of this Study

Marketing starts with the needs of the customer and ends with the satisfaction of the customer. In order to satisfy and attract the consumer, it is essential for the producer to understand the consumer behaviour. In Tamilnadu, cooking oil is an indispensable item in the daily food of people. So the study on consumer behaviour and his reaction to sales promotion is worth for the marketers of cooking oil as well as the people who are consuming cooking oil. Consumption of cooking oil is an integral part of human life.

Hence, everybody engaged in buying different kinds of cooking oil. Every consumer tries to obtain maximum satisfaction from the oil purchased by him. In the market different types of oils are available for cooking manufactured by small manufacturers (unbranded; loose oil), as well as big companies like Hindustan lever, Kaleeshwari (branded) etc. Consumers are influenced by the factors like price of the oil, quality of the oil, health aspects, brand name, consumer's income, consumer's attraction towards the oil, advertisement influence, discounts and free gifts, any other attractions etc. This study tries to find out the sales promotion factor which is most influential in selecting the cooking oil.

The understanding of consumer behaviour is essential for making better marketing campaigns. (e.g., timing of advertisement)

The understanding of consumer behaviour enables the firm to adopt the sales promotional strategy liked by the majority of consumers.

Studying consumer behaviour should make us better consumers. For example if you buy 5 liter of cooking oil pouch, you should pay less per liter than if you bought five one liter pouches. In practice, however you often pay a size premium by buying the large quantity. In other words, in this case, knowing this fact will sensitize you to the need to check the unit cost labels to determine if you are really getting a bargain.

Most of the companies have applied various elements of promotion mix. Promotion mix elements include advertising, publicity, sales promotion, personal selling and packaging.

Sales promotion is one of them and it is our concerned topic. In present competitive situation most of MNCs had developed sales promotion strategy in selection of parties, techniques and managing sales promotion techniques effectively and efficiently. This strategy provides competitive advantage to the companies in the market to grow, stabilize and excel in business performance. Therefore, sales promotion strategy is very significant for companies to earn bread and butter. This attracted me to select and study this topic.

1.11. Statement of the Problem

Oils are used daily in our life for cooking. Usage of oil for cooking is a very old one and its history is not traced. Today India have variety of oil used for cooking such as sunflower oil, sesame oil, ground nut oil, coconut oil, palm oil, rice bran oil and olive oil etc. There is a heavy competition among the brands as well as the non brands to get the attention of the customers. To attract the consumer it is essential for the marketers to understand the consumer's purchase behaviour. The marketers are discovering that advertising alone is not sufficient to attract a target market. The marketer must necessarily use sales promotional methods in conjunction with advertising.

Sales promotions like discount on prices, price pack deals, coupons, free gifts, contests and free samples must be offered to the consumers to remain competitive in the market. The aim of this investigation is to find out the perception and preference of the customers of Coimbatore city, towards sales promotional tools adopted by the manufacturers of cooking oil and answers to the following questions. Is sales promotion really influence the consumer towards the product? Which of the sales promotion is liked by the consumers?

Did the consumer change their behaviour for sales promotion at the time of purchase? The answers to the above questions will be helpful to the marketer in selecting the techniques of sales promotion that the customer would prefer. They can, then, adopt to use the same for their oils to effectively increase their sales and hence their profitability.

1.12. Objectives of the Study

1.12.1. To identify the predominant factors influencing the consumer towards the purchase of cooking oil.

1.12.2. To study the perception and preference of the customers to sales promotion offered by cooking oil companies.

1.12.3. To study the sales promotion particularly the consumer sales promotion.

1.12.4. To identify the most preferred oil for cooking by the consumers.

1.12.5. To focus on the different sales promotion techniques used by the cooking oil manufacturers and to identify the one that is effective.

1.12.6. To know the difference between the purchasing behaviour of rural and urban consumers.

1.12.7. To identify the brand awareness of the respondents in purchasing cooking oils.

1.12.8. To give valid suggestions to the manufacturers of cooking oil to understand the consumer behaviour for the betterment of their business.

1.13. Hypothesis

1.13.1. Based on the above objectives, the study has the following specific issues as hypothesis.

1.13.2. There are differences in the socio-economic characteristics between rural and urban consumer respondents.

1.13.3. There is no relationship between rural and urban consumer for cooking oil consumption.

1.13.4. Sales promotion techniques do not influence behaviour of respondents in rural and urban areas.

1.13.5. There is no difference between purchasing behaviour of consumer on the basis of age, income, occupation, educational qualification, family size, family type etc.

1.13.6. Sales promotions have contributed more to enable for high perception on cooking oil.

1.14. Research Methodology

Research methodology process includes a number of activities to be performed. These are arranged in proper sequence of timing for conducting research. One activity after another is performed to complete the research work. Research methodology includes the following steps.

1.14.1. Type of Research

The topic for the research study is consumer behaviour towards sales promotion tools and the nature of the topic is theoretical and descriptive. So to conduct the research study the type of research suitable is descriptive research only. The data are collected from the consumers of cooking oil, books, journals and websites. The descriptive research has met the requirement of research study.

1.14.2. Sources of Data

For the study purpose both primary and secondary data are used. The primary data are collected from consumers of cooking oil in northern Coimbatore. The secondary data are collected from records of the government institutions, books, journals, articles and websites. The primary and secondary data have been collected to cover every aspect of the study. The primary data are related to behaviour and response of consumers to sales promotional tools adopted by the cooking oil manufacturers. The secondary data are related to the understanding of consumer behaviour, sales promotion and the history of edible oil industry in India producing cooking oil. These data used in combination as per need of the study.

1.14.3. Primary Data

Primary data are information collected by a researcher specifically for a research assignment. In other words, primary data are information that a company must gather because no one has compiled and published the information in a forum accessible to the public. Companies generally take the time and allocate the resources required to gather primary data only when a question, issue or problem rises. Primary data are original in nature and directly related to the issue or problem and current data. Primary data are the data which the researcher collects through various methods like interviews, surveys, questionnaires etc.

1.14.4. Secondary Data

Secondary data are the data collected by a party not related to the research study but collected these data for some other purpose and at different time in the past. If the researcher uses these data then these become secondary data for the current users. These may be available in written, typed or in electronic forms. A variety of secondary information sources are available to the researcher gathering data on an industry, potential product applications and the market place.

Secondary data is also used to gain initial insight into the research problem. Secondary data is classified in terms of its source–either internal or external. Internal, or in-house data, is secondary information acquired within the organization where research is being carried out. External secondary data is obtained from outside sources.

1.15. Instruments for Data Collection

There are many instruments available for the data collection. They are questionnaire, telephone, mobile phone and facsimile, e-mail and Interview. Only two methods of data collection are used in this study. They are questionnaire and interview. They are explained below:

1.15.1. Questionnaire

Questionnaire is a set of questions has been prepared to ask a number of questions and collect answers from respondents related to the research topic. A number of questions are in printed or electronic form which is to be answered by the individuals. The forms often have blank spaces in which the answers can be written. Sets of such forms are distributed to groups and the answers are collected related to research topic. A questionnaire is a series of questions asked to individuals to obtain statistically useful information about a given topic.

When properly constructed and responsibly administered, questionnaires become a vital instrument by which statements can be made about specific groups or people or entire populations. In appropriate questions, incorrect ordering of questions, incorrect scaling or bad questionnaire format can make the survey valueless, as it may not accurately reflect the views and opinions of the participants. A useful method for checking a questionnaire and making sure it is accurately capturing the intended information is to pre-test it among a smaller subset of target respondents.

In a research or survey, questions are designed and asked to respondents to extract specific information.

It serves four basic purposes:

To

- Collect the appropriate data
- Make data comparable and amenable to analysis
- Minimise bias in formulating and asking question and
- To make questions engaging and varied.

For this study purpose a set of questions has been prepared to collect information related to the topic of the study. In this study a structured questionnaire has been used with different types of questions such as closed ended and open ended. Special care has been taken to select the scales for the questions for collection of responses from the respondents very effectively.

1.15.2. Interview

In this method the interviewer personally meets the informants and asks necessary questions to them regarding the subject of enquiry. Usually a set of questions or a questionnaire is carried by him and questions are also asked according to that. The interviewer efficiently collects the data from the informants by cross examining them. The interviewer must be very efficient and tactful to get the accurate and relevant data from the informants. [18] Interviews like personal interview/depth interview or telephone interview can be conducted as per the need of the study. About 10% of the respondents are interviewed personally with the help of questionnaire.

1.16. Research Methods

For collection of primary data for this research work, field research survey method has been used. Experimental method is not found suitable for this study because the topic is a theoretical topic and there is no need to have experiments. The survey method has been explained below:

1.16.1. Survey Method

Survey is used to collect quantitative information about items in a population. Surveys are used in different areas for collecting the data even in public and private sectors. A survey may be conducted in the field by the researcher. The respondents are contacted by the research person personally, telephonically or through mail. This method takes a lot of time, efforts and money but the data collected are of high accuracy, current and relevant to the topic. When the questions are administered by a researcher, the survey is called a structured interview or a researcher-administered survey. When the questions are administered by the respondent, the survey is referred to as a questionnaire or a self-administered survey. It is an efficient way of collecting information from a large number of respondents. Very large samples are possible. Statistical techniques can be used to determine validity, reliability and statistical significance. Surveys are flexible in the sense that a wide range of information can be collected. They can be used to study attitudes, values, beliefs and past behaviours. Because they are standardised, they are relatively free from several types of errors. There is an economy in data collection due to the focus provided by standardised questions. Only questions of interest to the researcher are asked, recorded, codified and analysed.

1.17. Sampling

The research is a systematic study to examine or investigate the issue or problem and find out the relevant information for solution. For research study data are to be collected from the respondents. It is not possible to collect data from everyone of the population.

Population is a very large number of persons or objects or items which is not feasible to manage. A population is a group of individuals, persons, objects or items from which samples are taken for measurement. For research purpose a part of the population is to be selected.

Sampling is the process in which a representative part of a population for the purpose of determining parameters or characteristics of the whole population is selected. This is called a sample. It is easier to contact a smaller part of the population for data collection. It can be done within a limited time, efforts and with minimum cost. For selection of a sample special care should be taken that the sample is proper representative of the whole population. Every segment of the population should be included but the number should not be very large which may become difficult to manage within the time and cost limits.

1.18. Sampling Methodology Used in this Research

The study is based on empirical analysis. Hence field survey method was adopted. As it covers both rural and urban areas, multi-stage random sampling procedure has been employed to select the area as well as respondents.

1.19. Selection of Area for the Study

The Coimbatore district has been selected purposively as a study area. However, the entire district has been divided into four zones namely:

(i) North

(ii) East

(iii) South and

(iv) Western Zone.

Out of which North Zone has been selected which comprises of 36 talukas. Northern City is divided into urban and rural areas. In Coimbatore northern region, there are 36 Taluka offices with the total population of 6, 41,021 with 3,21,922 males and 3,19,099 females according to the 2011 census. There were 991 women for every 1000 men. The North-Taluk had a literacy rate of 76.37. Child population in the age group below 6 was 28,302 males and 27,219 females.

Name of Thirty Six Places in North Taluka Were

1. graharasamakulam	9. Ganapathy	17. Kurudampalayam	25. Puliakulam	33. Vellakinar
2. Anaikattai North	10. Gudalur	18.Sanganur	26. Saravanampatti	34. Vellamadai
3. Anaikatti (South)	11. Idigarai	19. Naickenpalayam	27. Sarcarsamakulam	35. Vellanaipatti
4. Anupperpalayam	12. Kallipalayam	20. Nanjundapuram	28. Somayampalayam	36. Vilankurichi
5. Bilichi	13.Kavundampalayam	21. Pannimadai	29. Telungupalayam	
6. Chinnathadagam	14. Keeranatham	23.Narasimhanaickenpalayam	30.Thudiyalur	
7. Chinnavedampatti	15. Kondayampalayam	24. Kalapatti	31. Veerakeralam	
8. Coimbatore Corporation	16. Krishnarayapuram	22.Periyanaickenpalayam	32. Veerapandi	

1.19.1. Selection of Villages

Out of the 36 places in north taluka, 18 places were selected by using convenience sampling procedure for the study. Besides, an urban and rural center from each zone was selected on convenience basis for conducting field survey. In order to get equal representation from rural and urban areas 8 places from urban area and 10 places from rural areas were selected.

The details about talukas selected in north zone of the district are given in the Table-1.4.

Table 1.4: List of the Sample Villages of Rural and Urban Areas

Zone	S.No	Places in north taluk	Rural/urban
North	1.	Agraharasamakulam	Rural
	2.	Kalapatti	Urban
	3.	Bilichi	Rural
	4.	Periyanaickenpalayam	Urban
	5.	Gudalur	Rural
	6.	Veerakeralam	Urban
	7.	Kallipalayam	Rural
	8.	Thudiyalur	Urban
	9.	Idigarai	Rural
	10.	Saravanampatti	Urban
	11.	Naickenpalayam	Rural
	12.	Kavundampalayam	Urban
	13.	Vilankurichi	Rural
	14.	Pannimadai	Rural
	15.	Keeranatham	Rural
	16.	Narasimhanaickenpalayam	Urban
	17.	Vellamadai	Rural
	18.	Sarcarsamakulam	Urban

The following table 1.5 shows the population details of the sample areas selected.

Table 1.5: The Population Details of Sample Area Selected

S.NO	Places	Total Population	Male	Female
1.	Agraharasamakulam	3,879	1969	1910
2.	Kalapatti	22,034	11321	10713
3.	Bilichi	9,464	4,791	4,673
4.	Periyanaickenpalayam	22,921	11919	11002
5.	Gudalur	21,966	11280	10686
6.	Veerakeralam	19,994	10117	9877
7.	Kallipalayam	2,646	1279	1367
8.	Thudiyalur	21,004	10773	10231
9.	Idigarai	6333	3158	3175
10.	Saravanampatti	17737	9173	8564
11.	Naickenpalayam	5253	2662	2591
12.	Kavundampalayam	48276	24670	23606
13.	Vilankurichi	9124	4641	4483
14.	Pannimadai	10782	5494	5288
15.	Keeranatham	4229	2118	2111
16.	Narasimhanaickenpalayam	31,005	15813	15192
17.	Vellamadai	9772	4961	4811
18.	Sarkarsamakulam	7982	3958	4024
Total		2,74,401	1,40,097	1,34,304

Keeping in view, the proper representation of every segment of population and manageable size of the sample, the sample size selected is 720. The universe includes consumers of cooking oil belonging to all walks of life located in different parts of northern Coimbatore region.

1.19.2. Selection of Respondents

Since, the study intends to study on the consumer behaviour towards the sales promotional techniques adopted by cooking oil manufactures among the consumers; the sample for the study obviously would include both rural and urban member respondents. So far as the proportion of rural and urban members constituting the sample for the study is concerned, the state average figure related to coverage of consumer respondents' has been considered. It comes to around 75 percent. By adopting disproportionate to size sampling (Quota sampling), snow ball technique is used. Thus, 360 respondents, comprising of 36 respondents from each village (10X36) and remaining 360 respondents (8X45) from urban cities. Therefore, 720 members constitute the sample for the study.

1.19.3. Descriptive Analysis of the Sample

The sample on socio-economic factor is elaborated on by looking at simple descriptive statistics. Then, statistical concepts were applied to the data in hand to answer the hypotheses that were developed in this chapter. Results will be explained and interpreted. The questionnaire was issued to 1200 respondents in selected sample area who were the decision makers on the purchase of cooking oil. Only 720 questionnaires were received with full completion. Hundred respondents did not return the questionnaire. 380 questionnaires were received with partial completion as they didn't understand the objectives of the research and hence they are rejected. This yields a response rate of 60%. Although the response rate is relatively high, the data collection phase was harder than expected and it was a struggle to get respondents.

1.19.4. Tools and Techniques for Data Collection

As the issues to be addressed in the study are of qualitative and quantitative nature, different tools and techniques have been used. Besides, Personal Interview (PI) for administering the Structured Interview Schedule (SIS) among the respondents Focus Group Discussion (FGD) techniques has been used.

1.19.5. Personal Interview through Structured Interview Schedule (SIS)

A comprehensive SIS to be administered among households was prepared, pre-tested and finalised. The SIS consisted of questions pertaining to a wide range of information starting from demographic indicators such as age, gender, place of domicile (urban/rural) to socio-economic indicators such as educational attainment, income, occupation, savings, investment, participation in social organizations, exposure to mass media, contact with change agents. The SIS included a few statements to be responded in a seven point Likert's scale (strongly agree, agree, neither agree nor disagree, disagree, strongly disagree and do not know), meant for the consumer behaviour towards the sales promotional techniques adopted by cooking oil manufactures among the consumers.

1.19.6. Focus Group Discussion (FGD)

Qualitative research encompasses several different techniques. One of the important techniques for focus group has been used. Focus Group Discussion Guides (FGDG) were prepared, pre tested and finalised. FGD in general contained hints under three broader headings namely, Introduction, warm up session and Issue for focused discussions. The issues affecting the efficiency and effectiveness of the consumer behaviour towards the sales promotional tools adopted by cooking oil manufactures among the consumers through FGDs.

1.20. Data Analysis and Interpretation

SPSS (Statistical Package for Social Sciences) was used for data analysis. Besides, use of simple percentages and averages for interpretation of data, statistical tests such as test of significance, chi-square, zero-order correlation, linear multiple regression (LMR), factor Analysis and multivariate analysis were used for comprehension of the facts and information. The inferences of the FGD were drawn to supplement the inferences of quantitative analysis throughout the report. The purpose of using the statistical tools is to make the analysis more comprehensive and to draw meaningful inferences. A summary of key findings was made, based on inferences.

1.21. Period of the Study

This study was pertaining to the period from July 2012 to September 2013.

1.22. Scope of the Study

The focus of this study is on the behaviour of consumers of cooking oil towards the sales promotion in the edible oil industry manufacturing cooking oil. The perception and preference of the customer toward the sales promotion, the techniques adopted like price discounts, price pack deals, coupons, loyalty rewards program, free samples, extra quantity and free gifts have been taken as the main areas of this study.

1.23. Limitations of this Study

This study is based only on the responses to a comprehensive questionnaire, by a cross section of different strata of society who live in northern part of Coimbatore city.

Hence, the generalization of the study may not hold good for the entire universe.

- The study is confined to a finite period. Consumer's preference may change by the passage of time.
- The findings are based on the responses received for the questionnaire.
- The consumers were widely scattered in the study area. So the selection of sample, however done scientifically, may not represent the entire universe.

1.24. Details of Questionnaire Used

Part I: Personal Information

Part II: Frequency, Quantity of cooking oil purchased, place of purchase, years of usage and amount spent on cooking oil.

Part III: Factors influencing to change the cooking oil and level of satisfaction.

Part IV: Preferred Sales promotional activities.

Part V: Opinion about the sales promotion activities.

Part VI: Opinion about the media.

Part VII: Sales promotion factors influencing purchase.

1.25. Statistical Tools Used

- Simple percentage.
- Rank method.
- LMR Analysis.
- ANOVA.
- F-Test.
- KMO and Bartlett's test.
- Mean Average

1.26. Chapter Scheme

Chapter I: "Introduction and design of the study" presents the introduction of consumer behaviour and sales promotion, history, importance and usage of cooking oil in India, need for the study, statement of the problem, objectives of the study, limitations of the study, methodology and statistical tools used in the study.

Chapter II: This chapter devoted for "Review of literature" presents various studies conducted and published by the researchers and subject experts with respect to consumer behaviour and sales promotion on cooking oils and other fast moving consumer goods.

Chapter III: This chapter is allotted for "Theoretical perspective of consumer behaviour and sales promotion" gives the meaning of consumer behaviour; consumer behaviour roles played by a person in family, characteristics features of Indian consumers, consumer decision process, and various models of consumer behaviour, sales promotion methods and objectives of sales promotion.

Chapter IV: Fourth chapter denotes "Socio economic profile and behaviour of the consumers". This chapter analyse the socio economic profile of the consumers and behaviour of the consumers towards the cooking oils.

Chapter V: This chapter analyses the preference of consumers towards the sales promotion undertaken by the manufacturers of cooking oil.

Chapter VI: Final chapter devoted to "Summary of findings, suggestions and conclusion" lists exhaustively the important findings of the study.

References

[1]   Wayne D. Hoyer and Deborah J. Macinnis, "consumer behavior", Fifth edition mason, ohio: south-western cengage Learning, Pp. 13-16, 2010.

[2]   R.C. Anderson, D. Fell, R.L. Smith, E.N. Hansen and S. Gomon, "Current Consumer behaviour research in forest products", Forest Products Journal, Vol. 55, No. 1, Pp. 21-27, 2005.

[3]   R.S. Winer, "Marketing Management", Prentice Hall, Upper Saddle River, NJ, 2000.

[4]   Stephanine D. Kendall, "customer service from the customer's perspective", Fogli, Lawerence. Customer service delivery: Research and best practices. J-B SIOP professional practice series 20, 2007.

[5]   Jim Blythe, "Essentials of Marketing (4th ed)", Pearson education, 2008.

[6]   John Frain, "Customers and customer buying behaviour", Introduction to marketing (4th ed). Cengage Learning EMEA, 1999.

[7]   Richard C. Reizenstein, "customer" encyclopedia of health care management", Sage, 2004.

[8]   M. Solomon, "Consumer Behavior: Buying, Having. And Being", 5th ed, Prentice Hall. Upper Saddle River, NJ, 2002.

[9]   P. Kotler, "Marketing management analysis Planning and control", 9th ed. Prentice hall, 1976, Englewood Cliffs, N.JAssuncao, Joao L., Robert Meyer. 1993. The rational effect of price promotions."4,000-year-old 'kitchen' unearthed in Indiana" Archaeo News. January 26, 2006.

[10]   Dilip Kumar Jha, "Vegetable oil consumption likely to hit record high" articles in business standard dated 28th September 2010.

[11]   January 2009 Oilseeds: World Market and Trade. FOP 1-09. USDA, 2009-01-11., Table 03: Major Vegetable Oils: World Supply and Distribution at Oilseeds.

[12]   World Markets and Trade Monthly Circular, Corn Refiners Association, Corn Oil 5th Edition, 2006

[13]   Robin Dand, "The International Cocoa Trade", Woodhead Publishing, 1999.

[14]   "Dietary fats explained". Retrieved from internet May 4, 2012.

[15]   Bhattacharyya, "Research Methodology", 2nd Edition, Excel Books, New Delhi, 2006.

[16]   C.R. Kothari, "Research Methodology:Methods & Techniques", 2nd Edition, New age, New Delhi, 2009.

[17]   Donald R Cooper and Pamela S Schindler, "Business Research Methods", Tata McGraw Hill, New Delhi, 2007.

[18]   Sivkumar Krishnaswamy and Mathirajan, "Management Research Methodology", 2nd Edition, Pearson Pub, New Delhi, 2008.

[19]   Elangovan Mohan, "Research Methodology in Commerce", 1st Edition, Deep & Deep, New Delhi. of India , 2007.

CHAPTER II

REVIEW OF LITERATURE

2.1. Introduction to Review of Literature

"Review of literature" is an indispensible part of research which opens the eyes of the researcher to carry out his research in various dimensions of thinking. In this chapter reviews were collected about consumer behaviour, sales promotion and edible oils used for cooking.

2.2. Literature Pertaining to Consumer behaviour and Sales Promotion

John M.C Fall in his article titled "Priority Patterns and Consumer behaviour" find out that acquiring of goods in a priority pattern is not simply an individual process; it is also a group phenomenon.

Blattberg, Peacock, and Sen. (1976, 1978) describe 16 purchasing strategy segments based on three purchase dimensions: brand loyalty (single brand, single brand shifting, many brands), type of brand preferred (national, both national and private label) and price sensitivity (purchase at regular price, purchase at deal price). There are other variables that may be used to describe purchase strategies, examples are whether the household purchases a major or minor (share) national brand, store brand or generic or whether it is store-loyal or not.

McAlister (1983) and Neslin and Shoemaker (1983) use certain segments derived from those of Blattberg, Peacock and Sen. but add a purchase acceleration variable to study the profitability of product promotions.

A huge body of literature has examined consumer response to sales promotions, most importantly coupons (e.g. Sawyer and Dickson, 1984; Bawa and Shoemaker, 1987 and 1989; Gupta, 1988; Blattberg and Neslin, 1990; Kirshnan and Ram c.Rao, 1995; Leone and Srinivasan, 1996) [4, 5,6,7,8,9]. Apart from this, important gaps remain to be studied. It is commonly agreed that sales promotions are difficult to standardise because of legal, economic and cultural differences (e.g., Foxman, Tansuhaj, and Wong, 1988; Kashani and Quelch, 1990; Huff and Alden, 1998). [10, 11, 12] Multinational firms should therefore understand how consumer response to sales promotions differs between countries or state or provinces.

Mr.S Ramachander (1988) in his article in Economic and Political Weekly titled "Consumer Behaviour and Marketing towards an Indian Approach?" concludes that fresh study has to be made to understand the behaviour of Indian consumers due to the following reasons:

The degree of importance attached to the product in Indian households may be different from say, an American household. The kind of socio economic class which in India could afford and wish to buy the product may not be comparable with that of the American and British household. The advertisement which motivates a British or American housewife or teenager to buy a cosmetic or a pair of jeans (to take a concrete example) may not suit the socio- cultural background of an Indian target for the same product.

The 'execution' of the appeal and media environment in which the advertisement might appear may also be vastly different in this country, not to speak of the 'un-translatability' of many western colloquialisms and symbols into Indian languages, perhaps even into Indian English.

The role of the housewife in decision making is clearly different even with in India, across ethnic groups and regions. Any wrong assumption can easily lead to erroneous conclusions.

Marketers use various advertising and promotion tactics to attract customers and increase sales. Earlier research has shown that framing of promotion messages and presentation of price information influence consumers perception of prices and their willingness to buy (Das, 1992; Sinha, 1999; Sinha and Smith, 2000). [14, 15, 16]

However, Lan Xia and Kent B. Monroe (2008) had differentiated between consumers who have prior goals to buy the product relative to those who do not have such purchase goals. Further, they have added whether consumer's responses to different promotion message framing and price presentations differ when they do or do not have pre-purchase goals. Since the same promotion information may lead to variable perceptions as consumers goals vary (Shavitt, 1994), understanding how consumers with different purchase goals react to various promotion messages can help sellers design effective promotion programs.

In an analytical study, Assuncao and Meyer (1993) show that consumption is an endogenous decision variable driven by promotion and promotion-induced stockpiling resulting from forward-looking behaviour.

Adopting scarcity theory, Folkes (1993) show that consumers curb consumption of products when supply is limited because they perceive smaller quantities as more valuable.

Simonson, Carmon and O'Curry (1994) find that for products with unattractive premium promotions consumer preference decreases because consumers think they are paying extra for free gifts they do not want. The literal findings are that, "when consumers are uncertain about the values of products and about their preferences, such features and premiums provide reasons against buying the promoted brands and are seen as susceptible to criticism.

Suprihatini (1995a) investigated owners of small scale industries' attitudes towards characteristics of cooking oils. The results of the study showed that rancidity, price, efficiency, taste of fried food and clarity were perceived to be important attributes of cooking oils. However, some attributes such as colour, raw materials, freezing level, nutrient content, viscosity, cholesterol content and packaging were considered less important.

Suprihatini (1995b) examined attitudes towards red palm cooking oil attributes among 180 respondents. The majority of respondents (91%) showed positive responses towards palm cooking oils that contained vitamin A and E, and 85% also expressed positive feeling towards palm cooking oils that were non-Cholesterol. However, large majority of respondents (45%) had negative responses towards red palm cooking oil that had reddish colour. The study analysed respondents' intention to buy red cooking oil if the oils were available in the market, about 19% of respondents were interested to buy, 48% of respondents stated that they might be interested to buy and the rest of respondents expressed neutral intention. The study also examined the relationships among attitudes toward red palm cooking oil attributes and intention to buy red cooking oils.

Achiruddin (1997) surveyed 150 households to find out how householders' behave in the cooking oil usage. This study examined frequency of cooking oil buying, the places to buy cooking oil, the amount of cooking oil bought and the brands of cooking oils. The study also examined the relationships among characteristics of respondents and usage behaviour of cooking oil. Furthermore, the study also used cluster analysis to classify respondents based on the economic and demographic characteristics of respondents.

The evidence of short-term effects seems to be well documented in the literature. It is suggested that sales promotion can build brand awareness and motivate trial, provide more specific evaluation methods, as they are more immediate and operate in a specific time frame,(Pham, M.T., Cohen, J.B., Pracejus, J.W. & Hughes, G.D., 2001), influence sales, (Roberts, John H., 1995), expand the target market (Robertson, T.S., 1993) and achieve competitive advantage (Rothschild, M.L. & Gaidis, W.C., 1981). According to their purpose, sales promotions are often successful in inducing action, as they encourage consumers to act on a promotion while it is still available. Also, the strength of SP lies in its flexibility to quickly respond to competitor attacks contributed by Sandra Luxton (2001).

Throughout the world, consumer sales promotions are an integral part of the marketing mix for many consumer products. Marketing managers use price-oriented promotions such as coupons, rebates and price discounts to increase sales and market share, entice trial and encourage brand switching. Non-price promotions such as sweepstakes, frequent user clubs and premiums add excitement and value to brands and may encourage brand loyalty (e.g., Aaker 1991; Shea, 1996).

Donald E.Vinson, Jerome E.Scott and Lawrence M.Lamount in their research article titled "The roles of personal values in marketing and consumer behaviour" highlighted that consumer's react favourable for the concerns which hold truth in advertisement and follow honesty in representing the products.

Price and promotion strategies are closely related with each other. It is very hard to distinguish price variances which are caused by decisions derived from the price policy from those produced as a result of the promotion policy. Hence, proposal has been developed by Cummins (1998), according to which sales promotion has to stop being a part of the communication mix to become an autonomous variable.

When the promotion ends, sales are reduced even below the usual levels (without promotion). In the long term, the sales level tends to go back to a position near the initial position. Mela (1998) confirm that long-term price promotions make the consumer more sensitive to price and therefore their effectiveness is reduced with the subsequent negative effect on benefits. These results are coherent with those obtained by Mela (1997). However, we must clarify that the effects provoked by promotions vary according to multiple factors: the type of incentive, the amount of discount provided or the type of product to which the promotion is applied, among others.

Sumarwan (2000) examined the relationships among perceived popularity and quality of cooking oil brands and the brands of cooking oils used. The results of the study showed that BIMOLI was perceived the most popular brand of cooking oil, followed by FILMA. However, the brand perceived the best quality was FILMA. Al though, 50% of respondents had viewed BIMOLI as the most popular brand, but only 16% of respondents used BIMOLI.

Emerging literature in behavioural and economic theory has provided supporting evidence that consumption for some product categories responds to promotion. Using an experimental approach, Wansink (1996) establishes that significant holding costs pressure consumers to consume more of the product.

Wansink and Deshpande (2000) show that when the product is perceived as widely substitutable, consumers will consume more of it in place of its close substitutes. They also show that higher perishability increases consumption rates.

The results of research work by Suri (2000), detect the need to introduce promotions as explicit elements of the consumer buying behaviour.

Chandon and Wansink (2002), show that stockpiling increases consumption of high convenience products more than that of low-convenience products.

Price promotion characteristics can be grouped into four categories: price presentation, deal characteristics, situation factors and study effect (Krishna-2002). Price presentation research examines whether consumers perceptions of a promotion are influenced by how the promotion is communicated, e.g. framing. Research on deal characteristics studies the influence of factors such as deal percentage, free gift value and size of the bundle. Situation factors refer to the overall situation of the price promotion including types of stores, brands and whether the promotion information is received at home or in the store.

Finally, study effect addresses measurement issues including factors such as number of variables manipulated and number of participants. Different promotion characteristics influence current as well as future purchase intentions (Del Vecchio-2006).

Koen Pauwels (2002) has examined the permanent impact of sales promotion on accumulative annual sales for two product categories; storable and perishable products. It was found that perishable and storable product categories lack permanent effects of sales promotion. Furthermore, it is revealed that affects of sales promotion are short lived and persist only on an average of two weeks and up to eight weeks for both product categories, therefore confirming the short term impact of sales promotion.

Linda Harmina Teunter (2002) carried out research en-titled "Analysis of sales promotion effects on house hold purchase behaviour", by interviewing 206 respondents using six product categories (Candy bars, Soft-drinks, Fruit juice, Potato chips, Coffee and Pasta). The result of her study shows that:

- The promotion responsive households can be profiled as larger households consisting of older children and ($\geq$ 35 years of age) shopping responsible person that works out of the house and shops not very often, but purchases larger shopping baskets.

- Promotions can influence household purchase behaviour inside or outside the store. Some households scan newspapers and leaflets for interesting sales promotions, whereas other households only pay attention to promotions inside the retail store.

- The promotional quantity purchased is bigger for favourite brands. This seems to stress that promotions mainly result in purchases by consumers that would have bought the brand anyway. But for a specific brand, the number of regular consumers is most of the time much smaller than the number of non-regular consumers and promotions can drive these non-regular consumers to switch to the promoted brand, which is found to be 60 percent of the total promotional unit sales. Further, it is found that the probability to respond to a non-favourite brand promotion is larger for non-store loyal households than for store loyal-households.

- Among the different promotional types, price cut promotion is the most effective, about nine times as effective as a feature promotion without a price cut.

- The response to promotions is increased by displays.

- A sales promotion can influence household purchase behaviour such as switching brands, purchasing larger quantity than intended, purchasing at a different moment than intended, etc.

- Promotions are found to accelerate purchase timing for candy bar and pasta.

- The household postpone their post-promotional shopping for coffee and soft drinks.

- The quantity bought on promotions is increased for soft-drinks, fruit juice, potato chips and coffee. The increase ranges from 26 percent for soft drinks, up to 96 percent for coffee. Households do seem to adjust their pre and post-promotional purchase quantity downward for potato chips. Category expansion effects are found to be positive for all categories, but only significant for fruit juice (increase of 24%).

- Households use coffee promotions the most. On average, households made use of the available promotions during 44 percent of the promotional shopping trips for coffee (a promotional shopping trip is called promotional if both a household purchases from the specific category and there was a promotion within that specific category). Pasta promotions are used the least (8 percent). Promotion response differs across the product categories.

- Brand switching is significant for sales promotion of all six product categories ranging from 7 percent for soft drink promotions up to 47 percent for coffee promotions.

- Households make relatively more use of promotions in categories that have a higher average price level.

- Promotions within more impulse sensitive categories result in lower promotional purchased quantities than within less impulse sensitive product categories.

Sastri (2003) conducted a study by interviewing 100 respondents to find out the perceptions of cooking oil attributes. Respondents were asked to rank 15 attributes of cooking oils from the most important to the less important attributes. Using Thurston analysis, the study showed that the most important attribute (First Rank) of cooking oil was price, followed by non-cholesterol and nutrient fortification (such as Vitamin A, E and Omega9). The study also used cluster and CHAID analysis to classify respondents based on psychographic variables. Respondents were asked to express their agreement to series of questions related to respondents' activities, interests and opinions.

Ujang Sumarwan (April 2004) conducted a study by making face to face interview with 150 families from February to April 2004, to find out the attitudes of respondents toward the claims made by the cooking oil brands. He uses frequent analysis to present the characteristics of demographic and economic of respondents and to describe attitudes towards claims of cooking oil brands. He employed discriminant analysis to examine factors influencing attitudes towards claims of cooking oils. The result of the study showed that more than 50% of the respondents are neutral to three of the four claims made by the brand BIMOLI, 60% of respondents are neutral to two of the five claims made by the brand FILMA and TROPICAL, 60% of respondents are neutral to all claims made by brand AVENA and 40% of the respondents are neutral to three of the four claims made by the brand SANIA.

Derek D.Rucker and Richard E.Petty (March 2004) in their article titled "Emotion Specificity and Consumer behaviour: Anger, Sadness and preference for activity" find out that consumer's preference can be differently influenced by framing the activity level of the attributes associated with an attitude object to consistent with consumer's emotional state. Specifically, when individuals were induced to be angry, they indicated a preference for a vacation resort advertised as a place of activity over a vacation resort advertised as a place of relaxation. Conversely, when individuals were induced to be sad, they indicated a preference for a vacation resort advertised as a place of passivity over one advertised as a place of activity.

- Wuyang HU and Kevin Chen (2004), investigated consumer's purchase intention of vegetable oil that is made from genetically modified oil seeds in Beijing. In this research titled "Can Chinese consumers are persuaded?" They found that:
- Consumer's purchase intentions of genetically modified vegetable oil were found to be rather low, indicating a considerable skepticism towards genetically modified vegetable oil among Beijing residents.
- The more knowledgeable, older and better educated consumers were more likely to purchase genetically modified vegetable oil.
- The presence of favourable information was found to have a significantly positive impact on the consumer's intention to purchase genetically modified vegetable oil.

- The nutritional benefit of genetically modified vegetable oil can be slightly more effective for some consumers (0.3% better) or the slightly worse for the others (1.8% worse).

- Heterogeneity among consumer's perceptions and attitude is crucial for understanding the effectiveness of various types of information.

Besides the possibility that consumers do not want the premium promotions, people might draw inferences about this premium promotions rather than the promoted product, as argued by Raghubir (2004). People do not only draw inferences regarding the product they are buying, but possibly also about the quality and/or brand of the free gift attached to this product under premium promotion. "The fact that a manufacturer is providing a free gift along with purchase of their product, could either imply that the product itself was overpriced or that the free gift was of low value - that is, free gift promotions could lead to inferences about the cost and margin structure of the promoted product or the free gift or both".

Sales promotion when implemented effectively often results in an increase in short term sales figure. This explains the inclination of corporations to put in a large percentage of their funds in carrying out various sales promotion activities. However variations occur in effects of sales promotion based on the attractiveness of the concerned brand (Alvarez, 2005.

Lee, Leonard and Dan Ariely (2006) have articulated that goal evoking promotions were more effective in influencing consumer's behaviour when goals were less concrete, such as early in the shopping process.

Howard and Kerin (2006) found that consumers with different levels of involvement, operationalised by whether they are in the market for a particular product, have different information processing styles and hence respond to different price promotion cues.

Sales promotion in something considered as an activity of less importance but companies increasingly realise the importance of having a well planned and structured program for sales promotion. All business needs to communicate to the customer what they have to offer.

According to Mahavir Sherawet (2007), ease of carriage, package weight, simplicity, transparency and similarity of packaging have comparatively less impact on purchase decisions of rural consumers than urban ones. However, rural consumers are more critical about packaging as they strongly consider that it contributes to misleading buyers and is also an environmental hazard.

According to M.Foret and J.Padera (2007), in Czech Republic only a small growth in average consumption of edible oil and the consumption only reaches 9.3 liters per head per annum in

2005. In European Union the annual average is significantly higher – 21.5 liters per head per annum.

Klemann C.M.J.V conducted a research (October 2007) to find out "The effects of premium promotions on consumer's category incidence, brand choice and purchase quantity decisions". For this research, he gets the view of 88 respondents through e-mail questionnaire by selecting 9 brands of tooth paste. The result of his study shows that:

- The price and premium promotions lead to an increase in purchases of the tooth paste. The consequence of increased category purchases is that more people start re-buying certain product category which results in increased customers for a longer period of time.
- The consumers increase their brand choice for promoted brands more for price promotions as compared to premium promotions.
- The price promotion of 25% and the tooth brush premium promotions both increased the brand choice for promoted (low and high priced) brands almost to the same extent. The brand choice for promoted brands is almost equally affected by the price promotions of 25% and by the tooth brush premium promotion.
- The respondents increase their purchase quantity for premium promotions on low priced tooth paste.
- The managers should be very careful and suspicious towards premium promotions.

Prof. Philip Opar Donney (2007) a Marketing vice president of Asian companies from Afghanistan, basically he is from Kenya, has recommended the packed edible oil for regular diet by the customers than loose edible oil.

Prof. Purushootam Rao (2008), dean faculty of commerce and Head department of commerce, Osmania University Hyderabad from Andhra Pradesh highlighted in his research paper that, edible oil is the most important part of a food for human being. The Govt. must prevent the oil mixing practices done by the wholesalers and local retailers while they are selling loose oils to the consumers.

Prof. Reddy Bhagwan (2009) University of Tamil Nadu has recommended in his research article that the consumers must use the refined edible oil to prevent the fat in the human body. Heavy fat is the main cause of weight and stomach problems in the health of human beings.

Dr. B.K.Bhattacharya, West Bengal (2009) a eminent health physician advised and given important suggestions to his patients and consumers to use the less quantity of edible oil in the regular diet of the people, 30% of the Indian peoples were not conscious while using the edible oils in their diet, so the concentration must be given to the regular use of edible oils.

Prof. Merry George (2009), great academician from Malaysia analysed in her study that, the producers of edible oil mills are not taking care while producing the edible oils. The producers must avoid using the chemicals for getting bright colour and better transparency in edible oils. There must be strict rules and regulations in the production and selling of edible oils.

Dr. Simon Chippy (2007) Afghanistan a health specialist recommended to the patients to use Suffola and Sunflower packed edible oil in their regular food to avoid unwanted diseases from the use of regular edible oils.

Prof. Abdul Gilani, Pakistan (2009) has analysed in his research study that the customers or regular users of edible oils must avoid fatty edible oils in non-vegetarian food as well as vegetarian food.

Prof. James Berry U.S.A. (2009), said in her article that Govt. and different NGO's must come forward in public and try to create proper awareness in use of regular edible oils and save the life by health diseases.

Prof. Ramana Joof U.A.E. (2009) has found in her study that from Afghanistan, Iraq, Iran and Saudi Arabian people are using most fatty edible oils. She suggested to the regular users try to use less and refined edible oil in their regular food and easy diet.

Prof. H. Sulochana (2008), eminent female professor of Osmania University, Hyderabad highlighted in her article that, the consumers must care about the use of edible oil to avoid the health problems. In India 60% of the health problems are raised by not using the quality edible oil in their regular diet.

Mr.Surabhi Mittal (March2008) in his working paper number -209 titled "Demand- Supply Trends and Projections of Food in India", mentioned that between 1983-84 and 2004-20005, the per capita consumption of edible oil has almost doubled (i.e.) from 3.7 kilogram per head per annum in 1983 and 11 kilogram per head per annum in 2004-05. Further he projected that in 2026 the edible oil demand for India will be 40.9 Million Metric tonnes but the supply will be 13.9 Million Metric tonnes and the supply demand gap will be 26.99 Million Metric tones.

A scientific study on vanaspati and cooking oil brands available in the market revealed that most oil brands and almost all vanaspati brands are unfit for consumption owing to high tran's fatty acid contents.

The study released by the Centre for Science and Environment (CSE) had tested 30 available brands in the market, including desi ghee and butter, at its Delhi-based laboratory and arrived at the conclusions after conducting gas chromatography and other sophisticated tests."Through the tests, we had sought to find out the fatty acid profile of each brand and the injurious trans fat content in them," Associate Director of CSE, Chandra Bhushan said during a press briefing in Delhi.

According to the study, most brands resort to deceptive labeling of trans fat content in their products and are unable to substantiate health benefits as proclaimed in their advertisements. Tran's fatty acids are touted to increase heart risks as they reduce the content of good cholesterol in the body and increases risk of infertility in women, diabetes and Alzheimer's disease.

The tests recorded that trans fatty acid content in all vanaspati brands in the country are five to twelve times higher than the prescribed tran's fat standard for edible oil set in Denmark at two per cent of the total oil. Lowest amount of trans fatty acid content were found in desi ghee and Amul butter at 5.3 per cent and 3.7 per cent respectively. Mustard oil brands indicated tran's fat content within one per cent with good amount of essential fats like Omega 3, Omega 6 and Omega 9 in them. "The anomaly exist as the government chose to overlook the need to monitor trans fatty acid content in edible oils and thus ignoring the risk we are exposed to through our edible oils," CSE Director Sunita Narain said.

According to the WHO recommendations, the acceptable limit of Trans fatty acids in cooking oil is one per cent or below. Ratios for the presence of essential and saturated fats are also mentioned in the recommendations. Based on its study findings, the CSE, an NGO, on Tuesday sought better labeling regulation on trans fatty acid, stringent trans fatty standards, research on cooking oil, guidelines on advertising and marketing of edible oils and mandatory certification of all edible oils imported in the country. The NGO had also gathered minutes of a meeting between the Central Committee for Food Standards and its sub-committee on oil and fats through an RTI query.

The RTI response revealed that the sub-committee had recommended that trans fatty acid content in edible oils be brought down to the level of five percent by 2009 in a phased manner. Meanwhile, the government had sought more scientific data from the sub-committee and is awaiting the results. "If you consider what the Union Health ministry has issued in the name of labeling nutrition facts, you will know how our food is at risk. It literally allows companies to get away with anything–as long as it is on the label. This is just not acceptable," Narain said. Based on the study findings, the CSE researchers are of the opinion that not one oil type meets all body requirements and on such circumstances it is best to consume oil in moderation and switch frequently between oil varieties to get maximum nutritional value.

Dhinesh Babu.S and Venkateshwaran P.S (2010) in their review article titled "Marketing problems of edible oil industry in the state of Tamilnadu", found that, important marketing problems in edible oil markets are Finance (First problem),Customer (2), Competitors(3), and Intermediaries(4).

The marketing problems in finance are heavy marketing margin (0.8144), high credit period (0.7229), heavy requirement of working capital (0.6804) and requirement of heavy selling expenses (0.5968).

The marketing problems on customers are demand for products (0.8146), customer knowledge on products (0.7302), high switching behaviour among customers (0.6911), requirement of variety of products (0.6182) and frequent change in taste of consumer (0.5508).

The marketing problems from competitors are competitor's strategy (0.7943), price war in wholesale trade (0.6454) and unhealthy competition (0.5562).

The marketing problems in intermediaries are consistent searching of agents (0.8146), poor security on debts (0.7332) and more number of intermediaries (0.6561). [60]

Dr.Sarwade W.K Maharashtra, India (2011) conducted a research study to find out the Brand Preferences and Consumption pattern of Edible Oils in Maharashtra state by direct interviewing 1000 respondents through a detailed questionnaire. His study results showed that, in majority of families interviewed (87%) during this course, house wife is the decision maker for the brand and type of edible oil to used. Respondents considered health aspect (90%) and quality (88%) of a particular brand are the important factors in decision making. Majority of the respondents use sunflower oil (42%) followed by kardi (32%), ground nut (15%), soya bean (10%) and corn and kardi blend (1%). Branded oil is preferred than the loose oil in higher income class of consumers. Dhara has the maximum brand awareness (93%) followed by Suffola (92%), Fortune (82%) and Gemini (72%) respectively. Majority of the respondents (60%) prefer one liter and five liter package size. Majority of the respondents (43%) consume 2-4 liters of edible oils per month.

Dhadhal, Chitralekha H. (2011) in the PhD thesis titled, "A study of Brand loyalty and its effect on buying behaviour in case of selected cosmetic products in the state of Gujarat", found that:

- Majority (71.4% (571 among 800)) women skin care cosmetic buyers were found to be loyal to their favourite brand of skin care products.
- A vast majority (89% (713 out of 800 respondents)) were familiar with the word brand loyalty.

- Brand loyalty was highest with the least educated group of education less than SSC.

- Married women were found to be more brand loyal as compared to unmarried ones.

- Business women are found to be the most loyal and the students the least loyal of all.

Sindhu, Asha (2011) conducted a research study to find out the sales promotion strategy of selected companies of Fast Moving Consumer Goods sector in Gujarat region by interviewing 400 respondents through a detailed questionnaire.

Her study result shows that, customers frequently buy branded items in case of bath soaps, food products and tooth pastes. Branded beverages are purchased least. Advertisement and sales promotional methods attract more customers and personal selling is the least method that attracts customers. Price-off or discount is the most effective method followed by premium and extra quantity method to motivate customers to buy products. More than one third of the respondents get information about the sales promotion.[63]

Vaishnani, Haresh.B (2011) conducted a research to find out the "Effects of Sales promotions on Consumer preferences and brand equity perception": with special reference to FMCG products in the state of Gujarat. For this PhD research, they interviewed 460 respondents (281 males &179 females) through a structured questionnaire.

The result of their study shows that:

- The male and female attitudes toward the cash discount as one of the sales promotion schemes do not differ significantly. Both gender categories have same attitude towards cash discount. Also, it does not differ according to various employment statuses, family size (number of family members), family type (Joint or Individual) and marital status (Married or Unmarried) of the 460 respondents.

- There is significant difference in the attitude of the respondents towards cash discount based on the family income.

- Consumers prefer cash discount as a sales promotion schemes compare to free gift as a sales promotion scheme.

- There is no significant difference between consumer deal proness and gender, employment, status, educational qualification, family income, family size and family type.

- Deal proness differs according to marital status. Married one is more deal proness compared to unmarried. This is because unmarried may enjoy the freedom of spending without additional responsibilities of the family while married are deal prone may be because so many alternative of spending and additional responsibilities of family. Married respondents like to take the advantage of sales promotion schemes and ready to postpone the purchase to avail the benefits of the sales promotion schemes.

- The newspaper and point of purchase material preferred in knowing sales promotion schemes differ according to gender. Male respondents preferred to know about sales promotion schemes from newspaper while female respondents prefer to know from point of purchase display.
- Unemployed (262) respondents prefer television as a medium to know about sales promotion schemes.
- Graduate, Post-graduate and above post graduate respondents prefer internet as a medium of knowing the sales promotion scheme.
- Unmarried respondents prefer point of purchase material as medium of knowing sales promotion scheme.
- Males (281) prefer sales promotion scheme on national brand while female (179) prefer sales promotion scheme on international brand.
- Non-Government employees prefer sales promotion scheme on international brand through word of mouth, price-off and immediate type of benefits scheme.
- Awareness of sales promotion schemes through word of mouth, price-off and delayed benefits type scheme differs according to employment status.

N.Rajaveni and Dr. M.Ramasamy (2012) in their online research article titled "A study on Consumer brand preference on the consumption of cooking oil of various income groups in Chennai" finds out that:

- The brand immediately recalled by respondents were Supreme (22%; 47 respondents), Fortune (20%; 43 respondents), Gold winner (15%; 33 respondents), S.V.S (14%; 30 respondents), Roobini (13%; 28 respondents) and Saffola (10%; 21 respondents).
- 23% of the respondents are influenced by retailers to purchase a particular brand of oil, equal number of respondents (23%) are influenced by newspaper advertisements to purchase a particular brand of oil, while 18% of the respondents are influenced by television to purchase a particular brand of oil, nearly 15% of the respondents are influenced by internet to purchase a particular brand of oil, 13% of the respondents are influenced by Doctor's advice in purchasing a particular brand of oil and remaining 6% of the respondents are influenced by window display in purchasing a particular brand of oil.

- Nearly 61% of the respondents are not aware of nutritional benefits or the hazards caused by edible oils. Balance 39% of the respondents are aware of nutritional benefits or the hazards caused by edible oils.

- Nearly 70% of the respondents are ready to change their consumption habits when special awareness is created for pros/cons of edible oils through advertisements, only the remaining 30% of the respondents are not ready to change their consumption habits when special awareness is created for pros/cons of edible oils through advertisements.

- Nearly 26% of the respondents responded that retailers suggestion would be the best media to create an awareness about the edible oil, while 23% of the respondents responded that T.V would be the best media to create an awareness about the edible oil and another 26% of the respondents responded that news papers would be the best media to create an awareness about the edible oil, while 16% of the respondents responded that radio would be the best media to create an awareness about the edible oil and another 12% of the respondents responded that internet would be the best media to create an awareness about the edible oil.

- Nearly 65% of the respondents decide to purchase through the influence of spouse.

- Brand is influencing nearly 73% of the respondents in purchasing cooking oil.

Mrs.R. Prema in her research article titled "An Empirical study on Brand Preference towards edible oil in rural areas with special reference to Coimbatore district" finds out:

- Majority of respondents are aware of gold winner and ganapathy oil among various branded sunflower oil and ground nut oil. They are using gold winner and ganapathy sunflower oil for more than three years and they spent Rs.500-1000 per month and using 4-6 liters of edible oil per month for cooking.

- Majority of the respondents are purchasing edible oils in grocery shops.

- Quality influences the respondents to buy branded edible oil.

- Majority of the respondents are changing their brand when new brand is introduced in the market which is more advantageous and healthy.

- Minority of respondents are receiving complements at the time of purchase as gift.

- The majority of the respondents are recommending the branded edible oil to others.

- The majority of respondents stated that price of branded sunflower oil and groundnut oil is high and they satisfied with quality, attractive package, advertisement and availability.

- The majorities of the respondents are satisfied with Nature fresh, Gemini, Fortune, Poorna, Saffola and Sundrop heart sunflower oil and dissatisfied with Gold winner, Dhara, Usha sunflower oil.
- The majority of the respondents are satisfied with Idhyam Mantra, Ganapathy, Maharaja and Kalki Ground nut oil and dissatisfied with Dhara ground nut oil.
- The amount spent on edible oil decreases when income increases.

References

[1] John M.C. Fall, "Priority Patterns and Consumer behaviour", Journal of Marketing, Vol. 33, No. 4, Part 1, 1969.

[2] Robert Blattberg, Gary Eppen and Joshua Liebermann, "A Theoretical and Empirical Evaluation of Price Deals in Consumer Nondurables", Journal of Marketing, Vol. 45, Pp. 116-129, 1981.

[3] L. McAlister, "A Theory of Consumer Promotions: The Model", SSM Working Paper #1457-83, Massachusetts Institute of Technology, 1983.

[4] Alan G. Sawyer and Peter H. Dickson, "Psychological Perspectives on Consumer Response to Sales Promotion", Research on Sales Promotion: Collected Papers, Report No. 84-104, 1984.

[5] K. Bawa, and R.W. Shoemaker, "The effects of a direct mail coupon on brand choice behavior", Journal of Marketing Research, Vol. 24, Pp. 370-376, 1987.

[6] Sunil Gupta, "Impact of Sales Promotions on When, What, and How Much to Buy", Journal of Marketing Research, Vol. 25, Pp. 342-355, 1988.

[7] Robert C. Blatt Berg and Scott A. Neslin, "Sales Promotion: Concepts, Methods, and Strategies", Engiewood Cliffs, NJ: Prentice Hall, 1990.

[8] V. Kirshnan and Ram C. Rao, "Double Couponing and Retail pricing in a Couponed Product Category", Journal of Marketing Research, Vol. 32, No. 4, Pp. 419-432, 1995.

[9] R.P. Leone and S.S. Srinivasan, "Coupon face value: its impact on coupon redemptions, brand sales, and brand profitability", Journal of Retailing, Vol. 73, No. 3, Pp. 273-289, 1996.

[10] E.R. Foxman, P.S. Tansuhaj and J.K. Wong, "Evaluating Cross-National Sales Promotion Strategy: An Audit Approach", International Marketing Review, Vol. 5, No. 4, Pp. 7-15, 1988.

[11] Kashani, Kamran and John A. Quelch, "Can Sales Promotion Go Global?", Business Horizons, Vol. 33, No. 3, Pp. 37-43, 1990.

[12] L.C. Huff and D.L. Alden, "An investigation of consumer response to sales promotions in developing markets: a three country analysis", Journal of Advertising Research, Vol. 38, No. 3, Pp. 47-56, 1998.

[13] Economic and Political Weekly February 27, 1988.

[14] P.R. Das, "Semantic cues and buyer evaluation of promotional communication", Leone, R.P. and Kumar, V. (Eds), Enhancing Knowledge Development in Marketing, American Marketing Association, Chicago, IL, Pp. 12-17, 1992.

[15] I. Sinha, R. Chandran and S. Srinivasan, "Consumer evaluations of price and promotional restrictions–a public policy perspective", Journal of Public Policy & Marketing, Vol. 18, No. 1, Pp. 37-51, 1999.

[16] I. Sinha and M.F. Smith, "Consumers perceptions of promotional framing of price", Psychology & Marketing, Vol. 17, No. 3, Pp. 257-275, 2000.

[17] Lan Xia and Kent B. Monroe, "The influence of pre-purchase goals on Consumers perceptions of price promotions," International Journal of Retail & Distribution Management, Vol. 37, No. 8, Pp. 680-694, 2009.

[18] S. Shavitt, S. Swan, T.M. Lowrey and M. Wanke, "The interaction of endorser attractiveness and involvement in persuasion depends on the goal that guides message processing", Journal of Consumer Psychology, Vol. 3, No. 2, Pp. 137-162, 1992.

[19] J.L. Assuncao and R.J. Meyer, "The rational effect of price promotions on sales and consumption", Management Sci., Vol. 39, Pp. 517-535, 1993.

[20] V.S. Folkes, I.M. Martin and K. Gupta, "When to say when: Effects of supply on usage", J. Consumer Res., Vol. 20, Pp. 467–477, 1993.

[21] I. Simonson, Z. Carmon and S. O'Curry, "Experimental evidence on the negative effect of product features and sales promotions on brand choice", Marketing Science, Vol. 13, No. 1, Pp. 23–40, 1994.

[22] Suprihatini, "Preferences of Fried-Food Home Industries on Cooking Oil Characteristics: A case study at Ten Indonesian Home Industries in Bandung", The journal of Plantation Agri Business study, Vol. 1, No. 3, 1995. a.

[23] R. Suprihatini, "Concept test for the red palm Cooking Oil", The journal of Plantation Agri Business study, Vol. 1, No. 2, Pp. 25-35, 1995.b.

[24] Achiruddin, "An Analysis of Consumer Segmentation of Cooking Oil Based on Demographic Characteristics", Unpublished Master's thesis, Master of Management in Agri Business graduate school, Bogor Agricultural University, Bogor-Indonesia, 1997.

[25]   M.T. Pham, J.B. Cohen, J.W. Pracejus and G.D. Hughes, "Affect monitoring and the primacy of feelings in judgment", Journal of Consumer Research, Pp. 167-188, 2001.

[26]   John H. Roberts, "A Review of International Research into Promotional Effectiveness and Its Implications for an Australian Research Agenda", Australasian Journal of Market Research, Vol. 3, No. 2, Pp. 25-38, 1995.

[27]   T.S. Robertson, "How to reduce market penetration cycle times", Sloan Management Review, Vol. 35, Pp. 87-96, 1993.

[28]   M.L. Rothschild and W.C. Gaidis, "Behavioral learning theory: its relevance to marketing and promotions", Journal of Marketing, Vol. 45, Pp. 70–78, 1981.

[29]   Sandra Luxton, "Sales Promotion in the Australian Food Industry: A Review of Industry Practice and Its Implications", Journal of Food Products Marketing, Vol. 7, No. 4, Pp. 37-55, 2001.

[30]   D. Aaker, "Managing Brand Equity", New York: The Free Press, 1991.

[31]   C. Shea, "Playing to Win", Promo Magazine, 1996.

[32]   Donald E. Vinson, Jerome E. Scott and Lawerence M. Lamont, "The roles of personal values in marketing and consumer behaviour", Journal of Marketing, Vol. 41, No. 2, 1997.

[33]   J. Cummins, "Sales Promotion: How to Create and Implement Campaigns that Really Work", 2nd ed., Kogan Page, London, 1998.

[34]   C.F. Mela, S. Gupta and D.R. Lehmann, "The Long-Term Impact of Promotion and Advertising on Consumer Brand Choice", Journal of Marketing Research, Vol. 34, Pp. 248-261, 1997.

[35]   U. Sumarwan, "An Analysis of Perceived Popularity, Quality, Price, and their Relationship with the use of cooking oil brands", The Journal of Nutrition and family studies (Media Gizi dankeluarga), Vol. XXIV, Pp. 41-47, 2000.

[36]   Pierre Chandon and Brian Wansink, "A benefit congruency framework of sales promotion effectiveness", Journal of Marketing, Version: JM 4-5-2000.doc, 2000.

[37]   Suri R. Manchada and C.S. Kohli, "Brand evaluations: a comparison of fixed price and discounted price offers", The Journal of Product & Brand Management, Vol. 9 No. 3, Pp. 193-207, 2000.

[38]   Pierre Chandon and Brian Wansink, "When are stockpiled products consumed faster? A convenience-salience framework of post purchase Consumption incidence and quantity", J. Marketing Res., Vol. 39, Pp. 321–335, 2002.

[39]   A. Krishna, R. Briesch, D.R. Lehmann and H. Yuan, "A meta-analysis of the impact of price presentation on perceived savings", Journal of Retailing, Vol. 78, No. 2, Pp. 101-118, 2002.

[40]   D. DelVecchio, D.H. Henard and T.H. Freling, "The effects of sales promotion on post-promotion brand preference: a meta-analysis", Journal of Retailing, Vol. 82, No. 3, Pp. 203-213, 2006.

[41]   K. Pauwels, D.M. Hanssens and S. Siddarth, "The Long Term Effects of Price Promotions on Category Incidence, Brand Choice and Purchase Quantity", Journal of Marketing, Pp. 27-29, 2002.

[42]   Linda Harmina Teunter, "Analysis of sales promotion effects on the households purchase behaviour", Erasmus Research Institute of Management (ERIM). Erasmus university Rotterdam ERIM PhD series research in management, Pp. 195-204, 2002.

[43]   P.N. Sastri, "Consumer Behaviour Analysis of Cooking Oils and Its Implications of marketing strategy", Unpublished Master's thesis, Master of Management in Agri Business graduate school, Bogor Agricultural University, Bogor-Indonesia, 2003.

[44]   U. Ujang Sumarwan, "Factors Influencing Attitudes towards Claims of Cooking oil", Journal Manajemen don Agri bisnis, Vol. 2, No. 2, Pp. 81-91, 2005.

[45]   Derek D. Rucker and Richard E. Petty, "Emotion Specificity and Consumer behaviour: Anger, Sadness and preference for activity", Journal of Motivation and Emotion, Vol. 28, No. 1, Pp. 16-17, 2004.

[46]   H.U. Wuyang and Kevin Chen, "Can Chinese consumers be persuaded?", Department of Rural Economics University of Alberta, Edmonton Ag Bioforum, Vol. 7, No. 3, Pp. 124-132, 2004.

[47]   P. Raghubir, "Free gift with purchase: promoting or discounting the brand?", Journal of Consumer Psychology, Vol. 14, No. 1/2, Pp. 181-186, 2004.

[48]   B.A. Alvarez and R.V. Casielles, "Consumer evaluation of sales promotion: the effect on brand choice", European Journal of Marketing, Vol. 39, Pp. 54-70, 2005.

[49]   Leonard Lee and Dan Ariely, "shopping goals, goal concreteness and conditional promotions", Journal of consumer research, Vol. 33, No. 1, Pp. 60-71, 2006.

[50]   D.J. Howard and R. Kerin, "Broadening the scope of reference price advertising research: a field study of consumer shopping involvement", Journal of Marketing, Vol. 70, Pp. 185-204, 2006.

[51]   D. Jobber and G. Lancaster, "Selling and sales management (7th ed.)", Harlow: Pearson education, 2006.

[52]   Mahavir Sherawet and C. Kundu Subhash, "Buying behaviour of Rural and Urban consumers in India: the impact of packaging", International Journal of consumer studies, Vol. 31, No. 6, Pp. 630-638, 2007.

[53]   M. Foret and J. Padera, "Healthy Life style and buying behaviour in the Czech Republic", AGRIC.ECON-CZECH, 54 2008(7):307-313 supported by the ministry of education, Youth and Sports of the Czech Republic (grant no.MSM 6215648904), 2007.

[54]   C.M.J.V Klemann, "The effects of premium promotions on consumer's category incidence, brand choice and purchase quantity decisions", final PhD thesis, Universiteit Maastricht, Pp. 62-66, 2007.

[55]   www.responservice.com

[56]   www.superhaat.com

[57]   A. Wilson, V.A. Zeithaml, M.J. Bitner and D.D. Gremler, "Services marketing: Integrating customer focus across the firm", Mc Graw Hill, 2012.

[58]   Mr.Surabhi Mittal, "Demand- Supply Trends and Projections of Food in India", Indian Council for Research on International Economic Relations, Pp. 5-7, 2008.

[59]   The Indian Express news paper, Tuesday February 3, 2009.

[60]   S. Dhinesh Babu, and P.S. Venkateshwaran, "Marketing problems of edible oil industry in the state of Tamilnadu", Asian Journal of Management Research, Pp. 61-62, 2010.

[61]   Dr.W.K. Sarwade, "Brand Preferences and Consumption Pattern of Edible Oils in Maharashtra State", International Conference on Economics and Finance Research IPEDR, Pp. 323-333, 2011.

[62]   H. Dhadhal, Chitralekha, "A study of Brand loyalty and its effect on buying behaviour in case of selected cosmetic products in the state of Gujarat", thesis PhD, 2011.

[63]   Asha Sindhu, "Sales promotion strategy of selected companies of FMCG sector in Gujarat region", PhD thesis, Saurashtra university, Pp. 291-292, 2011.

[64]   H.B. Vaishnani, "Effects of Sales promotions on Consumer preferences and brand equity perception: with special reference to FMCG products", PhD thesis Saurashtra university, Pp. 338-343, 2011.

[65]   N. Rajaveni and Dr.M. Ramasamy, "A study on Consumer brand preference on the consumption of cooking oil of various income groups in Chennai", Sathyabama University, Chennai. Source: http://ssrn.com/abstract=1894093, 2012.

[66]   R. Prema, "An Empirical study on Brand Preference towards edible oil in rural areas with special reference to Coimbatore district", Indian Journal of Applied Research, Vol. 3, No. 3, Pp. 224-226, 2013.

CHAPTER III

CONCEPTUAL FRAME WORK OF CONSUMER BEHAVIOUR AND SALES PROMOTION

3.1. Meaning of Consumer Behaviour

Consumer behaviour can be defined as the decision-making process and physical activity involved in acquiring, evaluating, using and disposing of goods and services. This definition clearly brings out that it is not just the buying of goods/services that receives attention in consumer behaviour but, the process of it starts much before the goods have been acquired or bought. A process of buying starts in the minds of the consumer, which leads to the finding of alternatives between products that can be acquired with their relative advantages and disadvantages. This leads to an internal and external research. Then follows a process of decision-making for purchase and using the goods and then the post purchase behaviour which is also very important, because it gives a clue to the marketers whether his product has been a success or not.

3.2. Marketing Strategy and Consumer Behaviour

3.2.1. Marketing Analysis

Market analysis requires an understanding of the 4-Cs which are consumer, conditions, competitor and the company. A study is undertaken to provide superior customer value, which is the main objective of the company. For providing better customer value we should learn the needs of the consumer, the offering of the company, vis-a-vis its competitors and the environment which is economic, physical, technological, etc.

A consumer is anyone who engages himself in physical activities of evaluating, purchasing, using or disposing of goods and services. A customer is one who actually purchases a product or service from a particular organisation or a shop. A customer is always defined in terms of a specific product or company. However, the term 'consumer' is a broader term which emphasises not only the actual buyer or customer, but also its users, i.e. consumers. Sometimes a product was purchased by the head of the family and used by the whole family, i.e. a refrigerator or a car. There are some consumer behaviour roles which are played by different members of the family.

The following table 3.1 shows the role played by the consumers and the description of that role.

Table 3.1: Behavioural Roles Played by the Consumers

Role	Description
Initiator	The person who determines that some need or want is to be met (For ex., a daughter indicating the need for a colour TV).
Influencer	The person or persons who intentionally or unintentionally Influence the decision to buy or endorse the view of the initiator.
Buyer	The person who actually makes a purchase
User	The person or persons who actually use or consume the product.

All the consumer behaviour roles are to be kept in mind but, the emphasis is on the buyer whose role is overt and visible.

3.2.2. Consumer

To understand the consumer, researches are made. Sometimes motivational research becomes handy to bring out hidden attitudes, uncovered emotions and feelings. Many firms send questionnaires to customers to ask about their satisfaction, future needs and ideas for a new product. On the basis of the answers received, a change in the marketing mix is made and advertising is also streamlined. The study of the characteristic features leads to a better understanding of the consumer and his needs. The following table 3.2 will shows the characteristic features of Indian consumers.

Table 3.2: Characteristic Features of Indian Consumers

1. Geography 2. Population 3. Urban-Rural 4. Sex 5. Age factor 6. Literacy level 7. Incentive level 8. Linguistic diversity 9. Religion 10. Dress, food	Indian consumers

3.2.3. The External Analysis (Company)

The external analysis may be done by the feedbacks from the industry analyst and by marketing researches. The internal analysis is made by the firm's financial conditions, the quantum of the sales, quality of work force and other factors within the company.

3.2.4. Competition

In the analysis of the market, a study of the strengths and weaknesses of the competitors, their strategies, their anticipated moves and their reaction to the companies' moves and plans are to be made. The company will react accordingly with the result of information and changes its marketing mix and the offering which can out do the competitor. This is a very difficult process and it is easier say than do. To have correct information about the competitors and to anticipate their further moves is the job of the researcher.

3.2.5. Condition

The conditions under which the firms are operating have also to be seriously considered. The factors to be studied are the economy, physical environment, government regulations, technological developments, etc. These Factors will affect the consumer needs, i.e. the deterioration of the environment and its pollution may lead to the use and innovation of safer products. People are health conscious and are concerned with their safety. Hence, in this case, safer products have a better chance with the consumer. In case of recession, the flow of money is restricted greatly. This leads to the formulation of different marketing strategies.

3.2.6. Marketing Segmentation

The market is divided into segments which are a portion of a larger market whose needs are similar and they are homogeneous in themselves. Such segments are identified with similar needs.

3.2.7. Identify Product Related Needs (Need Set)

By need set, it is meant that there are products which satisfy more than one need. An automobile can fill the transportation needs, status need, fun needs or time saving needs. So the company tries to identify the need sets which its product can fulfill. Then we try to identify the groups who have similar needs, i.e. some people need economical cars, others may go for luxury cars.

3.2.8. Group Customers with Similar Need Sets

The customers with similar need sets are grouped.

3.2.9. Describe Each Group based on Demographic and Psychographic Characteristics

The groups are identified and they are described in terms of their demographic and psychographic characteristics. The company finds out how and when the product is purchased and consumed.

3.2.10. Select Target Market

After all the above preliminary work is done, the target customer group known as the target segment is chosen, keeping in mind how the company can provide superior customer value at a profit. The segment which can best be served with the company's capability at a profit is chosen. It has to be kept in mind that different target segments require different marketing strategies and with the change in the environmental conditions the market mix has to be adjusted accordingly. Attractiveness of the segment can be calculated by marking the various criterions on 1 to 10 scales as given below:

Table 3.3: Attractiveness of the Market Segment

1 2 3 4 5 6 7 8 9 10

Criterion	Score on 1 to 10 scale with company being most favorable
Segment size.	---
Segment growth rate.	---
Competitor strength.	---
Customer satisfaction	--- with the existing product.
Fit with company image.	---
Fit with company objectives.	---
Fit with company resources.	---
Fit with other segments.	---
Investment required.	---
Stability/Periodic ability.	---
Zest to serve.	---
Sustainable advantage available.	---
Leverage to other segments/markets.	---
Other factors.	---

3.2.11. Marketing Strategy

Strategies are formulated to provide superior customer value. In formulating market strategies, the 4-ps are directed at the target market. The following figure 3.1 will show the 4-ps of marketing.

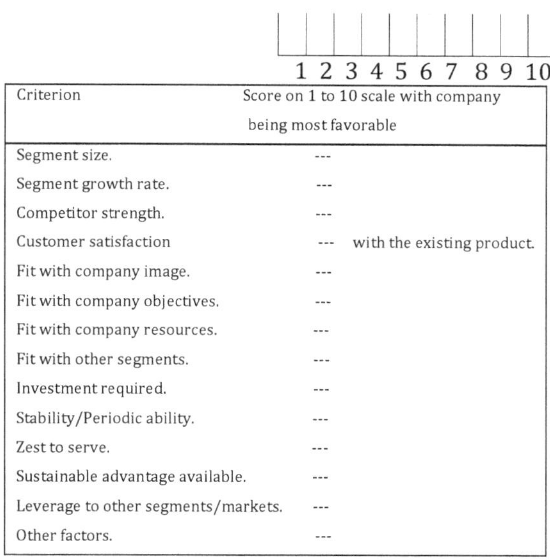
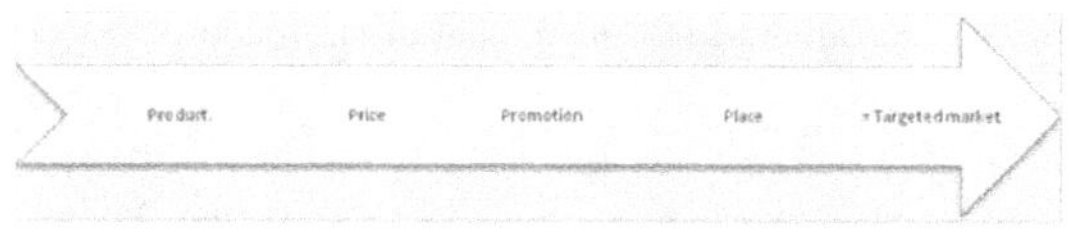

Figure 3.1: Four Ps of Marketing

3.2.12. Product

Product is anything that is offered to the consumer which is tangible and can satisfy a need and has some value.

3.2.13. Price

Price is the amount of money one must pay to obtain the right to use the product.

3.2.14. Distribution

The goods can be distributed by many channels. They could be retailers, wholesalers, agents or by direct selling. Distribution outlets play an important role in reaching the goods to the consumer. They provide time, place and possession utilities. Some goods need to be marketed through the channels or the middleman.

Others can be marketed directly by the company to the actual consumer.

3.2.15. Communication (Promotion)

Promotion is the means of changing the attitudes of the consumer, so that it becomes favourable towards the company's products. Various means of promotion are advertising, personal selling, sales promotion and publicity.

3.2.16. Service

Service refers to auxiliary service that enhances the value of the product or the service. For instance, while buying a car, free services are provided over a certain period of time. Checkups are free and maintenance is also covered on the charge of an adequate amount along with the product purchased. These auxiliary services are provided at a cost with money. These provide value to the product or the customer. These services give an advantage to the customer and he is free from the botheration of occasional checkups or risk. The risk is considerably reduced and the customer derives satisfaction with his decision to purchase.

3.2.17. Consumer Decision Process

The consumer buying process is a complex matter as many internal and external factors have an impact on the buying decisions of the consumer. When purchasing a product there are several processes, which consumers go through. They are as follows:

3.2.18. Problem Recognition

The consumer will purchase a product whenever he feels that the product is needed for him. So the consumer must feel the need before he buys the product.

3.2.19. Information Search-Internal, External

In this stage the consumer has to decide whether to continue the same product or to change from it. For taking this decision he needs information. Sources of information could be family, friends, neighbours who may have the product consumer have in mind, alternatively he may ask the sales people or retailer or read specialist magazine about the product.

3.2.20. Alternative Evaluation

If the consumer wants to purchase sunflower oil, he has to decide which brand to purchase? Shall it be Gold winner, Sundrop or Suffola? Consumers allocate attribute factors to certain products, almost like a point scoring system which they work out in their mind over which brand to purchase. This means that consumers know what features from the rivals will benefit them and they attach different degrees of importance to each attribute. For example, price may be better on Suffola but taste and health are better in Gold winner, but taste and health are more important to them than price.

Consumers usually have some sort of brand preference with companies as they may have had a good history with a particular brand or their friends may have had a reliable history with one, but if the decision falls between the Suffola or Gold winner, then which one shall it be?

In this case review is needed on particular brand.

3.2.21. Purchase Decision

Through the evaluation process as mentioned above, consumers will reach their final purchase decision and they reach the final process of going through the purchase action e.g. The process of going to the shop to buy the product, which for some consumers can be as just as rewarding as actually purchasing the product. Purchase of product can either be through the store or over the phone.

3.2.22. Post Purchase behaviour

Every consumer has doubts about the product after he purchases it. This is called as post purchase behaviour and research shows that it is a common trait amongst purchasers of products. Manufacturers of products clearly want recent consumers to feel proud of their purchase; it is therefore just as important for manufacturers to advertise for the sake of their recent purchaser so consumers feel comfortable that they own a product from a strong and reputable organization. This limits post purchase behaviour. i.e., consumers feel reassured that he own the latest advertised product.

3.3.   Factors Influencing the behaviour of Buyers

Consumer behaviour is affected by many uncontrollable factors. Just think, what influences us before we buy a product or service? Our friends, our upbringing, our culture, the media, a role model or influences from certain groups?

Culture is one factor that influences behaviour. Simply culture is defined as our attitudes and beliefs. But how are these attitudes and believes developed? As an individual growing up, a child is influenced by their parents, brothers, sisters and other family member who may teach them what is wrong or right. They learn about their religion and culture, which help them develop these opinions, attitudes and beliefs (AIO). These factors will influence their purchase behaviour however other factors like groups of friends or people they look up to may influence their choices of purchasing a particular product or service.

Reference groups are particular groups of people. Some people may look up towards to other persons that have an impact on consumer behaviour. So they can be simply a band like the spice girls or our immediate family members. Opinion leaders are those people that we look up, because we are respecting their views and judgments and these views may influence consumer decisions. So it may be a friend who works with the Information Technology trade who may influence our decision on which computer to buy. The economical environment also has an impact on consumer behaviour. Do consumers have a secure job and a regular income to spend on goods? Marketing and sales promotion obviously influenced the consumers in trying to evoke them to purchase a particular product or service.

People's social status will also impact their behaviour. What is their role within the society? Are they actors or Doctors or Office goers? Clearly being parents affects their buying habits depending on the age of the children, the type of job they had mean them need to purchase formal clothes, the income which is earned has an impact. The life style of someone who earns Rs.10,00,000 per annum would clearly be different from someone who earns Rs.10,000 per annum; also characters will have an influence on buying decisions. Whether the person is extrovert (outgoing and spends on entertainment) or introvert (keeps to themselves and purchases via on-line or phone) again has an impact on the types of purchases made.

3.4.   Types of Buying behaviour

There are four typical types of buying behaviour based on the type of products that intends to be purchased. They are:

3.4.1 Complex Buying behaviour

Complex buying behaviour is where the individual purchases a high value brand and seeks a lot of information before the purchase is made.

3.4.2   Habitual Buying behaviour

Habitual buying behaviour is where the individual buys a product out of habit .e.g. a daily news paper, liquor or cigarette.

3.4.3   Variety Seeking Buying behaviour

Variety seeking buying behaviour is where the individual likes to shop around and experiment with different products. So an individual may shop around for different breakfast cereals because he/she wants variety in the mornings.

3.4.4   Dissonance Reducing Buying behaviour

Dissonance reducing buying behaviour is when buyer is highly involved with the purchase of the product, because the purchase is expensive or infrequent. There is little difference between existing brands, an example would be buying a diamond ring, there is perceived little difference between existing diamond brand manufacturers. The following table 3.4 will depict the Black box model of consumer behaviour.

Table 3.4

Environmental Factors		Buyers Black Box		
Marketing stimuli	Environmental stimuli	Buyer characteristics	Decision process	Buyers Response
Product	Economic	Attitudes	Problem recognition	Product choice
	Technological	Motivation	Information search	Brand choice
Price	Political	Perceptions	Alternative evaluation	Dealer choice
	Cultural	Personality	Purchase decision	Purchase timing
Place	Demographic	Life style	Post purchase behaviour	Purchase amount
Promotion	Natural	Knowledge		

3.4.5   Black Box Model of Consumer Behaviour

This black box model shows the interaction of stimuli, consumer characteristics, decision process and consumer responses. It can be distinguished between interpersonal stimuli (between people) or intrapersonal stimuli (within people).The black box model is related to the black box theory of behaviorism. The marketing stimuli are planned and processed by the companies, whereas the environmental stimulus is given by social factors, based on the economical, political and cultural circumstances of a society. The buyer's black box contains the buyer characteristics and the decision process, which determines the buyer's response.

The black box model considers the buyers response as a result of a conscious, rational decision process, in which it is assumed that the buyer has recognised the problem. However, in reality many decisions are not made in awareness of a determined problem by the consumer.

The study of consumers helps firms and organisations improve their marketing strategies by understanding issues such as how

- The psychology of how consumers think, feel, reason and select between different alternatives (e.g., brands, products and retailers).
- The psychology of how the consumer is influenced by his or her environment (e.g., culture, family, signs, media).
- The behaviour of consumers while shopping or making other marketing decisions;
- Limitations in consumer knowledge or information processing abilities influence decisions and marketing outcome.
- How consumer motivation and decision strategies differ between products that differ in their level of importance or interest that they entail for the consumer; and
- How marketers can adapt and improve their marketing campaigns and marketing strategies to more effectively reach the consumer.
- One official definition of consumer behaviour is "The study of individuals, groups or organisations and the processes they use to select, secure, use and dispose of products, services, experiences or ideas to satisfy needs and the impacts that these processes have on the consumer and society."

3.5. Different Segments of Indian Consumers

The behaviour of the Indian consumer is influenced to a great extent by their social class, social status and the income earned by them. Hence it is necessary for us to know about the different segments of the consumers for the better understanding of Indian consumer behaviour.

3.5.1 The Socialites

Socialites belong to the upper class. They prefer to shop in speciality stores, go to clubs on weekends and spend a good amount on luxury goods. They are always looking for something different. They are the darlings of exclusive establishments. They go for high value, exclusive products. Socialites are also be very brand conscious and would go only for the best known in the market.

3.5.2   The Conservatives

The conservatives belong to the middle class. The conservative segment is the reflection of the true Indian culture. They are traditional in their outlook, cautious in their approach towards purchases, spend more time with family than in party and focus more on savings than spending, slow in decision making; They seek a lot of information before making any purchase. They look for durability and functionality but at the same time they also been image conscious. They prefer high value consumer products, but often have to settle for the more affordable one. These habits in turn affect their purchasing habits where they are trying to go for the middle and upper middle level priced products.

3.5.3   The Working Women

The working women segment is the one, which has seen a tremendous growth in the late nineties. This segment has opened the flood gates for the Indian retailers. The working women today have grown out of her longstanding image of being the home maker. Today, she is rubbing shoulders with men, proving herself to be equally good, if not better. Working women have their own mind in decision to purchase the products that appeal to them.

3.5.4   India's Rich

India's rich can be categorized to five major categories as follows:

3.5.4.1. The Rich

The rich have greater income of more than US dollars 11,000 per annum. Total household having such incomes are 10, 58,961. These people are upwardly mobile. Some of them in this category are double income and no kids (DINK) households. They spend more on leisure and entertainment activities than on future investments. Across the category, backgrounds are distinctly middle class. They aspire, therefore, to attain the super rich status.

3.5.4.2. The Super Rich

The super rich have income greater than US Dollar 22,000 per annum. Total number of households is 3,20,900. There are less DINK families here than in the rich category. The super rich are mainly professionals and devoted to consumerism. They buy many durables and are status conscious.

3.5.4.3. The Ultra Rich

The ultra rich have income greater than US Dollar 44,000 per annum. The number of households in this category is 98,289. There is no typical profile of the ultra rich. There are some DINK households of middle level executives. Some single earning households are of first generation entrepreneurs. Some rich farmers, who have been rich for a long time, belong to this category.

3.5.4.4. The Sheer Rich

The sheer rich are made up by households having income exceeding US Dollar 1,10,000 per annum. Such households are 20,863. They do not have a homogenous profile. There are joint families as well as nuclear families in this category. They consume services greatly. They own multiple cars and houses. They aspire to social status and power.

3.5.4.5. The Obscenely Rich

The obscenely rich were made up of households having income exceeding US Dollar 2,22,000 per annum. There are hardly 6,515 such households in India. They are first-generation entrepreneurs who have made it big. Some of them are techies. A variety of people belong to this category. They are just equivalent to the rich in the developed countries. They crave for exclusivity in what they buy. Most premium brands are relevant to them.

3.5.4.6. The Rural Consumer

About three quarters of the Indian population are in the rural areas and with the growing middle class, especially in the Indian cities; the spillover effect of the growing urban middle class is also felt in the rural areas. The Indian rural market has been growing at 3-4% per annum, adding more than one million new consumers every year and now accounts for close to 50% of the volume consumption of fast-moving consumer goods (FMCG) in India. The market size of the fast moving consumer goods sector is projected to more than double to US Dollar 23.25 billion by 2014 from the present US Dollar 11.16 billion. As a result, it is becoming an important market place for fast moving consumer goods as well as consumer durables.

3.6.   Five Myths of Consumer Behaviour

3.6.1   Myth 1: Consumers behave the Same in All Markets

The problem: The whole process of creating and introducing a new technology product is littered with guesswork that leaves the product designers in a revolutionary frame of mind-even after the product starts shipping and the information starts to flow. Designers believe that consumers will flock to their new technology product, service or web site because it provides a similar value or copies a concept provided in an established market. In the end, consumers don't understand the offering and don't use it.

The following figure 3.2 shows the consumer adaptation S curve.

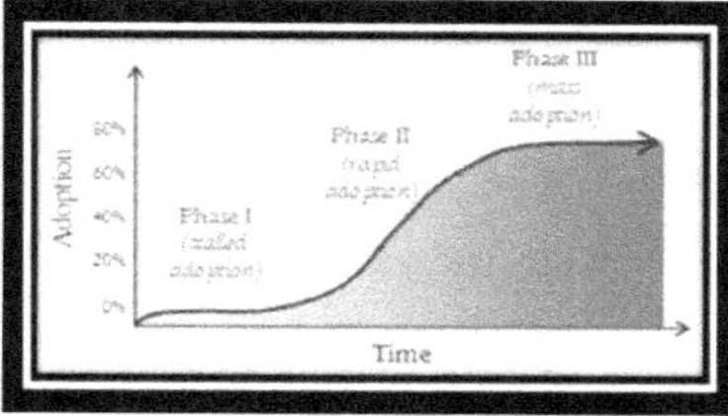

Figure 3.2: Consumer Adoption S Curve

The reality: Consumers behave differently in new markets than in established markets.

The ***Consumer Adoption S-Curve*** demonstrates how consumers change their behaviour as they progress through a product's growth phases. It shows why new products in Phase I require a different focus than a similar product that has already progressed to Phase III.

The solution: New products are more successful when designers analyse usage patterns earlier to determine the product's key success factors. Once identified, these key success factors should be optimised and streamlined to create a consumer-grade experience that will attract mass consumer success.

3.6.2   Myth 2: The More Consumers see it, the More Successful it Will Be

The problem: Many companies believe in their product so much that they can't understand why it isn't successful. They assume that the problem is that others don't know about the product, so they increase their marketing budget. However, they soon spend themselves out of business because consumers attracted to the product don't stay to become long-term loyal users. The following figure 3.3 shows the consumer adoption funnel.

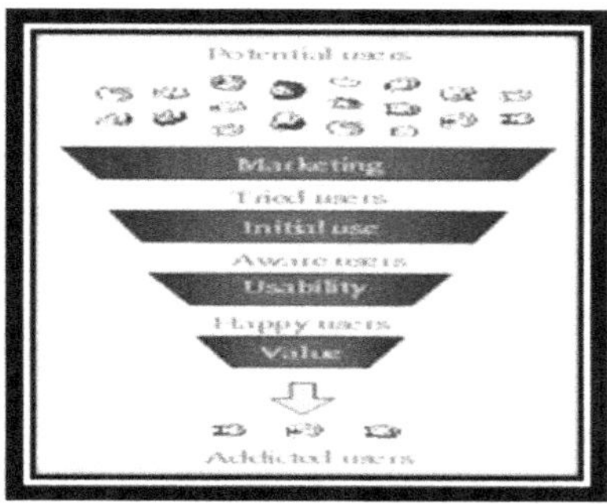

Figure 3.3: Consumer Adoption Funnel

The reality: If the offering isn't attractive, there is no point in getting more users to see it.

The **_Consumer Adoption Funnel_** demonstrates how users progress through their experience with a new product or service.

The solution: Using marketing to attract more users won't change how these users behave once they arrive-marketing is only the first gate of four in the _Consumer Adoption Funnel._ You can coax users into trying your product or service, but you can't compel them to use it long term. _Stickiness_ (value versus cost) must be optimised before users will increase their usage.

3.6.3   Myth 3: If I'll Use it, My Users will

The problem: It is often hard for designers of a new technology product or service to differentiate themselves from their users. They think that new users will fall in love with the product just as they have. They find it very difficult to understand why users reject their offerings.

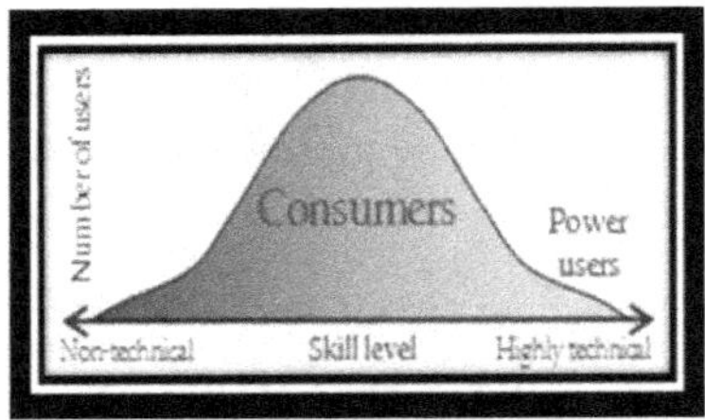

Figure 3.4: Consumer Bell Curve

The reality: Consumers don't have your knowledge or your motivation when trying your product.

The Consumer Bell Curve describes where the bulk of users are relative to their skill levels and willingness to proactively find value in a product.

The solution: Study the average consumer behaviour and accept that it won't match our behaviour. Understand that we are a power user, while most of our consumers are not. Look for unnecessary complexities and customisation requirements or long installation processes that are probably hurting our product's success. Don't add settings or preferences to our product as a way to solve design disputes. Design for the users' skill levels, not our skill level.

3.6.4   Myth 4: Consumers will Find a Product's Value

The problem: Most companies feel that it is best to have lots of features so that users can navigate to and use whichever features fit their needs. These companies are usually disappointed, as users don't look for the features they want. Instead, users struggle to find value and give up.

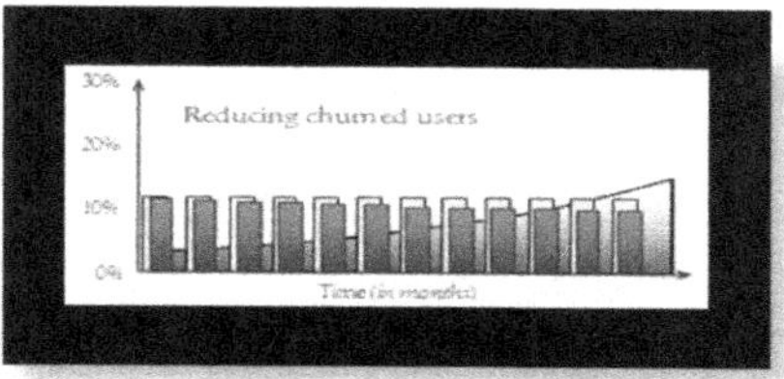

Figure 3.5: Consumer Churn Graph

The reality: The value must find the user.

The Consumer Churn Graph demonstrates how focusing on improving a user's ability to find value in a product will increase a user's success with the product.

The solution: Instead of focusing on how to get more users to your product or trying to design more features for more segments of users, focus on removing or hiding rarely used features and highlighting your key features and value.

3.6.5 *Myth 5: Consumers Want More Features*

The problem: As an idea turns into a product and starts shipping, its designers and engineers seem to have an unlimited number of new ideas for new features to include in the next version, each feature designed to make the product "more complete". However, in the eyes of the consumer, the exact opposite is happening. The early users are wondering why the key feature is so hard to use, buggy or incomplete.

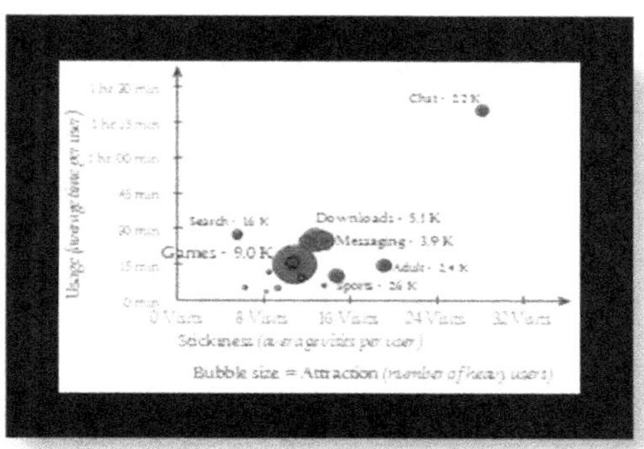

Figure 3.6: Consumer Behaviour Bubble Chart

The reality: Consumers only want a few key features, and they want them to work well.

The Consumer Behavior Bubble Chart enables comparisons of different features or services to determine how many consumers use each feature (Attraction), how much time consumers spend with each feature (Usage), and how often they return to use the feature again in the future (Stickiness).

The solution: Before shipping a product, all you have is your professional training and experience to aid you in designing a product. But once you have built and shipped the product, you have access to a wealth of consumer usage information that can help drive future design decisions. Use this data to tell you where your value really is and focus on continuously improving that value.

3.7.   Knowledge of Consumers

The human behaviour is complex, replete with controversies and contradictions and comes as no surprise to marketing academicians as well as practioners. There is a widespread recognition that consumer behaviour is the key to contemporary marketing success (Hawkins, 2003).

Consumer behaviour has been legitimised in marketing for it provides the conceptual framework and strategic thinking for carrying out successful segmentation of markets (Schiffman and Kanuk 2000).

There have been a number of debates between positivistic and interpretive consumer researchers (Hudson and Ozanne 1988). In this way, the field of consumer behaviour has been characterised by diversity of viewpoints; as a result, the entire field now is based on an interdisciplinary science (Kassarjian 1995).

3.7.1. Consumer Behaviour Approaches

The understanding of consumer behaviour appeals to a set of different areas of knowledge/factors: Psychological, cultural social psychological, physio-pyschological, genetics anthropology. One of them is the psychology since consumer behaviour deals with emotions, beliefs and attitudes. Research on emotions within marketing has evolved three approaches: the categories approach, the dimensions approach and the cognitive appraisals approach (Watson and Spence, 2007).

The categories approach groups emotions around exemplars and considers their different effects on consumption related behaviour.

The dimensions approach uses the affective dimensions of valence and level of arousal to distinguish between emotions and the effects they have on consumer behaviour. The cognitive appraisals approach has used emotions' underlying motivational and evaluative roots to explain their influences on consumption related behaviours. This approach supposes that underlying evaluations of a situation (e.g. its desirability, certainty, etc.) combine to elicit specific emotions. This approach may be used to explain how an extensive range of emotions, including those with similar valence and arousal levels, are elicited and how they lead to different behavioural responses. The cognitive approach has been considered relevant for understanding the emotional responses of consumers in the marketplace (Johnson and Stewart, 2005: 3).

Bagozzi (1999) propose that the cognitive appraisals approach offers a more complete explanation of consumers' behavioural responses to emotions than other one. What is apparent from the new learning, however, is that we potentially miss those beliefs and attitudes held at the unconscious or implicit level that can be crucial to determining consumer behaviour. Also the memory that people hold on their consumer experiences will drive both aversion and preference towards products. Aversion behaviour is our avoidance of certain things (brands or marketing offers) made to us as consumers.

The importance of the implicit memory in terms of its capacity to process and store information cannot be understated. The implicit memory registers vast amounts of input from our surrounding environment as we move through life. Millions of experiences that we had throughout our entire lives are stored away in a particular part of our memory system and can be instantly accessed to help us develop an intuitive 'feeling' about what we should, or should not do. The critical issue, however, is that most of the associations that drive intuition reside in the unconscious part of our brain. They are brought into play automatically, and are not the subject of conscious awareness. We can't normally articulate the basis of our intuitions. So consumers often make brand choices intuitively, and cannot tell why they made that choice.

Fishbein's (1967) attitudinal model has also been widely used in the marketing context (Lilien, 1992) [16] and this paradigm provides researchers with a useful lens for examining the factors explaining consumer purchasing intention and adoption. According to this model, behaviour is predominantly determined by intention. Other factors like attitudes, subjective norms and perceived behavioural control also are shown to be related to an appropriate set of salient behavioural, normative and control beliefs about the behaviour.

However, Fishbein's model stops at the adoption level and does not capture other important factors that explain and predict consumer continuance behaviour (repurchase).

The expectation-confirmation model (Oliver, 1980), on the other hand, focuses on the post-purchase behaviour. It is a widely used model in the consumer behaviour literature, particularly in explaining consumer satisfaction and repeat purchase. Satisfaction is the central notion of this model, which is formed by the gap between expectation and perceived performance. The expectation confirmation theory suggests that if the perceived performance meets one's expectation, confirmation is formed and consumers are satisfied.

Bhattacherjee (2001) stated that satisfied users are more likely to continue purchasing the same products.

3.8. Influence of Culture on Consumer Behaviour

As regards cultural it is the main external factors that shape human behaviour. It represents living style, which came into being after adjustments to the environment, people and things through generations. The effect of culture on people's life is so great that it will even affect the motives and choices when consuming or shopping (Chang, 2005).

Otts (1989) defined culture as "All technologies, beliefs, knowledge and fruits that people share and transfer to next generations."

Taylor (1958) believed that culture was everything that an individual learns in society. It is a combination of knowledge, beliefs, arts, morals, laws, customs and any other capabilities.[21] Culture is one of the main factors to determine behaviour. The two external factors (culture and physical environment) and two internal factors (physiological and psychological factors) interact and form the basic factors to determine human behaviour. Culture also

Includes three parts namely culture, subculture and social class. Culture is the most basic deciding factor of human desire and behaviour. Everyone is included in many smaller subculture groups, which provide a clearer sense of identification and social process. Basically, subculture can be divided into four types: nationality groups, religious groups, racial groups and geographical regions. Many subcultures can form some important market segments and provide the decision reference on product designs and marketing campaigns for marketing personnel to serve the demands of consumers (Jen, 1990).

Through the interactions of the group, different people's experience and individual characteristics were combined. During the combination process, individuals would seek someone highly matched to him in order to form a subgroup or small group together. Schein (1985) believed the subgroup could form a common history through a certain time development, by sharing experiences, attitudes, communication methods and individual personalities, and, in doing so, give birth to subculture. The individual life style is affected by the interaction of internal factors such as value and personality characteristics and external factors such as society and culture and also reflects on daily life activities. According to the paradox of personality in marketing, we all have a personality, but we do not know how it is systematically related to our consumer behaviour (Albanese, 1989).

3.8.1. *Psychology of Consumer Behaviour*

Social psychology is another knowledge field that helps to understand consumer behaviour. The social psychology focus on the understanding of individual's behaviour in the presence of other individuals or groups. Concepts such as social perceptions, social influence, social rewards, peer pressure, social cues, social sanctions, etc. all shed light on the mysteries of consumer behaviour. Approaches to understanding consumer behaviour have emphasised external influences on consumption-related acts. The whole idea behind this reasoning is that consumer behaviour takes place within the context of groups and other individuals' presence which influences consumer's processing of information and decision making (Engel . 1968).

Another area of knowledge that has been used to a better understanding of consumer behaviour is the physio-pyschological one. Physiological psychology is the study of the interaction of the body with the mind. It is the study of the extent to which behaviour is caused by physical and chemical phenomena in the body (Morris1996).

Kroeber-Riel (1980) pointed out that cognitive and psychological processes originate from physiological ones. This field holds many promises for explaining consumer behaviour. For instance, the hypothalamus is that center of the brain which mainly controls consumption (Zimbardo and Gerrig 1996). The chemical changes due to the use/eat of the first product results in a blood borne input to the brain to activate further consumption. Thus, the individual would order one more product to use/eat. Such behaviour is explained based on the research findings on the functions of the hypothalamus and other related areas of the brain (Valenstein, 1970; Zhang, 1994) [29&30]

Physio-psychology provides fascinating ways to help understand consumer behaviour without looking into the consumer's "black box" for hypothetically based variable explanations.

To explain consumer behaviour further, new frontiers in science were introduced such as genetics and anthropology (Demirdjian, and Senguder, 2004).

According to genetics approach our genes direct our consumption behaviour. Perhaps humans are all programmed to act in certain ways in their consumptive and consumer-related behaviour. Is the presence of certain genes that compel us to consume certain kind of products? Genetic science may very well come up with definite findings to explain consumer behaviour and thus we may strike a vein of truth in finding explanations and laws of consumer behaviour (Ferber, 1977).

3.8.2. *Business Anthropology in Consumer Behaviour*

Business anthropology and its implementation in consumer behaviour studies have demonstrated to the business world that anthropological approach as new perspective will bring a new era for the consumer science.

The applied anthropologists will become the hottest candidates for business related research jobs given the fact that anthropological methods are becoming more widely acceptable in the business world in general and in consumer studies particular (Demirdjian and Senguder, 2004).

3.8.3. *Consumer Behaviour Attitude*

Attitude is an important factor that influences consumer decision. The concept of attitude is closely related to belief, concept and behaviour. Mowen and Minor (1998) stated that the term consumer attitude formation described relationships among belief, attitude and behaviour. Belief, attitude and behaviour are also related to the concept of product attributes. Product attributes are characteristics of product. Consumers usually have belief toward product attributes. Consumer belief is consumer knowledge about an object, its attributes and benefits (Mowen and Minor, 1998). Therefore consumer knowledge is closely related to the attitude concept.

The traditional Tri-component of attitudes (Schifman and kanuk,2000) described that attitude has three components: cognitive, affective and conative. The cognitive component represents a consumer's knowledge and belief about an object (an object may be a specific branded product, packaging, company or other object). The affective component is a person's feeling about a specific object. The conative component represents an intention to behave towards a specific object.

Andress Hasslinger, Selma Hodzic and Claudio Opazo (2007) have attempted to examine the factors responsible for influencing the behaviour of the consumers. They have identified price, trust and convenience were important factors. Price was considered to be the most important factor for a majority of the consumers. Furthermore, they have three segments such as high spenders, price easers and bargain seekers.

3.9.   Consumer Behaviour Model

Stochastic models of consumer behaviour usually start out by postulating a probability law to represent purchase behaviour at the individual customer level and then aggregating over the customer population by assuming that model parameters of the process follow a certain probability distribution. Lilien (1974) was the first person who undertakes the research studies involving stochastic models which incorporate the effects of marketing mix variables, in which he proposes a modification in the Linear Learning Model to account for differences in consumer responsiveness to premium and regular gasoline brands. He postulates that the probability of choosing the premium brand is the weighted sum of two terms. One term is determined by the Linear Learning Model and the other one is the value of a "price consciousness function" which is determined by the difference between the retail prices of the premium brand and the regular brands. To account for heterogeneity he assumes that the weight and the initial choice probability of the Linear learning Model follow a Beta Distribution over the population.

Leeflang and Boonstra (1982) generalise this model to include any number of decision variables. However, they find that the parameter estimation for their model is very cumbersome. Thus they conclude that ". . . the application (of Linear Learning Models) will become extremely difficult when controllable marketing variables are included through the development of the modified Linear Learning Models. The development of models which represent the effect of controllable marketing variables in some more parsimonious manner seems worthy of future re-search".

According to Sadaomi Oshikawa (1969), Cognitive dissonance theory is applicable to very limited areas of consumer behaviour. He also provides suggestions regarding the circumstances under which dissonance reduction may be useful in increasing the repurchase probability of a purchased brand.

Previous research has demonstrated this value construct to be cognitively separate but functionally related to an individual's system of global values and descriptive and evaluative beliefs.

Concept in the marketing is to deal with understanding the buyer behaviour. The attitude of Indian consumers has undergone a major transformation over the last few years. The Indian consumer today wants to lead a life full of luxury and comfort. He wants to live in present and does not believe in savings for the future. An important and recent development in India"s consumerism is the emergence of the rural market for several basic consumer goods.

The Indian middle class has provided a big boost to the consumer culture during the recent past and it is hoped that their buying behaviour will continue to change in the coming future. Due to fast growth of the services sector per capita income of people of India is also increasing. The number of middle class is increasing due to another fact that people are fast shifting from agriculture to the services and industry sector where growth prospects are reasonably high as compared to the agriculture sector which is showing slow growth. The consumption pattern of a country depends on liberalization of economic policies, buying habits of the younger generation, financial independence at a young age, increase in number of nuclear families and increase in media exposure of the people. The tastes and preferences of the current generation are changing rapidly. The current generation does not mind paying extra for better facilities and ambience. Another major factor that has led to increased consumerism is the growth of credit culture in India. The Indian consumer does not feel shy to purchase products on credit and pay tomorrow for what they use or buy today. This tendency has led to a tremendous increase in purchase of homes, cars, two-wheelers and consumer goods. The market for luxury products in India is also climbing at an astonishing rate as compared to a decade ago when it was almost negligible. The reason behind this is that the purchasing power of people of India is rising very steeply. The Indian consumer today is highly aware about the product, price, quality and the options available with him. The purchasing is done by keeping all these factors in mind. Today, price is not the only consideration as it was a few years back when prices played a major role in purchasing. Marketers are trying hard to capture this ever increasing Indian middle class as they form the bulk of Indian consumers.

To manage the post-purchase stage, the marketing team must convince the potential customer that the product will live up to the benefit offerings made and so the sales people must never 'over-promise' and so build too high expectations to obtain the sale. The customer should be constantly reassured that he or she has made the right decision both during and after the sale. Excellent products, quality processes and skilled staff with a deep knowledge of human nature will help overcome these problems. It's a fact of life that a unsatisfied customer will tell many others, a satisfied customer just a few.

- Small levels of difficulty–very simple routine evaluation processes, for example buying the weekly groceries. Problem-solving difficulties can vary even at this level according to whether the purchase is on impulse, a product or brand perhaps not bought before or the use of a different supermarket.

- Medium levels of difficulty–this involves the purchase of relatively expensive products or services that are only needed occasionally, e.g. new refrigerator, carpet or three-piece suit. Consumer involvement level will vary according to such things as to whether it is a known brand or not, more features on offer and the price levels under consideration.

- High levels of difficulty–high expenditure, high emotional risk, high stress levels, e.g. buying a house, a car or making long-term large money investments. High-quality, reassuring information is needed on a constant basis, overcoming objections, countering competition offerings and spelling out benefit offering and default safeguards.

3.10. Sales Promotion

Sales Promotion is the activity that aims directly to influence buyers to buy products and increase sales. In sales promotion mainly three parties are involved i.e. consumers, traders and sales force. Sales promotion refers to many kinds of incentives and techniques that are directed towards consumers, traders and sales force with the intention to increase sales in short term.

"Sales promotions include incentive offering and interest creating activities which are generally short term marketing events other than advertising, personal selling, publicity and direct marketing. The purpose of sales promotion is to stimulate, motivate and influence the purchase and other desired behavioural responses of the firm's customers".[40]

Sales promotion offers a direct inducement to act by providing extra worth over and above what is built into the product at its normal price. These temporary inducements are offered usually at a time and place where the buying decision is made. Not only are sales promotions very common in the current competitive market conditions, they are increasing at a fast pace. These promotions are direct inducements. In spite of the directness, sales promotions are fairly complicated and a rich tool of marketing with innumerable creative possibilities limited only by the imagination of promotion planners. Sales promotion is often referred to by the names of 'extra purchase value' and 'below-the-line selling'.

The main objective of sales promotion is to increase the sales of products in short term by influencing behaviour of buyers. Sales promotion methods are many and these are selected as per the target groups. For this purpose, a sales promotion strategy is to be prepared to achieve the objectives effectively. The strategy is a game plan that is needed to perform the tasks effectively and get competitive advantages over others in market. Sales promotion strategy directs the manager in selection of parties, methods of sales promotion, implementation of methods and measuring effectiveness of whole efforts regarding sales promotion. In competitive situation, it is very difficult to increase sales or profit. But with sales promotion strategy sales can be increased in short–term. Strategy is the game plan to achieve the targets as per planning. It explains what, when, where, who and how to do, so that objectives of the planning are achieved. Without the strategy the task may not be completed effectively. Sales promotion strategy would help to neutralize the effect of competition and defend the company in the market in performing the sales related tasks. The importance of sales promotion strategy is increasing day by day and in future higher level of competition, it would increase further.

Indian industry is a fast developing industry. Fast Moving Consumer Goods (FMCG) are more in demand and frequently purchased by customers. These goods include all consumable goods (other than pulses and grains) and consumers buy at regular intervals in small quantities. Main items in this category are detergents, soaps, shaving products, shampoos, toothpastes and brushes, packed food stuffs, household accessories, creams, oils, tea, coffee, etc. Every family spends a large portion of monthly budget on FMCG products. Contribution of FMCG sector in every economy is significant. Now, due to globalisation, every economy is facing tough competition. Entries of MNCs and cheaper import have made the situation more difficult. To carry out the business in this sector, it has become very difficult. Every company has to spend a large portion of their budget on promotional efforts.

3.10.1. Objectives of Sales Promotion

3.10.1.1.To introduce new products and to acquaint the customers how to use the Product.

3.10.1.2.To acquaint the customers about the utility of the product.

3.10.1.3. To effect spot buying and to attract new customers.

3.10.1.4.To increase sales during slack periods and to increase profits of the firm.

3.10.1.5.To improve the public image/goodwill of the firm.

3.10.2. The Important Sales Promotion Methods are

3.10.2.1 Distribution of Free Samples

Distribution of free samples is an expensive but powerful tool of sales promotion used to gain consumer acceptance and to popularise the product. It is an effective device of sales promotion as the consumers can test the product before buying it. The sample may be delivered door to door, offered in retail stores or fairs. This device is suitable for introducing new products such as soaps, drugs, cosmetics, perfumes, tea, cooking oil, etc.

3.10.2.2 Coupons

Coupon is a certificate that entitles its holder to a specified saving or discount on the purchase of a particular product. The customers present their coupons to retailers and get the product at a much reduced price. Coupons may be issued by the manufacturers either directly by mail or through the dealers. They are also issued through newspapers and magazines.

3.10.2.3 Premium

Premium is the offer of an article free of cost or at a nominal price on the purchase of a specified product. It helps to increase the immediate sales.

3.10.2.4 Trading or Bonus Stamps

Trading or bonus stamps are issued by retailers to customers who buy goods from them and its purpose is to increase customer loyalty. The number of stamps given to a buyer depends upon the amount of purchases made by him.

3.10.2.5 Point of Purchase Materials

Point of purchase materials includes banners, signs, photos, posters and other in-store promotional tools. They are demonstrated or displayed at the place where the customer makes actual purchases as they remind them about the brand name and promote impulsive buying.

3.10.2.6 Price Contests

Under price contests, consumers are given rewards for analytical or creative thinking about the products in the form of slogan writing, sentence completion, problem solving quiz, etc. It helps to create consumers' interest in the products, provide new ideas for advertising and may reveal buying motives.

3.10.2.7 Trade Fairs and Exhibition

Trade fairs and exhibitions are an important technique of sales promotion as they have wide appeal .These helps in introducing the firms and their products to the public at large. Under this, business firms are allotted stalls wherein they display or demonstrate their products.

3.10.2.8 Merchandising Aids

Merchandising aids refer to the services provided to induce commercial buyers to purchase goods in large quantities. It includes training in stores layout and inventory control, advertising, product demonstration, etc.

3.10.2.9 Clearance Sale

Clearance sale at reduced prices may be organised on important festivals or other occasions. (Ex. Discounts in the Tamil month of Aadi). Such sales attract a large number of customers and help to clear accumulated stocks.

3.10.2.10   Freebies

Freebies are free samples that companies give away to interest consumers in their products. Unlike sweepstakes, receiving freebies is not a matter of luck; as long as supplies last, every qualified person who requests a freebie will get one. Freebies might include printable board games, sample-sized beauty lotions, mini boxes of cereal and much more.

3.10.3. Consumer Sales Promotion Techniques

3.10.3.1 Price deal: A temporary reduction in the price, such as 50% off.

3.10.3.2 Loyal Reward Program: Consumers collect points, miles or credits for purchases and redeem them for rewards.

3.10.3.3 Cents-off deal: Offers a brand at a lower price. Price reduction may be a percentage marked on the package.

3.10.3.4 Price-pack deal: The packaging offers a consumer a certain percentage more of the product for the same price (for example, 25 percent extra).

3.10.3.5 Coupons: Coupons have become a standard mechanism for sales promotions.

3.10.3.6 Loss Leader: the price of a popular product is temporarily reduced in order to stimulate other profitable sales

3.10.3.7 Free-standing insert (FSI): A coupon booklet is inserted into the local newspaper for delivery.

3.10.3.8 On-shelf couponing: Coupons are present at the shelf where the product is available.

3.10.3.9 Checkout dispensers: On checkout the customer is given a coupon based on products purchased.

3.10.3.10   On-line couponing: Coupons are available online. Consumers print them out and take them to the store.

3.10.3.11   Mobile couponing: Coupons are available on a mobile phone. Consumers show the offer on a mobile phone to a salesperson for redemption.

3.10.3.12   Online interactive promotion game: Consumers play an interactive game associated with the promoted product.

3.10.3.13   Rebates: Consumers are offered money back if the receipt and barcode are mailed to the producer.

3.10.3.14   Contests/sweepstakes/games: The consumer is automatically entered into the event by the product.

3.10.4. Point-of-sale Displays

3.10.4.1.   Aisle interrupter: A sign that juts into the aisle from the shelf.

3.10.4.2.   Dangler: A sign that sways when a consumer walks by it.

3.10.4.3.   Dump bin: A bin full of products dumped inside.

3.10.4.4.   Glorifier: A small stage that elevates a product above other products.

3.10.4.5.   Wobblers: A sign that jiggles.

3.10.4.6.   Lipstick Board: A board on which messages are written in crayon.

3.10.4.7.   Necker: A coupon placed on the 'neck' of a bottle.

3.10.4.8.   YES unit: "your extra salesperson" is a pull-out fact-sheet

3.10.4.9.   Electroluminescent: Solar-powered, animated light in motion.

3.10.5. Electroluminescent Point of Purchase Signs

3.10.5.1.Kids eat free specials: Offers a discount on the total dining bill by offering 1 free kid's meal with each regular meal purchased.

3.10.6. Trade Sales Promotion Techniques

3.10.6.1.Trade allowances: Short term incentive offered to induce a retailer to stock up on a product.

3.10.6.2.Dealer loader: An incentive given to induce a retailer to purchase and display a product.

3.10.6.3.Trade contest: A contest to reward retailers that sell the most products.

3.10.6.4.Point-of-purchase displays: Used to create the urge of "impulse" buying and selling your product on the spot.

3.10.6.5.Training programs: Dealer employees are trained in selling the product.

3.10.6.6.Push money: also known as "spliffs". An extra commission paid to retail employees to push products.

3.10.6.7.Trade discounts (also called functional discounts): These are payments to distribution channel members for performing some function.

3.10.6.8.Retail Mechanics

Retailers have a stock number of retail 'mechanics' that they regularly roll out or rotate for new marketing initiatives.

- Buy x get y free a.k.a. BOGOF for Buy One Get One Free
- Three for two
- Buy a quantity for a lower price.

3.11. Political Issues

Sales promotions have traditionally been heavily regulated in many advanced industrial nations, with the notable exception of the United States. For example, the United Kingdom formerly operated under a resale price maintenance regime in which manufacturers could legally dictate the minimum resale price for virtually all goods; this practice was abolished in 1964. Most European countries also have controls on the scheduling and permissible types of sales promotions, as they are regarded in those countries as bordering upon unfair business practices. Germany is notorious for having the strictest regulations. Famous examples include the car wash that was barred from giving free car washes to regular customers and a baker who could not give a free cloth bag to customers who bought more than 10 rolls.

3.12. Sales Promotion Strategies

There are three types of sales promotion strategies: *Push*, *Pull*, or a *combination* of the two. A push strategy involves convincing trade intermediary channel members to "push" the product through the distribution channels to the ultimate consumer via promotions and personal selling efforts. The company promotes the product through a reseller who in turn promotes it to yet another reseller or the final consumer. Trade-promotion objectives are to persuade retailers or wholesalers to carry a brand, give a brand shelf space, promote a brand in advertising and/or push a brand to final consumers. Typical tactics employed in push strategy are: allowances, buy-back guarantees, free trials, contests, specialty advertising items, discounts, displays and premiums.

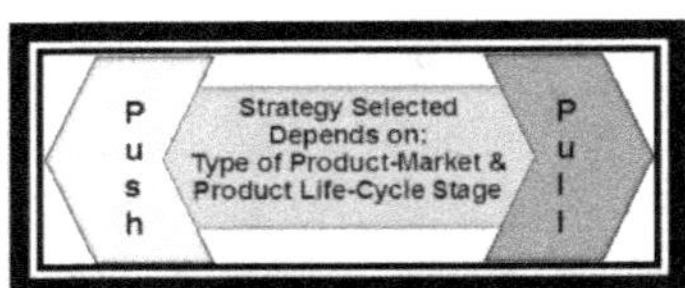

Figure 3.7: Push and Pull Strategy

A pull strategy attempts to get consumers to "pull" the product from the manufacturer through the marketing channel. The company focuses its marketing communications efforts on consumers in the hope that it stimulates interest and demand for the product at the end-user level. This strategy is often employed if distributors are reluctant to carry a product because it gets as many consumers as possible to go to retail outlets and request the product, thus pulling it through the channel. Consumer-promotion objectives are to entice consumers to try a new product, lure customers away from competitors' products, got consumers to "load up" on a mature product, hold & reward loyal customers and build consumer relationships. Typical tactics employed in pull strategy are: samples, coupons, cash refunds and rebates, premiums, advertising specialties, loyalty programs/patronage rewards, contests, sweepstakes, games and point-of-purchase (POP) displays.

Car dealers often provide a good example of a combination strategy. If you pay attention to car dealers' advertising, you will often hear them speak of cash-back offers and dealer incentives. The ratio of sales promotion and advertising in 1940 is 40:60 Growth in sales promotion since 1940 is 9% and growth in advertising is 6%.

3.13. Sales Promotion: Advantages & Disadvantages

The main advantages associated with promotional sales are an easy way to learn customer response and it work fast. It is also an inexpensive marketing technique. Sales promotion does not always bring positive impact to business, sometime this type of promotion cause negative brand impact to customers mind in the long-term.

So, a promotional campaign needs to be designed taking into account the consequences of losing brand value. A PIMS study of 1991 suggests that overuse of sales promotion brings low ROI, almost 15% less, in comparison to balanced and calculated promotional offers. It is advisable not to use sales promotion as a tool of brand imaging; advertising is always the best way as far as branding is concerned. So, marketers need to be careful and must understand the difference between the sales promotion and advertising.

3.14. Promotion and Monetary Savings

Are monetary savings the only explanation for consumer response to a sales promotion?

According to Pierre Chandon, Brain Wansink (2000), there are monetary and non monetary promotions provide consumers with different levels of three hedonic benefits (opportunities for value-expression, entertainment and exploration), and three utilitarian benefits (savings, higher product quality and improved shopping convenience). They have also described that for high-equity brands, monetary promotions are more effective for utilitarian products than for hedonic products.

According to Buzzell, Quelch and Salmon (1990), marketers and academics often view the reliance on sales promotions, especially monetary promotions, as a sub-optimal consequence of price competition caused by myopic management.

According to Abraham and Lodish (1990) and Kahn and McAlister (1997), in the short-run, the proliferation of monetary promotions erodes their capacity to rent market share, which explains why so many are unprofitable.

According to Mela Gupta and Lehman (1997), in the long run, it is feared that sales promotions increase price sensitivity and destroy brand equity-both with retailers and consumers. As a result, many industry experts are calling for more effective and cost-efficient promotions that rely less on price (Promotion Marketing Association of America 1994) and some go so far as to recommend eliminating most promotions by switching to an everyday-low-price policy (Kahn and McAlister 1997; Lal and Rao 1997).

3.14.1. Promotion and Consumption

Emerging literature in behavioural and economic theory has provided supporting evidence that consumption for some product categories responds to promotion. Using an experimental approach, Wansink (1996) establishes that significant holding costs pressure consumers to consume more of the product. There are some recent empirical papers addressing the promotion effect on consumer Stock piling behaviour under price or promotion uncertainty.

3.14.2. Sales Promotion and Consumer Response/Preference

Consumer promotions are now more pervasive than ever. Witness 215 billion manufacturer coupons distributed in 1986, up 500% in the last decade (Manufacturers Coupon Control Center 1988) and manufacturer expenditures on trade incentives to feature or display brands totaling more than $20 billion in the same year, up 800% in the last decade.

3.15. Conclusion

From the above theoretical perspective, we will be able to know about the importance of studying consumer behaviour and sales promotion effectiveness.

References

[1]   R.L. Sandhusen, "Marketing", 2000. Cf. S. 218,219 ("http://en.wikipedia.org/w/index.php?title=Consumer_behaviour&oldid=453 453142335" on 30 September 2011 at 01:17.)

[2]   http://www.newagepublishers.com

[3]   W.D. Hoyer and Deborah J. Macinnis, "consumer behavior", Fifth edition mason, ohio: south-western cengage Learning, Pp. 13-16, 2010.

[4]   J. Howard and J.N. Sheth, "Theory of Buyer Behavior", J. Wiley & Sons, New York, NY, 1968.

[5]   http://www.consumer psychologist.com/

[6]   http://www.edms.matrade.gov.my/...nsf/.../ (October 2005: product market study)

[7]   Paul Allen Smethers and Alaistair France in the deep business intelligence analysis project titled "Five myths of consumer behaviour: Create technology product consumers will love"

[8]   D.I. Hawkins, R.J. Best and K.A. Coney, "Consumer Behaviour: Building Marketing Strategy", Boston, Massachusetts: Irwin McGraw-Hill, 2003.

[9]   L.G. Schiffman, and L.L. Kanuk, "Comportamento do Consumidor", 6ª Edição.Rio de Janeiro: Editorial LTC, 2000.

[10]   L.A. Hudson and J.L. Ozanne, "Alternative Ways of seeking Knowledge in Consumer Research", Journal of Consumer Research, Vol. 14, No. 4, Pp. 508-521, 1988.

[11]   H.H.Kassarjian, "Some Recollections from a Quarter Century Ago", Advances in Consumer Research, 1995.

[12]   L. Watson and M.T. Spence, "Causes and consequences of emotions on consumer behaviour A review and integrative theory cognitive appraisal", European Journal of Marketing, Vol. 41, No. 5, Pp. 587-511, 2007.

[13]   A.R. Johnson and D.W. Stewart, "A reappraisal of the role of emotion in consumer behaviour: traditional and contemporary approaches", Malhotra, N.K. (Ed.), Review of Marketing Research, Vol. 1, Pp. 3-33, 2005.

[14]   R.P. Bagozzi, M. Gopinath and P.U. Nyer, "The role of emotions in marketing", Journal of the Academy of Marketing Science, Vol. 27, No. 2, Pp. 184-206, 1999.

[15]   M. Fishbein, "Attitude and prediction of behaviour", M.Fishbein (Ed.), Readings in attitude theory and measurement, Pp. 477-492, 1967.

[16]   G.L. Lilien, K. Philip and M.K. Sridhar, "Marketing Models", New Jersey: Prentice Hall, 1992.

[17]   R.L. Oliver, "A cognitive model for the antecedents and consequences of satisfaction", Journal of Marketing Research, Vol. 17, Pp. 460-469, 1980.

[18]   A. Bhattacherjee, "Understanding information systems continuance: An expectation confirmation model", MIS Quarterly, Vol. 25, No. 3, Pp. 351-370, 2001.

[19]   L.C. Chang, "The Study of Subculture and Consumer Behaviour: An Example of Taiwanese University Students Consumption Culture", Journal of American Academy of Business, Cambridge. Hollywood, Vol. 7, No. 2, Pp. 258-265, 2005.

[20]   J.S. Otts, "The organizational culture perspective", Chicago: Dorsey Press, 1989.

[21]   E.B. Tylor, "Primitive culture", New York: Harper, 1958.

[22]   Y. Jen, "Culture and self: perspectives of easterners and westerners", first edition, Taipei, Yuen-Liu Press Co., Ltd, 1990.

[23]   E.H. Schein, "Organizational culture and leadership: A dynamic view", San Francisco, CA: Jossey-Bass, 1985.

[24]   P.J. Albanese, "The Paradox of Personality in Marketing: A New Approach to the Problem", Bloom, P. et al. (Eds), Enhancing Knowledge Development in Marketing, American Marketing Association, Chicago, IL, Pp. 245-249, 1989.

[25]   J.F. Engel, D.T. Kollat and R.D. Blackwell, "Consumer Behavior", Holt, Rinehart and Winston, 1968.

[26]   C.G. Morris, "Psychology: An Introduction", Upper Saddle River, New Jersey: Prentice Hall, 1996.

[27]   Werner Kroeber-Riel, "Konsumentenverhalten", second Edition, Vahlen, Munchen, Germany, 1980.

[28]   P. Zimbardo and R.J. Gerrig, "Psychology and Life", New York, N.Y.: Harper Collins College Publishers, 1996.

[29]   E.V. Valenstein, Cox and J. Kakolewski, "Reexamination of the Role of the Hypothalamus in Motivation", Psychological Review, Vol. 77, Pp. 16-31, 1970.

[30]   Y.R. Zhang, M. Proenca, M. Maffel, L.L. Barone and J. Friedman, "Positional Cloning of the Mouse Obese Gene and Its Human Homologue", Nature, Vol. 372, Pp. 425-432, 1994.

[31]   Z.S. Demirdjian and T. Senguder, "Perspectives in Consumer Behaviour: Paradigm Shifts in Prospect", Journal of American Academy of Business, Cambridge, Vol. 4, No. ½, Pp. 348-356, 2004.

[32]   R. Ferber, "Selected Aspects of Consumer Behaviour: A Summary from the Perspective of Different Disciplines", Washington: U.S. Government Printing Office, 1997.

[33]   J.C. Mowen and M. Minor, "Consumer behaviour", 5th edition page, New Jersey: prentice hall, 1998.

[34]   L.J. Schiffman and L.L. Kanuk, "consumer behaviour", 7th edition page-144 New Jersey: prentice hall, 2000.

[35]   Andress Hasslinger, Selma Hodzic & Claudio Opazo, "Consumer behaviour in shopping", working paper number:11(26), Department of Business studies, Kristianstad university, Sweeden, Pp. 16-19, 2007.

[36]   G.L. Lilien, "Application of a Modified Linear Learning Model of Buyer Behavior", Journal of Marketing Research, Vol. 11, Pp. 279-285, 1974.

[37]   P.S. Leeflang & Anne Boonstra, "Some Comments on the Development and Application of Linear Learning Models", Management Science, Vol. 28, Pp. 1233-1246, 1982.

[38]   Sadaomi Oshikawa, "Can Cognitive Dissonance Theory Explain Consumer Behavior?", Journal of Marketing, Vol. 33, No. 4, Pp. 44-49, 1969.

[39]   Wright 01381_1844 refer

[40]   B. Kazmi, "Advertising & Sales Promotion", 1st Edition, Excel Books, New Delhi, 2007.

[41]   Stuart Mitchell, "Resale price maintenance and the character of resistance in the conservative party: 1949-64", Canadian Journal of History, Vol. 40, No. 2, Pp. 259-289, 2005.

[42]   P. Kotler, "Marketing management analysis planning and Control", 9th Ed prentice hall, Englewood cliffs, Pp. 122-175, 1967.

[43]   Anonymous, "Handcuffs on the high street", The Economist 355, no. 8170 62, 2000.

[44]   Pierre Chandon and Brian Wansink, "A benefit congruency framework of sales promotion effectiveness", Journal of Marketing, 2000.

[45]   Robert Buzzell, John Quelch and Walter Salmon, "The Costly Bargain of Trade Promotion", Harvard Business Review, Pp. 141-149, 1990.

[46]   M.M. A braham, and L.M. Lodish, "Getting the Most out of Advertising and Promotion", Harvard Business Review, Pp. 50-63, 1990.

[47]   C.F. Mela, Sunil Gupta and Donald R. Lehmann, "The Long-Term Impact of Promotion and Advertising on Consumer Brand Choice", Journal of Marketing Research, Vol. 34, Pp. 248-261, 1997.

[48]   Promotion Marketing Association of America, Inc (1994), Winning with Promotion Power: The Reggie Awards Winners. Ravenswood, IL: Dartnell Corporation.

[49]   Kahn and Leigh McAlister, Grocery Revolution, "The New Focus on the Consumer-Reading", Massachusetts: Addison-Wesley, 1997.

[50]   Brian Wansink, "Does package size accelerate usage volume?", J. Marketing, Pp. 601–614, 1996.

CHAPTER IV

SOCIO-ECONOMIC PROFILE AND BEHAVIOUR OF THE CONSUMERS-AN ANALYSIS

4.1. Definition of Demographic Factors

Socio economic characteristic of a population expressed statistically, such as age, sex, income level, marital status, occupation, religion, birth rate, death rate, average size of a family, average age at marriage. A census is a collection of the demographic factors associated with every member of a population.

4.1.1. Meaning of Demographic Factors

Demographics are the quantifiable statistics of a given population. Demographics are also used to identify the study of quantifiable subsets within a given population which characterise that population at a specific point of time. These types of data are used widely in public opinion polling and marketing. Commonly examined demographics include gender, age and ethnicity, knowledge of languages, disabilities, mobility, home ownership, employment status and even location. *Demographic trends* describe the historical changes in demographics in a population over time (for example, the average age of a population may increase or decrease over time). Both distributions and trends of values within a demographic variable are of interest. Demographics are essential on the population of a region and the culture of the people there.

4.1.2. Demographic Profiles in Marketing

Marketers typically combine several variables to define a demographic profile. A demographic profile (often shortened to "a demographic") provides enough information about the typical member of this group to create a mental picture of this hypothetical aggregate. For example, a marketer might speak of the single, female, middle-class, *age 18 to 24*, college educated demographic.

Researchers typically have two objectives in this regard: first to determine what segments or subgroups exist in the overall population; secondly to create a clear and complete picture of the characteristics of a member of each segment. Once these profiles are constructed, they can be used to develop a marketing strategy and marketing plan. The five types of demographics for marketing are age, gender, income level, race and ethnicity.

4.1.3. *Demographic Indicators*

Age and Gender: Age is an important factor used by all for role assignments *(Elizabeth B. Hurlock 1974)*. It is an important symbol of self. To create the impression of identity and belongingness, people make use a few symbols of age such as appearance, degree of autonomy and activities engaged in *(Lundberg 1958)*. Thus age is an important acquired status which influences on the socio-economic and cultural behaviour of an individual. Similarly 'gender' is an important ascribed factor which determines the status, roles and responsibilities of an individual in the family, community and society and on the socio-economic and cultural behaviour.

Table 4.1: Gender of the Respondents

Gender	Rural	Urban	Total
Male	132 (36.67%)	78 (21.67%)	210 (29.17%)
Female	228 (63.33%)	282 (78.33%)	510 (70.83%)
Total	360(100%)	360 (100%)	720(100%)

Table 4.1 reveals the gender of rural and urban respondents. From the above table, it was evident that among gender of the respondents, women were the decision makers in the majority of the family both in rural and urban areas. In urban areas more than 78 percent of the women are decision makers in purchasing cooking oil, whereas, in rural areas more than 63 percent of the women were decision makers in purchasing cooking oil. Only 36.67 percent of male in rural areas and 21.67 percent of male in urban areas were the decision makers in purchasing cooking oil. Overall 70.83 percent of the female respondents were decision makers in purchasing cooking oil and only 29.17 percent of male respondents involved in the decision of purchasing cooking oil. The following chart 4.1 will graphically explain the above table.

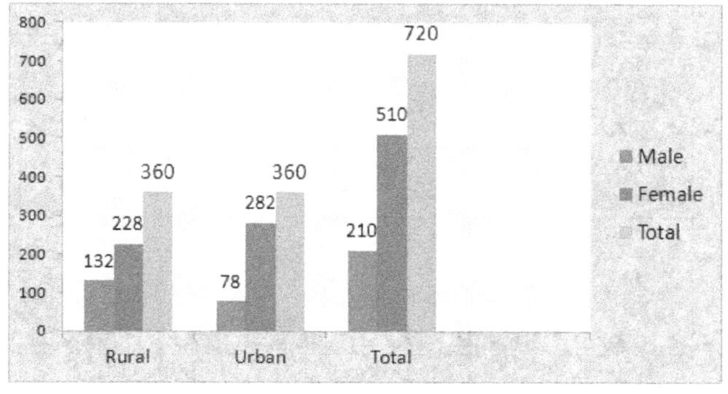

Chart 4.1: Gender of Rural and Urban Respondents

Table 4.2: Age of the Respondents

Age	Rural	Urban	Total
Below 30 years	27 (7.5)	31 (8.61)	58 (8.05)
31 to 40 years	109 (30.28)	136 (37.78)	245 (34.03)
41- 50 years	205 (56.94)	163 (45.28)	368 (51.11)
Above 50 years	19 (5.28)	30 (8.33)	49 (6.81)
Total	360 (100)	360 (100)	720 (100)

Table 4.2 presents the age of the rural and urban respondents. From the table, it was inferred that majority (51.11 percent) of the respondents fall between the age category of 41-50 years, followed 31-40 years (34.03 percent). The percent of respondent's falls below the age of 30 years is 8.05 percent and above 50 years is 6.81 percent. In rural area 56.94 percent of the respondents fall between the age category of 41-50 years whereas, in urban areas 45.28 percent of the respondents fall between the age category of 41-50 years.

In urban areas 37.78 percent of the respondents and in rural areas 30.28 percent of the respondents were in the age category of 31-40 years. In urban areas 8.61 percent of the respondents and in rural areas 7.5 percent of the respondents were below the age of 30 years. In urban areas 8.33 percent of the respondents and in rural areas 5.28 percent of the respondents were above the age of 50 years. The following chart 4.2 graphically explains the age of the respondents.

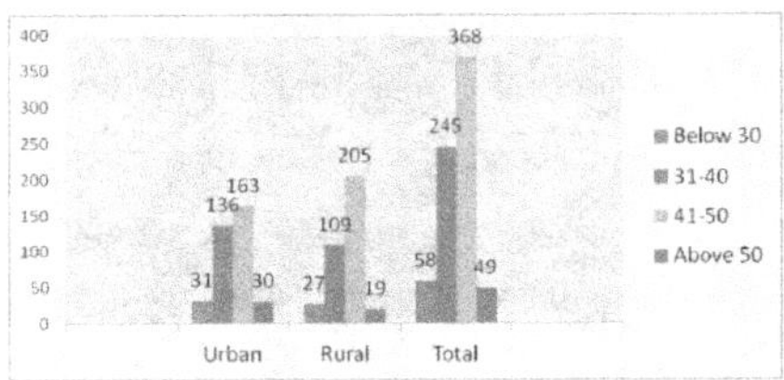

Chart 4.2: Age of Urban and Rural Respondents

Table 4.3: Age and Gender of Rural and Urban Respondents

| Age Category | Rural | | | Urban | | | Grand Total |
	Male	Female	Total (I)	Male	Female	Total (ii)	(I+II)
Below 30 years	8	19	27	13	18	31	58
31 to 40 years	46	63	109	29	107	136	245
41- 50 years	71	134	205	27	136	163	368
Above 50 years	7	12	19	9	21	30	49
Total	132	228	360	78	282	360	720
Mean Age	42.82	43.76	43.04	42.67	42.33	42.61	

Table 4.3 reveals the gender and age of the respondents. The table shows that mean age of male rural respondents were 42.82 percent and female rural respondents were 43.76 percent and overall average was 43.04 percent. The mean age of male urban respondents was 42.67 percent and female urban respondents were 42.33 percent and overall average was 42.61 percent. The following chart 4.3 will explain the age and gender of rural and urban respondents statistically.

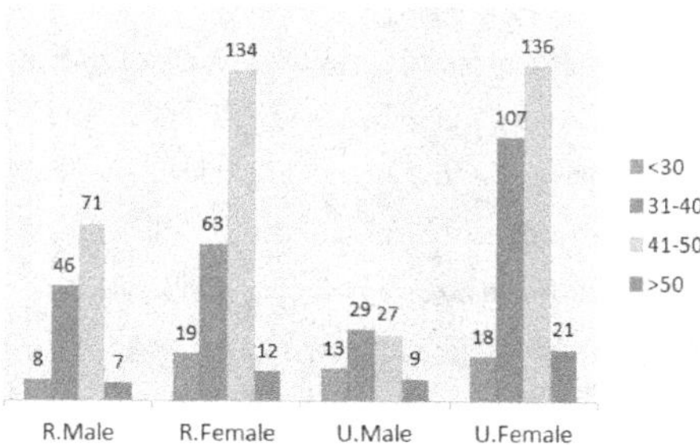

Chart 4.3: Age and Gender of Rural and Urban Respondents

4.2. Level of Education

Education is one of the primary needs of all human societies *(Sumner and Keller 1946, Ghosh 1987, Debrata Das 2002)*. Education is the social process by which an individual learns the necessary things to fit him or her in the society. It is synonymous to socialisation. So far, in the study respondents were identified on the basis of their level of formal education such as primary, secondary, collegiate and professional education and those who did not have formal education were termed as illiterates.

Table 4.4: Educational Status of the Respondents

Category	No. of. Respondents		
Education level	Rural (N=360)	Urban (N=360)	Total (N=720)
Illiterate	10 (2.78)	2 (0.55)	12 (1.67)
Primary Level	35 (9.72)	26 (7.22)	61 (8.47)
Secondary level	49 (13.61)	68 (18.89)	117 (16.25)
Higher secondary	87 (24.17)	54 (15)	141 (19.58)
Diploma / ITI	36 (10)	17 (4.73)	53 (7.36)
Higher Education (UG/ PG)	107 (29.72)	190 (52.78)	297 (41.25)
Professional Education	36(10)	3 (0.83)	39 (5.42)
Mean average	3.4111	1.6583	2.0200

Table 4.4 reveals the education of the respondents. From the table, it was inferred that majority of the respondents (41.25 percent) finished their higher education i.e. Graduate or Post Graduate. 19.58 percent of the respondents finished their higher secondary,16.25 percent of respondents finished SSLC and 8.47 percent of the respondents finished only the primary level education. 7.36 percent of the respondents were diploma or I.T.I holders. 5.42 percent of the respondents completed their professional degree. Only 1.67 percent of the respondents were illiterate. 52.78 percent of the urban respondents and 29.72 percent of the rural respondents finished their higher education (Graduate or Post Graduate). 24.17 percent of the rural respondents and 15 percent of the urban respondents finished their higher secondary education (+2). 18.89 percent of the urban respondents and 13.61 percent of the rural respondents finished their secondary level education (SSLC). 10 percent of the rural respondents and 4.73 percent of the urban respondents were diploma or I.T.I holders. 10 percent of the rural respondents and 0.83 percent of the urban respondents completed their professional degree (either doctor or lawyer or teacher or auditor.etc). 9.72 percent of the rural respondents and 7.22 percent of urban respondents completed only their primary level education. 2.78 percent of the rural respondents and 0.55 percent of the urban respondents were illiterate. The educational mean average of rural respondents was 3.4111 and an urban respondent was 1.6583.

The following chart 4.4 shows the educational qualifications of the respondents.

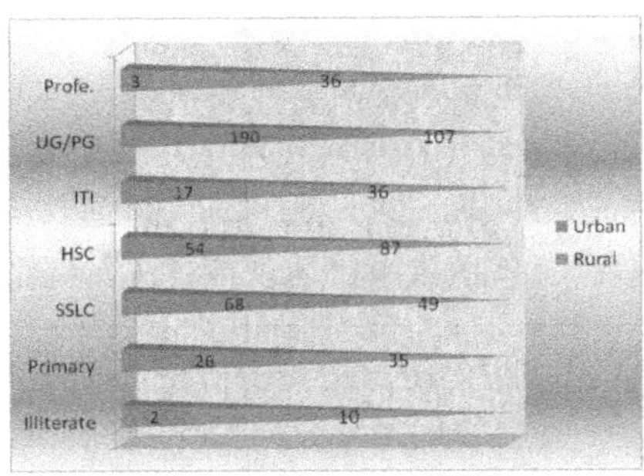

Chart 4.4: Educational Status of the Respondents

4.3. Community

In the social hierarchy next to religion, community forms the major aspects. Community touches everything today. It decides one's health, wealth, occupation, social and economic behaviour and the status. It exerts greater influence on the perception of an individual towards the objects *(Ghurye 1950)*. An attempt is made to find out any significant difference in behaviour based on community between the respondents.

Table 4.5: Community of the Respondents

| Category | No. of. Respondents | | |
Community	Rural (N=360)	Urban (N=360)	Total (N=720)
OC	13 (3.61)	14 (3.89)	27 (3.75)
BC	165 (45.83)	176 (48.89)	341 (47.36)
MBC	115 (31.95)	133 (36.94)	248 (34.44)
SC/ST	67 (18.61)	37 (10.28)	104 (14.45)
Mean average	2.6556	2.5361	

Table 4.5 illustrates the community of the respondents. From the table, it was clear that majority of the respondents (47.36 percent) belong to backward class and 34.44 percent of the respondents belong to most backward class category. 14.45 percent of the respondents belong to SC or ST category and only 3.75 percent of the respondents come under the open category. 48.89 percent of the urban respondents and 45.83 percent of the rural respondents belong to backward class category. 36.94 percent of the urban respondents and 31.95 percent of the rural respondents belong to most backward class category. 18.61 percent of the rural respondents and 10.28 percent of the urban respondents belongs to SC/ST category. 3.89 percent of the urban respondents and 3.61 percent of the rural respondents belong to open category. The mean average of community was 2.6556 and 2.5361 for rural and urban respondents respectively.

The following chart 4.5 shows the community of the rural and urban respondents.

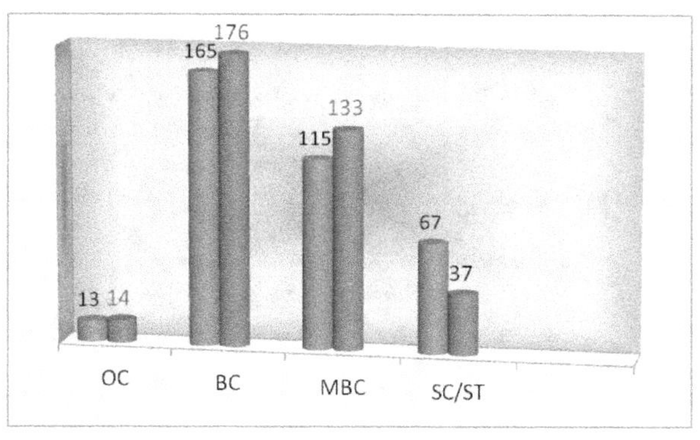

Chart 4.5: Community of the Rural and Urban Respondents

4.4. Religion

Religion refers to belief and reverence for a supernatural power or powers regarded as creator and governor of the universe. Religion is a personal or institutionalised system grounded in such belief and work ship. Religion is set of beliefs, values, and practices based on the teachings of a spiritual leader. It is a cause, principle or activity pursued with zeal or conscientious devotion.

Table 4.6: Religious Status of Respondents

Category	No. of. Respondents		
Religion	Rural (N=360)	Urban (N=360)	Total (N=720)
Hindu	186 (51.67)	187 (51.94)	373 (51.80)
Muslim	70 (19.44)	94 (26.11)	164 (22.78)
Christian	104 (28.89)	79 (21.95)	183 (25.42)
Mean average	1.7722	1.7000	

** Chi-square value between religions and of the respondents is 10.325 which is not significant at 00.001 level*

Table 4.6 portrays the religion followed by the respondents. From the table, it was evident that majority of the respondents (51.80 percent) were Hindus. 25.42 percent of the respondents were Christians and 22.78 percent of the respondents were Muslims. 51.94 percent of the urban respondents and 51.67 percent of the rural respondents were Hindus. 28.89 percent of the rural respondents and 21.95 percent of the urban respondents were Christians. 26.11 percent of the urban respondents and 19.44 percent of the rural respondents were Muslims. The religious mean average of rural and urban respondents was 1.7722 and 1.7000 respectively.

The following chart 4.6 shows the religion of the rural and urban respondents.

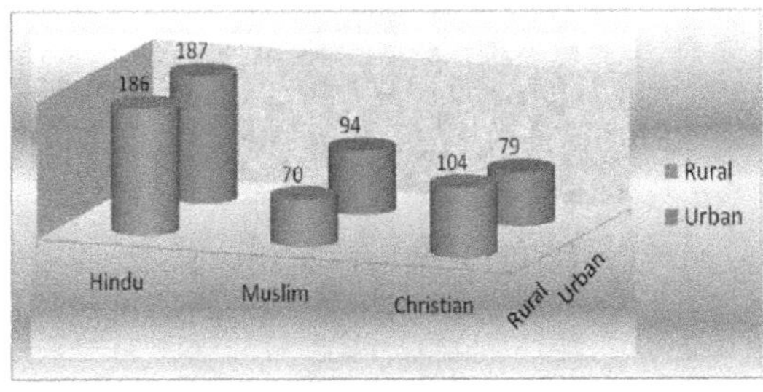

Chart 4.6: Religion of the Rural and Urban Respondents

Table 4.7: Marital Status of Respondents

Category	No. of. Respondents		Total
Marital status	Rural (N=360)	Urban (N=360)	Total (N=720)
Married	277 (76.94)	241 (66.94)	518 (71.94)
Unmarried	83 (23.06)	119 (33.06)	202 (28.06)
Mean average	1.2306	1.3306	

Chi-square value between marital and of the respondents 8.918 which is significant at 00.05 level

Table 4.7 portrays the marital status of the respondents. From the table, it was inferred that majority (71.94 percent) of the respondents were married, while minority of them (28.06 percent) were unmarried. In rural areas 76.94 percent of the respondents and in urban areas 66.94 percent of the respondents were married. In urban areas 33.06 percent of the respondents and in rural areas 23.06 percent of the respondents were unmarried. The mean average of marital status of urban and rural respondents was 1.3306 and 1.2306 respectively.

The following chart 4.7 shows the marital status of the rural and urban respondents.

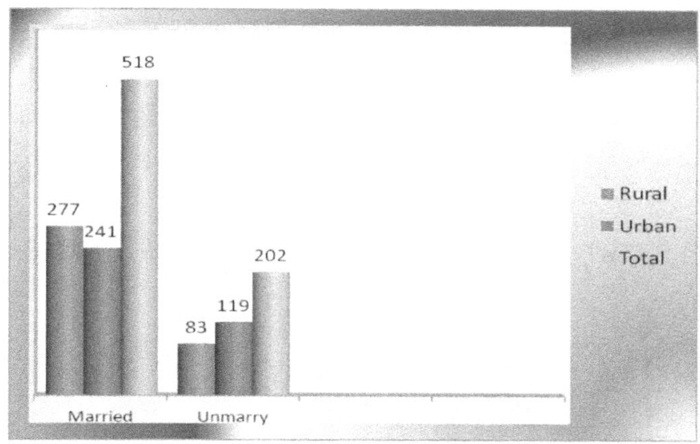

Chart 4.7: Marital status of Rural and Urban Respondents

4.5. Type and Size of Family

Family is a social institution forms very basis for determining the social interactions like marriage and such other social aspects of individuals *(Green Arnold 1956)*. The type and size of family also determines income level, the pattern of expenditure and standard of living.

Table 4.8: Family Size of the Respondents

Category	No. of. Respondents		
Family size	Rural (N=360)	Urban (N=360)	Total (N=720)
Small (Up to 3 members)	164 (45.55)	191 (53.06)	355 (49.31)
Medium (Up to 5 members)	153 (42.50)	151 (41.94)	304 (42.22)
Big (above 5 members)	43 (11.95)	18 (5)	61 (8.47)
Mean average	1.6639	1.5194	

Chi-square value between family size and of the respondents 12.313 which is significant at 0.001 level

Table 4.8 presents the family size of the respondents. From the table, it was inferred that majority (49.31 percent) of the respondents were having the family size of only 3 members, slightly more than 42 percent of the respondents were having the family size up to 5 members. Only 8.47 percent of the respondents were having the family size more than 5 members. In urban areas, 53.06 percent of the respondents and in rural areas 45.55 percent of the respondents were having the small family of only 3 members. 42.50 percent of the rural respondents and 41.94 percent of the urban respondents were having the medium family between 4-5 members. 11.95 percent of the rural respondents and 5 percent of the urban respondents were having the big family of above 5 members. The family size mean average of rural and urban respondents was 1.6639 and 1.5194 respectively.

The following chart 4.8 shows the family size of the rural and urban respondents.

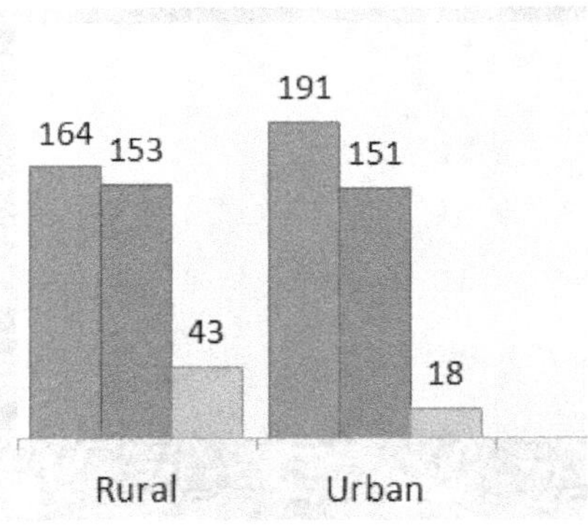

Chart 4.8: Family Size of Rural and Urban Respondents

Table 4.9: Type of Family of the Respondents

Category	No. of. Respondents		
Type of family	Rural (N=360)	Urban (N=360)	Total (N=720)
Nuclear	275 (76.39)	211 (58.61)	486 (67.5)
Joint	85 (23.61)	149 (41.39)	234 (32.5)
Mean average	1.2361	1.4139	

Chi-square value between type of family and of the respondents 25.932 which is not significant at 00.05 level

Table 4.9 explains the type of family of respondents. From the table, it was evident that majority (67.5 percent) of the respondents belong to nuclear family. Only 32.5 percent of the respondents belong to joint family.76.39 percent of the rural respondents and 58.61 percent of the urban respondents belong to nuclear family. 41.39 percent of urban respondents and 23.61 percent of rural respondents belong to joint family. The family type mean average was 1.2361 and 1.4139 for rural and urban areas respectively.

The following chart 4.9 shows the family type of the rural and urban respondents.

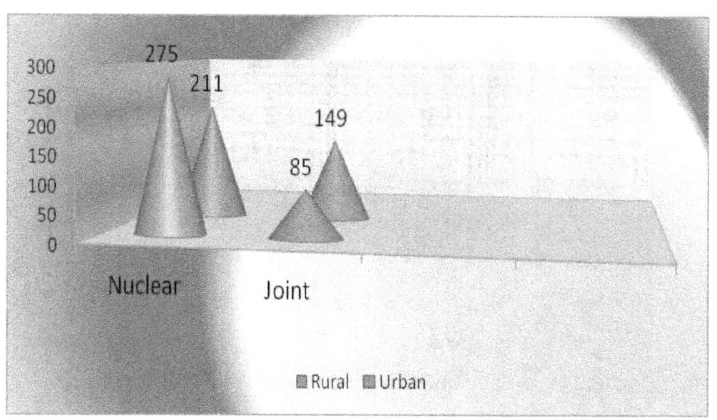

Chart 4.9: Type of Family of Rural and Urban Respondents

4.5.1 Occupation

Occupation refers to a person's usual or principal work or business, especially as a means of earning a living. Everybody in this world is with some occupation. However, the nature and type as well as status of the occupation were determined by one's demographic, social, economic, cultural and other bio–psychographics and agro-geographic factors. The occupation will also influence the behaviour of the consumers.

Table 4.10: Occupation Status of Respondents

Category Occupation	No. of. Respondents		Total
	Rural (N=360)	Urban (N=360)	(N=720)
Professional	3 (0.83)	18 (5)	21 (2.92)
Government	31 (8.61)	17 (4.72)	48 (6.67)
Private	197 (54.72)	181 (50.28)	378 (52.5)
Business	17 (4.72)	8 (2.22)	25 (3.47)
House wife	86 (23.89)	128 (35.56)	214 (29.72)
Retired	26 (7.23)	8 (2.22)	34 (4.72)
Mean average	3.6389	3.6528	

Chi-square value between occupation and of the respondents 36.487 which is significant at 0.001level.

Table 4.10 presents the occupation of the respondents. From the table, we can understand that majority (52.5 percent) of the respondents were working with private concerns. 29.72 percent of the respondents were house wives. 6.67 percent of the respondents were government employees. 4.72 percent of the respondents were retired from their job. 3.47 percent of the respondents were having their own business. Only 2.92 percent of the respondents were professionals (either doctor or teacher or lawyer or auditor etc.). 54.72 percent of the rural respondents and 50.28 percent of the urban respondents were private employees. 35.56 percent of urban respondents and 23.89 percent of rural respondents were house wives. 8.61 percent of rural respondents and 4.72 percent of urban respondents were government employees. 7.23 percent of rural respondents and 2.22 percent of urban respondents retired from their jobs. 4.72 percent of rural respondents and 2.22 percent of urban respondents were doing their own business. 5 percent of urban respondents and 0.83 percent of rural respondents were professionals. The mean average of occupation was 3.6389 and 3.6528 for rural and urban respondents respectively. The following chart 4.10 shows the occupation of the rural and urban respondents.

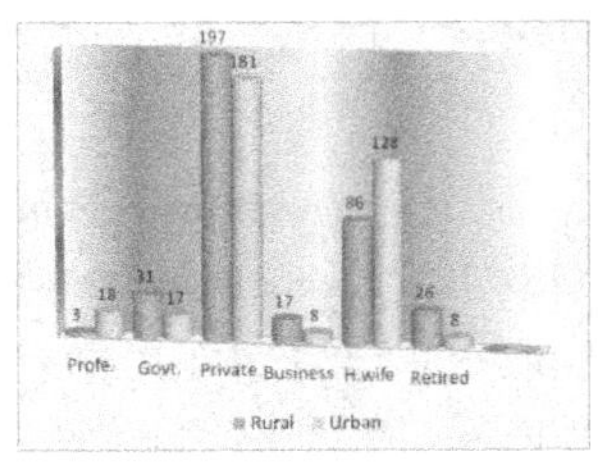

Chart 4.10: Occupations of Rural and Urban Respondents

4.6. Family Annual Income

Income is the most important deciding factor of standard of living. Access to food and shelter, economic comforts and social appreciations etc., greatly depend upon one's income level.

Table 4.11: Income Status of Respondents

Category Income Rs .in. lakhs	No. of. Respondents		Total (N=720)
	Rural (N=360)	Urban (N=360)	
Below 2 lakhs	61 (16.94)	55 (15.28)	116 (16.11)
2 lakhs to 4 lakhs	168 (46.67)	208 (57.78)	376 (52.22)
4 lakhs to 6 lakhs	23 (6.39)	18 (5)	41 (5.69)
6 lakhs to 8 lakhs	53 (14.72)	34 (9.44)	87 (12.08)
8lakhs to 10 lakhs	37 (10.28)	31 (8.61)	68 (9.45)
Above 10 lakhs	18 (5)	14 (3.89)	32 (4.45)
Mean average	2.6972	2.5000	

Chi-square value between income and of the respondents 10.354 which is significant at 00.05 level

Table 4.11 presents the annual income of the respondents. From the table, it was inferred that majority (52.22 percent) of the respondents were having an annual income from Rs. 2 lakhs to 4 lakhs. 16.11 percent of the respondents annual income falls below Rs.2 lakhs. 12.08 percent of the respondents were having an annual income from Rs.6 lakhs to 8 lakhs. 9.45 percent of the respondents were having an annual income from Rs.8 lakhs to 10 lakhs. 5.69 percent of the respondents were having an annual income from Rs.4 lakhs to 6 lakhs. 4.45 percent of the respondents were having an annual income of above 10 lakhs. 57.78 percent of the urban respondents and 46.67 percent of the rural respondents annual income were between Rs.2 lakhs and 4 lakhs. 16.94 percent of the rural respondents and 15.28 percent of the urban respondents annual income were below Rs.2 lakhs. 14.72 percent of the rural respondents and 9.44 percent of the urban respondents annual income were between Rs.6 lakhs and 8 lakhs. 10.28 percent of the rural respondents and 8.61 percent of the urban respondent's annual income were between Rs.8 lakhs and 10 lakhs. 6.39 percent of the rural respondents and 5 percent of the urban respondents annual income were between Rs.4 lakhs and 6 lakhs. Only 5 percent of the respondents in rural area and 3.89 percent of the respondents in urban area were having annual income more than Rs.10 lakhs. The mean average of income was 2.6972 and 2.5000 for rural and urban respondents respectively. The following chart 4.11 shows the annual income of the rural and urban respondents.

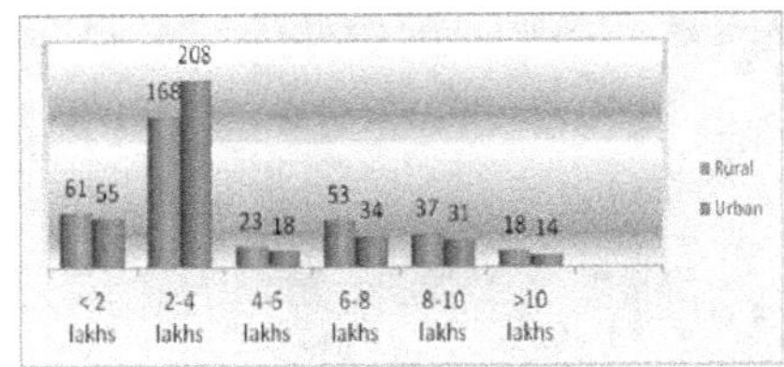

Chart 4.11: Annual Income of Rural and Urban Respondents

Table 4.12: Place of Purchase of Cooking Oil by the Respondents

Place of Purchase	Rural	Urban	Total
Grocery shop	151(41.94)	134(37.22)	285 (39.58)
Departmental store	178 (49.44)	182(50.56)	360 (50.0)
Wholesale stores	31 (8.62)	18(5.0)	49 (6.81)
Others	0 (0)	26(7.22)	26 (3.61)
Total	360 (100)	360 (100)	720 (100)

Table-4.12 shows the place of purchase of cooking oil by the respondents. From the table, it was evident that majority (50 percent) of the respondents were making their purchase at departmental stores followed by the purchase at grocery shop (39.58 percent). Only 6.81 percent of the respondents and 3.61 percent of the respondents were making their purchase at wholesale stores and other shops respectively. 50.56 percent of the urban respondents and 49.44 percent of the rural respondents were making their purchase at departmental stores. 41.94 percent of the rural respondents and 37.22 percent of the urban respondents were making their purchase at grocery shop. 8.62 percent of the rural respondents and 5 percent of the urban respondents were making their purchase at wholesale stores. No respondents in rural areas and 7.22 percent of respondents in urban areas were making their purchase at other places like exhibition, local markets and in mobile vans. The following chart 4.12 will statistically explain the place of purchase of rural and urban respondents.

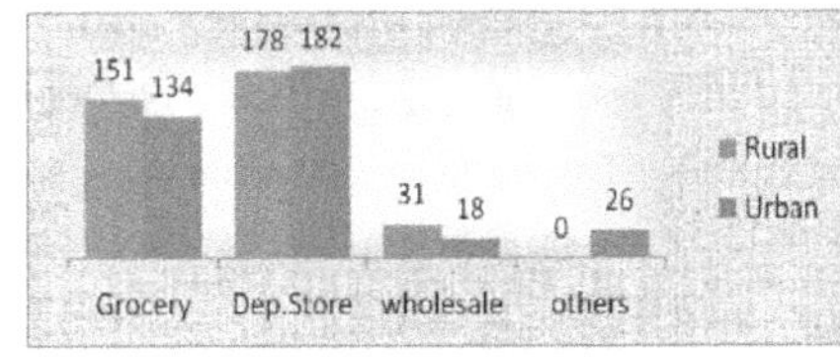

Chart 4.12: Place of purchase by Rural and Urban Respondents

Ho: There was no significant difference between rural and urban respondents with that of place of purchase.

H1: There was a significant difference between rural and urban respondents with that of place of purchase.

Table 4.13

ANOVA					
Type of respondents					
	Sum of Squares	d.f	Mean Square	F	Sig.
Between Groups	7.627	3	2.542	10.560	.000
Within Groups	172.373	716	0.241		
Total	180.000	719			

From the above table 4.13, it was inferred that in one way ANOVA, the total variation was partitioned in to two components, between groups represent variation of the group means around the overall mean and within groups represent variation of the individual scores around their respective group means. Significance indicates the significance level of the F-test. Small significance value (<.05) indicates group difference. In the above table, the significance level (0.000) was observed to be less than 0.05. Hence, null hypothesis (H0) was rejected and we can conclude that there is significant difference observed between rural and urban groups with that place of purchasing cooking oil.

Table 4.14: Type of Oil Purchased by the Respondents

Type of oil	Rural (N=360)	Urban (N=360)	Total (N=720)
Sun flower oil	68 (18.89)	117 (32.5)	185 (25.69)
Sesame oil	42 (11.67)	30 (8.33)	72 (10)
Palm oil	104 (28.89)	23 (6.39)	127 (17.64)
Vanaspathi	25 (6.94)	42 (11.67)	67 (9.31)
Olive oil	57 (15.83)	38 (10.55)	95 (13.19)
Ground nut oil	25 (6.94)	60 (16.67)	85 (11.81)
Coconut oil	28 (7.78)	42 (11.67)	70 (9.72)
Rice bran oil	06 (1.67)	07 (1.94)	13 (1.81)
Other oil	05 (1.39)	01 (0.28)	06 (0.83)
Mean average	3.5778	3.6787	3.7834

Table 4.14 shows the type of cooking oil purchased by the respondents. It was understood from the table, that majority (25.69 percent) of the respondents were purchasing sunflower oil for their cooking followed by the purchase of palm oil (17.64 percent). The 13.19 percent of the respondents were purchasing olive oil, 11.81 percent were purchasing groundnut oil, 10

percent were purchasing sesame oil, 9.72 percent were purchasing coconut oil, 9.31 percent were purchasing vanaspathi oil, 1.81 percent were purchasing rice bran oil and 0.83 percent of the respondents were using other oils such as suffola, corn oil etc for their cooking. Thus, the total mean average was 3.7834.

32.5 percent of the urban respondents and 18.89 percent of the rural respondents were purchasing sunflower oil. 28.89 percent of the rural respondents and 6.39 percent of the urban respondents were purchasing palm oil. 16.67 percent of the urban respondents and 6.94 percent of the rural respondents were purchasing groundnut oil. 15.83 percent of the rural respondents and 10.55 percent of the urban respondents were purchasing olive oil. 11.67 percent of the urban respondents and 7.78 percent of the rural respondents were purchasing coconut oil. 11.67 percent of the urban respondents and 6.94 percent of the rural respondents were purchasing vanaspathi. 11.67 percent of the rural respondents and 8.33 percent of the urban respondents were purchasing sesame oil. 1.94 percent of the urban respondents and 1.67 percent of the rural respondents were purchasing rice bran oil. 1.39 percent of the rural respondents and 0.28 percent of the urban respondents were purchasing other oils such as suffola, corn oil for their cooking. The mean average of rural and urban areas was 3.5778 and 3.6787 respectively. The following chart 4.13 will statistically explain the above findings.

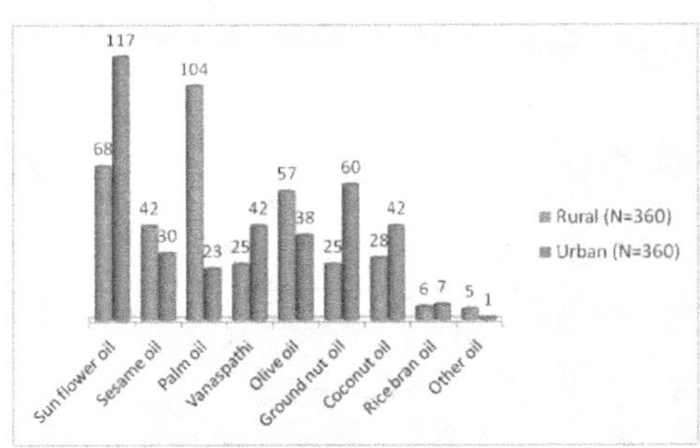

Chart 4.13: Type of Oil Preferred by the Rural and Urban Respondents

Ho: There was no significant difference between type of oil purchased and socio demographic factors such as age, gender of the respondents, educational status and marital status, Family Size, Type of family, Community, Religion, Occupation and income.

H1: There was a significant difference between type of oil purchased and socio demographic factors such as age, gender of the respondents, educational status and marital status, Family Size, Type of family, Community, Religion, Occupation and income.

Table 4.15: ANOVA

		Sum of Squares	d.f	Mean Square	F	Sig.
Age	Between Groups	2.225	3	.742	1.366	.052
	Within Groups	388.575	716	.543		
	Total	390.800	719			
Gender of the respondents	Between Groups	3.063	3	1.021	5.017	.002
	Within Groups	145.687	716	.203		
	Total	148.750	719			
Educational status	Between Groups	31.833	3	10.611	4.477	.004
	Within Groups	1697.054	716	2.370		
	Total	1728.888	719			
Marital status	Between Groups	3.293	3	1.098	5.533	0.001
	Within Groups	142.035	716	.198		
	Total	145.328	719			
Family Size	Between Groups	4.671	3	1.557	3.828	.010
	Within Groups	291.279	716	.407		
	Total	295.950	719			
Type of family	Between Groups	4.432	3	1.477	6.885	.000
	Within Groups	153.412	716	.215		
	Total	157.844	719			
Community	Between Groups	9.360	3	3.120	5.244	0.01
	Within Groups	426.027	716	.595		
	Total	435.388	719			
Religion	Between Groups	1.934	3	.645	.916	.433
	Within Groups	503.927	716	.704		
	Total	505.861	719			
Occupation	Between Groups	48.456	3	16.152	11.920	.000
	Within Groups	970.232	716	1.355		
	Total	1018.688	719			
Income	Between Groups	25.773	3	8.591	4.573	.004
	Within Groups	1345.226	716	1.879		
	Total	1370.999	719			

From the above ANOVA Table 4.15, we can find that there was significance difference between the variables gender (0.002), education (0.004), marital status (0.001), family size (0.010), type of family (0.000), community (0.01), occupation (0.000), age (0.52) and income (0.004) with type of oil purchased as the significance level was less at 1 percent level. Hence the null hypothesis (H0) was rejected in the case of gender, education, marital status and family size, type of family, community, occupation and income with that of type of oil purchased and alternative hypothesis (H1) was accepted.

The table 4.15 also concludes that there was no significant difference between religions (0.433) with that of type of oil purchased as the significance level was greater at 1 percent level. Hence the null hypothesis (H0) was accepted and alternative hypothesis (H1) was rejected.

Ho: There was no significant difference between rural and urban respondents with the type of oil purchased.

H1: There was a significant difference between rural and urban respondents with the type of oil purchased.

Table 4.16

ANOVA					
Type of respondents					
	Sum of Squares	d.f	Mean Square	F	Sig.
Between Groups	7.627	3	2.542	10.560	0.000
Within Groups	172.373	716	.241		
Total	180.000	719			

From the above table 4.16, it could be inferred that there was a significant difference between rural and urban respondents with the type of oil purchased as the significance level was 0.000 which was less at 1 percent level. Hence the null hypothesis (H0) was rejected and alternative hypothesis (H1) is accepted.

Table 4.17: Quantity of oil Purchased by Respondents

Quantity Purchased per month	Rural (N=360)	Urban (N=360)	Total (N=720)
Below 2 liters	220 (61.11)	213 (59.17)	433 (60.14)
2-3 liters	120 (33.33)	112 (31.11)	232 (32.22)
Above 3 liters	20 (5.56)	35 (9.72)	55 (7.64)

Table 4.17 shows the quantity of cooking oil purchased by the respondents. From the table, it was clear that majority (60.14 percent) of the respondents were purchasing below two liters of cooking oil per month. 32.22 percent of the respondents were purchasing two to three liters of cooking oil per month. 7.64 percent of the respondents were purchasing above three liters of cooking oil per month. 61.11 percent of the rural respondents and 59.17 percent of the urban respondents were purchasing below two liters of cooking oil per month. 33.33 percent of the rural respondents and 31.11 percent of the urban respondents were purchasing two to three liters of cooking oil per month.9.72 percent of the urban respondents and 5.56 percent of the rural respondents were purchasing above three liters of cooking oil per month.

The following chart 4.14 will statistically explain the above findings.

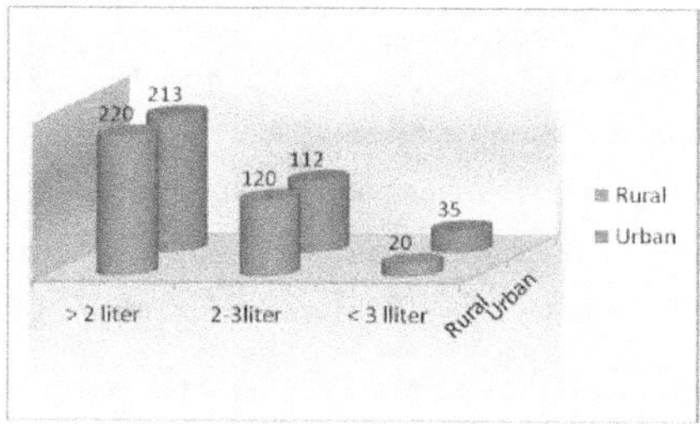

Chart 4.14: Quantity of Oil Purchased by Rural and Urban Respondents

Table 4.18: Quantity of Sunflower Oil Purchased by the Respondents

Quantity Purchased per month	Rural (N=68)	Urban (N=117)	Total (N=185)
Below 2 liters	41(60.29)	77 (65.81)	118 (63.78)
2-3 liters	25 (36.77)	28 (23.93)	53 (28.65)
Above 3 liters	02 (2.94)	12 (10.26)	14 (7.57)

Table 4.18 presents the quantity of sunflower oil purchased by the respondents. From the table, it was clear that among the sunflower oil purchasing respondents majority (63.78 percent) were purchasing below two liters of sunflower oil per month, 28.65 percent of the respondents were purchasing two to three liters of sunflower oil per month and 7.57 percent of the respondents were purchasing above three liters of sunflower oil per month. Among the urban sunflower oil purchasing respondents 65.81percent and among the rural sunflower oil purchasing respondents 60.29 percent were purchasing below two liters of sunflower oil per month. 36.77 percent of the rural sunflower oil purchasing respondents and 23.93 percent of the urban sunflower oil using respondents were purchasing between two to three liters of oil per month. 10.26 percent of the urban sunflower oil using respondents and 2.94 percent of the rural sunflower oil using respondents were purchasing above three liters of oil per month.

Table 4.19: Quantity of Sesame Oil Purchased by the Respondents

Quantity Purchased per month	Rural(N=42)	Urban(N=30)	Total(N=72)
Below 2 liters	10 (23.80)	24 (80)	34 (47.22)
2-3 liters	22 (52.40)	04 (13.33)	26 (36.11)
Above 3 liters	10 (23.80)	02 (6.67)	12 (16.67)

Table 4.19 presents the quantity of sesame oil purchased by the respondents. From the table, it was clear that among the sesame oil purchasing respondents majority (47.22 percent) were purchasing below two liters of sesame oil per month, 36.11 percent of the respondents were purchasing two to three liters of sesame oil per month and 16.67 percent of the

respondents were purchasing above three liters of sesame oil per month. Among the urban sesame oil purchasing respondents 80 percent and among the rural sesame purchasing respondents 23.80 percent were purchasing below two liters of sesame oil per month. 52.40 percent of the rural sesame oil using respondents and 13.33 percent of the urban sesame oil using respondents were purchasing between two to three liters of oil per month. 23.80 percent of the rural sesame oil using respondents and 6.67 percent of the urban sesame oil using respondents were purchasing above three liters of oil per month.

Table 4.20: Quantity of Palm Oil Purchased by the Respondents

Quantity Purchased per month	Rural (N=104)	Urban (N=23)	Total (N=127)
Below 2 liters	63 (60.58)	01 (4.35)	64 (50.39)
2-3 liters	40 (38.46)	16 (69.56)	56 (44.09)
Above 3 liters	01 (0.96)	06 (26.09)	07 (5.52)

Table 4.20 illustrates the quantity of palm oil purchased by the respondents. From the table, it was understood that among the palm oil purchasing respondents majority (50.39 percent) were purchasing below two liters of palm oil per month, 44.09 percent of the respondents were purchasing two to three liters of palm oil per month and 5.52 percent of the respondents were purchasing above three liters of palm oil per month.

Among the urban palm oil purchasing respondents 69.56 percent and among the rural palm oil purchasing respondents 38.46 percent were purchasing two to three liters of palm oil per month. 60.58 percent of the rural palm oil using respondents and 4.35 percent of the urban palm oil using respondents were purchasing below two liters of oil per month. 26.09 percent of the urban palm oil using respondents and 0.96 percent of the rural palm oil using respondents were purchasing above three liters of oil per month.

Table 4.21: Quantity of Vanaspathi Oil Purchased by the Respondents

Quantity Purchased per month	Rural (N=25)	Urban (N=42)	Total (N=67)
Below 2 liters	20 (80)	18 (42.86)	38 (56.72)
2-3 liters	04 (16)	20 (47.62)	24 (35.82)
Above 3 liters	01 (4)	04 (9.52)	05 (7.46)

Table 4.21 illustrates the quantity of vanaspathi oil purchased by the respondents. From the table, it was inferred that majority (56.72 percent) of the vanaspathi oil purchasing respondents were purchasing below two liters of oil per month, followed by two to three liters (35.82 percent) per month. Only 7.46 percent of the vanaspathi oil purchasing respondents were purchasing above three liters of oil. 80 percent of the rural and 42.86 percent of the urban vanaspathi oil purchasing respondents were purchasing below two liters of oil per month. 47.62 percent of the urban and 16 percent of the rural vanaspathi oil purchasing

respondents were purchasing two to three liters of oil per month. 9.52 percent of the urban and 4 percent of the rural vanaspathi oil purchasing respondents were purchasing above three liters of oil per month.

Table 4.22: Quantity of Olive Oil Purchased by the Respondents

Quantity Purchased per month	Rural (N=57)	Urban (N=38)	Total (N=95)
Below 2 liters	40 (70.18)	33 (86.84)	73 (76.84)
2-3 liters	15 (26.31)	05 (13.16)	20 (21.05)
Above 3 liters	02 (3.51)	0	02 (2.11)

Table 4.22 explains the quantity of olive oil purchased by the respondents. From the table, it was clear that among olive oil purchasing respondents 76.84 percent were purchasing below two liters of oil per month, 21.05 percent were purchasing two to three liters of oil per month and 2.11 percent were purchasing above three liters per month. 86.84 percent of the rural and 70.18 percent of the urban olive oil purchasing respondents were purchasing below two liters of oil per month. 26.31 percent of the rural and 13.16 percent of the urban olive oil purchasing respondents were purchasing two to three liters of oil per month. 3.51 percent of the rural olive oil purchasing respondents were purchasing above three liters of olive oil and no respondents in urban areas were purchasing more than three liters of olive oil.

Table 4.23: Quantity of Ground Nut Oil Purchased by the Respondents

Quantity Purchased per month	Rural (N=25)	Urban (N=60)	Total (N=85)
Below 2 liters	15 (60)	20 (33.33)	35 (41.18)
2-3 liters	07 (28)	30 (50)	37 (43.53)
Above 3 liters	03 (12)	10 (16.67)	13 (15.29)

Table 4.23 presents the quantity of ground nut oil purchased by the respondents. It was understood from the table, that, among the ground nut oil purchasing respondents, 43.53 percent were purchasing two to three liters of oil per month. 41.18 percent of ground nut oil purchasing respondents were buying below two liters of oil per month. Only 15.29 percent of ground nut oil purchasing respondents were purchasing above three liters of oil per month. 60 percent of the rural ground nut oil purchasing respondents and 33.33 percent of urban ground nut oil purchasing respondents were purchasing below two liters of oil per month. 50 percent of the urban ground nut oil purchasing respondents and 28 percent of rural ground nut oil purchasing respondents were purchasing two to three liters of oil per month. 16.67 percent of the urban ground nut oil purchasing respondents and 12 percent of rural ground nut oil purchasing respondents were purchasing above three liters of oil per month.

Table 4.24: Quantity of Coconut Oil Purchased by the Respondents

Quantity Purchased per month	Rural (N=28)	Urban (N=42)	Total (N=70)
Below 2 liters	24 (85.71)	33 (78.57)	57 (81.43)
2-3 liters	04 (14.29)	08(19.05)	12 (17.14)
Above 3 liters	0	01 (2.38)	01 (1.43)

Table 4.24 explains the quantity of coconut oil purchased by the respondents. It was inferred from the table, that among the coconut oil purchasing respondents, 81.43 percent were purchasing below two liters of oil per month. 17.14 percent of coconut oil purchasing respondents were purchasing two to three liters of oil per month. 1.43 percent of coconut oil purchasing respondents were buying above three liters of oil per month. 85.71 percent of the rural coconut oil purchasing respondents and 78.57 percent of urban coconut oil purchasing respondents were purchasing below two liters of oil per month. 19.05 percent of the urban coconut oil purchasing respondents and 14.29 percent of rural coconut oil purchasing respondents were purchasing two to three liters of oil per month. 2.38 percent of the urban coconut oil purchasing respondents and no respondents from rural area were purchasing above three liters of coconut oil per month.

Table 4.25: Quantity of Rice Bran Oil Purchased by the Respondents

Quantity Purchased per month	Rural (N=06)	Urban (N=07)	Total (N=13)
Below 2 liters	06(100)	06 (85.71)	12 (92.31)
2-3 liters	0	01 (14.29)	01 (7.69)

Table 4.25 presents the quantity of rice bran oil purchased by the respondents. From the table, it was evident that majority (92.31 percent) of rice bran oil purchasing respondents were purchasing below two liters of oil per month. 7.69 percent of the rice bran oil purchasing respondents were purchasing two to three liters per month. 100 percent of the rural and 85.71 percent of the urban rice bran oil purchasing respondents were purchasing below two liters of oil per month. 14.29 percent of the rural rice bran oil purchasing respondents were purchasing two to three liters of oil per month.

Table 4.26: Quantity of Other Oil Purchased by the Respondents

Quantity Purchased per month	Rural (N=05)	Urban (N=01)	Total (N=06)
Below 2 liters	01(20)	01 (100)	02 (33.33)
2-3 liters	03(60)	0	03 (50)
Above 3 liters	01(20)	0	1 (16.67)

Table 4.26 reveals the quantity of other oil purchased by the respondents. It was understood from the table, that 50 percent were purchasing two to three liters, 33.33 percent were purchasing below two liters and remaining 16.67 percent were purchasing above three liters of oil per month. 100 percent of the urban and 20 percent of the rural respondents

purchasing other oil were purchasing below two liters of oil. 60 percent of the rural respondents using other oil were purchasing two to three liters of other oil. 20 percent of the rural respondents using other oil were purchasing above three liters of other oil.

Ho: There was no significant difference between Age and Quantity of oil purchased

H1: There was a significant difference between Age and Quantity of oil purchased

Table 4.27: ANOVA

		Sum of Squares	d.f	Mean Square	F	Sig.
Sunflower oil Qty. purchase	Between Groups	0.293	3	0.098	.195	.900
	Within Groups	357.435	716	0.499		
	Total	357.728	719			
Sesame oil Qty. purchase	Between Groups	1.595	3	0.532	1.701	.165
	Within Groups	223.733	716	0.312		
	Total	225.328	719			
Palm oil Qty. purchase	Between Groups	3.313	3	1.104	3.226	.025
	Within Groups	42.104	123	0.342		
	Total	45.417	126			
Vanspathi.Qty.purchase	Between Groups	2.692	3	0.897	2.395	.077
	Within Groups	23.606	63	0.375		
	Total	26.299	66			
Olive oil Qty.pruchase	Between Groups	4.999	3	1.666	3.311	.024
	Within Groups	45.801	91	0.503		
	Total	50.800	94			
Ground Nut oil Qty.pruchase	Between Groups	2.025	3	0.675	1.221	.308
	Within Groups	44.798	81	0.553		
	Total	46.824	84			
Coconut oil Qty. Purchase	Between Groups	.951	3	0.317	.688	.563
	Within Groups	30.421	66	0.461		
	Total	31.371	69			
Rice bran oil. Qty. Purchase (00.05 level)	Between Groups	.423	1	0.423	1.034	.331
	Within Groups	4.500	11	0.409		
	Total	4.923	12			

From the above ANOVA Table 4.27, it was inferred that there was no significant difference between the age and quantity of sunflower oil purchased as the significance level was 0.900 which was greater at 5 percent level. There was no significant difference between age and quantity of Vanaspathi purchased as the significance level was 0.077 which was greater at 1 percent level. There was no significant difference between age and quantity of ground nut oil purchased as the significance level was 0.308 which was greater at 1 percent level. There was no significant difference between age and quantity of coconut oil purchased as the significance level was 0.563 which was greater at 1 percent level. There was no significant difference between age and quantity of rice bran oil purchased as the significance level was 0.331 which was greater at 1 percent level. Hence, the null hypothesis (H0) was accepted in the case of sunflower oil, vanaspathi, ground nut oil, coconut oil and rice bran oil and the alternative hypothesis was rejected.

There was a significant difference between age and quantity of sesame oil purchased as the significance level was 0.165 which was less at 5 percent significance level. There was a significant difference between age and quantity of palm oil purchased as the significance level was oil 0.025 which was less at 1 percent level. There was a significant difference between age and quantity of olive oil purchased as the significance level was 0.024 which was less at 1 percent level. Hence, the null hypothesis (H0) was rejected in the case of sesame oil, palm oil and olive oil and the alternative hypothesis was accepted.

Ho: There was no significant difference between Gender and Qty of oil purchased

H1: There was a significant difference between Gender and Qty of oil purchased

Table 4.28: ANOVA

		Sum of Squares	d.f	Mean Square	F	Sig.
Sunflower oil Qty. purchase	Between Groups	1.874	1	1.874	3.777	.052
	Within Groups	355.717	717	.496		
	Total	357.591	718			
Sesame oil Qty. purchase	Between Groups	.028	1	.028	.091	.763
	Within Groups	221.944	717	.310		
	Total	221.972	718			
Palm oil Qty. purchase	Between Groups	1.758	1	1.758	5.017	.027
	Within Groups	43.456	124	.350		
	Total	45.214	125			
Vanspathi.Qty.purchase	Between Groups	.037	1	.037	.092	.062
	Within Groups	26.261	65	.404		
	Total	26.299	66			
Olive oil Qty.pruchase	Between Groups	.186	1	.186	.342	.560
	Within Groups	50.614	93	.544		
	Total	50.800	94			
Ground Nut oil Qty.pruchase	Between Groups	.004	1	.004	.007	.934
	Within Groups	46.806	82	.571		
	Total	46.810	83			
Coconut oil Qty. Purchase	Between Groups	.029	1	.029	.062	.803
	Within Groups	31.343	68	.461		
	Total	31.371	69			
Rice bran oil. Qty. Purchase	Between Groups	.173	1	.173	.401	.540
	Within Groups	4.750	11	.432		
	Total	4.923	12			

From the above ANOVA table 4.28, it was inferred that there was no significant difference between gender and quantity of sesame oil purchased as the significance level was 0.763 which was greater at 5 percent level. There was no significant difference between gender and quantity of vanaspathi oil purchased as the significance level was 0.062 which was greater at 1 percent level. There was no significant difference between gender and quantity of ground nut oil purchased as the significance level was 0.934 which was greater at 1 percent level. There was no significant difference between gender and quantity of coconut oil purchased as the significance level was 0.803 which was greater at 1 percent level. There was no significant difference between gender and quantity of rice bran oil purchased as the significance level was 0.540 which was greater at 1 percent level. There was no significant difference between gender and quantity of sunflower oil purchased as the significance level was 0.052 which was greater at 5 percent level. Hence, the null hypothesis (H0) was accepted in the case of sesame oil, vanaspathi, olive oil, ground nut oil, coconut oil, sunflower oil and rice bran oil and the alternative hypothesis was rejected. There was a significant difference between gender and quantity of palm oil purchased as the significance level was 0.027 which was less at 1 percent level. Hence, the null hypothesis (H0) was rejected in the case of palm oil and the alternative hypothesis was accepted.

Ho: There was no significant difference between marital status and Qty of oil purchased.

H1: There was a significant difference between marital status and Qty of oil purchased.

Table 4.29: ANOVA

		Sum of Squares	d.f	Mean Square	F	Sig.
Sunflower oil Qty. purchase	Between Groups	.199	1	.199	.399	.028
	Within Groups	357.529	718	.498		
	Total	357.728	719			
Sesame oil Qty. purchase	Between Groups	.123	1	.123	.392	.531
	Within Groups	225.205	718	.314		
	Total	225.328	719			
Palm oil Qty. purchase	Between Groups	.584	1	.584	1.629	.204
	Within Groups	44.833	125	.359		
	Total	45.417	126			
Vanspathi.Qty.purchase	Between Groups	.138	1	.138	.344	.560
	Within Groups	26.160	65	.402		
	Total	26.299	66			
Olive oil Qty.pruchase	Between Groups	.587	1	.587	1.088	.300
	Within Groups	50.213	93	.540		
	Total	50.800	94			
Ground Nut oil Qty.pruchase	Between Groups	.039	1	.039	.070	.792
	Within Groups	46.784	83	.564		
	Total	46.824	84			
Coconut oil Qty. Purchase	Between Groups	2.800	1	2.800	6.664	.012
	Within Groups	28.571	68	.420		
	Total	31.371	69			
Rice bran oil. Qty. Purchase	Between Groups	.006	1	.006	.014	.907
	Within Groups	4.917	11	.447		
	Total	4.923	12			

From the above ANOVA Table 4.29, it was inferred that there was no significant difference between marital status and quantity of sesame oil purchased as the significance level was 0.531 which was greater at 5 percent level. There was no significant difference between marital status and quantity of palm oil purchased as the significance level was 0.204 which was greater at 1 percent level. There was no significant difference between marital status and quantity of vanaspathi purchased as the significance level was 0.560 which was greater at 1 percent level. There was no significant difference between marital status and quantity of olive oil purchased as the significance level was 0.300 which was greater at 1 percent level. There was no significant difference between marital status and quantity of ground nut oil purchased as the significance level was 0.792 which was greater at 1 percent level. There was no significant difference between marital status and quantity of rice bran oil purchased as the significance level was 0.907 which was greater at 1 percent level. Hence, the null hypothesis (H0) was accepted in the case of sesame oil, palm oil, vanaspathi, olive oil, ground nut oil and rice bran oil and the alternative hypothesis was rejected.

There was a significant difference between marital status and quantity of sunflower oil purchased as the significance level was 0.028 which was less at 5 percent level. There was a significant difference between marital status and quantity of coconut oil purchased as the significance level was 0.012 which was less at 1 percent level. Hence, the null hypothesis (H0) was rejected in the case of sunflower oil and coconut oil and the alternative hypothesis was accepted.

Ho: There was no significant difference between Education and Qty of oil purchased

H1:   There was a significant difference between Education and Qty of oil purchased

From the below ANOVA table 4.30, it was inferred that there was a significant difference between educational qualification and quantity of sunflower oil purchased as the significance level was 0.098 which was less at 5 percent level. There was a significant difference between educational qualification and quantity of sesame oil purchased as the significance level was 0.081 which less at 5 percent level. Hence, the null hypothesis (H0) was rejected in the case of sunflower oil and sesame oil and the alternative hypothesis was accepted.

There was no significant difference between educational qualification and quantity of palm oil purchased as the significance level was 0.06 which was greater at 1 percent level. There was no significant difference between educational qualification and quantity of vanaspathi purchased as the significance level was 0.663 which was greater at 1 percent level.

Table 4.30: ANOVA

		Sum of Squares	d.f	Mean Square	F	Sig.
Sunflower oil Qty. purchase	Between Groups	2.674	6	.446	.895	.098
	Within Groups	355.054	713	.498		
	Total	357.728	719			
Sesame oil Qty. purchase	Between Groups	3.522	6	.587	1.887	.081
	Within Groups	221.806	713	.311		
	Total	225.328	719			
Palm oil Qty. purchase	Between Groups	3.316	6	.553	1.575	.060
	Within Groups	42.101	120	.351		
	Total	45.417	126			
Vanspathi.Qty.purchase	Between Groups	1.685	6	.281	.685	.663
	Within Groups	24.613	60	.410		
	Total	26.299	66			
Olive oil Qty.pruchase	Between Groups	2.619	6	.436	.797	.575
	Within Groups	48.181	88	.548		
	Total	50.800	94			
Ground Nut oil Qty.pruchase	Between Groups	.697	5	.139	.239	.944
	Within Groups	46.126	79	.584		
	Total	46.824	84			
Coconut oil Qty. Purchase	Between Groups	2.089	6	.348	.749	.613
	Within Groups	29.283	63	.465		
	Total	31.371	69			
Rice bran oil. Qty. Purchase	Between Groups	.123	3	.041	.077	.971
	Within Groups	4.800	9	.533		
	Total	4.923	12			

There was no significant difference between educational qualification and quantity of olive oil purchased as the significance level was 0.575 which was greater than at 1 percent level. There was no significant difference between educational qualification and quantity of groundnut oil purchased as the significance level was 0.944 which was greater at 1 percent level. There was no significant difference between educational qualification and quantity of coconut oil purchased as the significance level was 0.613 which was greater at 1 percent level. There was no significant difference between educational qualification and quantity of rice bran oil purchased as the significance level was 0.971 which was greater at 1 percent level. Hence, the null hypothesis (H0) was accepted in the case of palm oil, vanaspathi, olive oil, ground nut oil, coconut oil and rice bran oil and the alternative hypothesis was rejected.

Ho: There was no significant difference between Income and Qty of oil purchased

H1: There was a significant difference between Income and Qty of oil purchased

Table 4.31: ANOVA

		Sum of Squares	d.f	Mean Square	F	Sig.
Sunflower oil Qty. purchase	Between Groups	2.777	5	.555	1.117	.050
	Within Groups	354.951	714	.497		
	Total	357.728	719			
Sesame oil Qty. purchase	Between Groups	2.122	5	.424	1.357	.238
	Within Groups	223.206	714	.313		
	Total	225.328	719			
Palm oil Qty. purchase	Between Groups	2.866	5	.573	1.630	.157
	Within Groups	42.551	121	.352		
	Total	45.417	126			
Vanspathi.Qty.purchase	Between Groups	3.477	5	.695	1.859	.115
	Within Groups	22.821	61	.374		
	Total	26.299	66			
Olive oil Qty.pruchase	Between Groups	9.491	5	1.898	4.089	.002
	Within Groups	41.309	89	.464		
	Total	50.800	94			
Ground Nut oil Qty.pruchase	Between Groups	1.606	5	.321	.561	.729
	Within Groups	45.218	79	.572		
	Total	46.824	84			
Coconut oil Qty. Purchase	Between Groups	3.670	5	.734	1.696	.148
	Within Groups	27.701	64	.433		
	Total	31.371	69			
Rice bran oil Qty. Purchase	Between Groups	1.256	5	.251	.480	.782
	Within Groups	3.667	7	.524		
	Total	4.923	12			

From ANOVA Table 4.31, it was understood that there was no significant difference between income and quantity of palm oil purchased as the significance level was 0.157 which was greater at 1 percent level. There was no significant difference between income and quantity of vanaspathi purchased as the significance level was 0.115 which was greater at 1percent level. There was no significant difference between income and quantity of ground nut oil purchased as the significance level was 0.729 which was greater at 1 percent level. There was no significant difference between income and quantity of coconut oil purchased as the significance level was 0.148 which was greater at 1percent level. There was no significant difference between income and quantity of rice bran oil purchased as the significance level was 0.782 which was greater at 1percent level. Hence, the null hypothesis (H0) was accepted in the case of palm oil, vanaspathi, ground nut oil, coconut oil and rice bran oil and the alternative hypothesis was rejected. There was a significant difference between income and quantity of sunflower oil purchased as the significance level was 0.050 which was less at 5 percent level. There was a significant difference between income and quantity of sesame oil purchased as the significance level was 0.238 which was less at 5 percent level. There was a significant difference between income and quantity of olive oil purchased as the significance level was

0.002 which was less at 1 percent level. Hence, the alternative hypothesis (H1) was accepted in the case of sunflower oil, sesame oil and olive oil and the null hypothesis (H0) were rejected.

Table 4.32: ANOVA

		Sum of Squares	d.f	Mean Square	F	Sig.
Sunflower oil Qty. purchase	Between Groups	.640	2	.320	.643	.026
	Within Groups	357.088	717	.498		
	Total	357.728	719			
Sesame oil Qty. purchase	Between Groups	.038	2	.019	.060	.942
	Within Groups	225.290	717	.314		
	Total	225.328	719			
Palm oil Qty. purchase	Between Groups	.189	2	.095	.259	.072
	Within Groups	45.228	124	.365		
	Total	45.417	126			
Vanspathi.Qty.purchase	Between Groups	.088	2	.044	.107	.098
	Within Groups	26.211	64	.410		
	Total	26.299	66			
Olive oil Qty.pruchase	Between Groups	.569	2	.284	.521	.596
	Within Groups	50.231	92	.546		
	Total	50.800	94			
Ground Nut oil Qty.pruchase	Between Groups	.596	2	.298	.529	.591
	Within Groups	46.228	82	.564		
	Total	46.824	84			
Coconut oil Qty. Purchase	Between Groups	.640	2	.320	.698	.501
	Within Groups	30.731	67	.459		
	Total	31.371	69			
Rice bran oil. Qty. Purchase	Between Groups	1.266	2	.633	1.731	.226
	Within Groups	3.657	10	.366		
	Total	4.923	12			

Ho: There was no significant difference between Family size and Qty of oil purchased

H1: There was a significant difference between Family size and Qty of oil purchased

From ANOVA table 4.32 it was inferred, that there was no significant difference between family size and quantity of sesame oil purchased as the significance level was 0.942 which was greater at 5 percent level. There was no significant difference between family size and quantity of palm oil purchased as the significance level was 0.072 which was greater at 1 percent level. There was no significant difference between family size and quantity of vanaspathi purchased as the significance level was 0.098 which was greater at 1 percent level. There was no significant difference between family size and quantity of olive oil purchased as the significance level was 0.596 which was greater than at 1 percent level. There was no significant difference between family size and quantity of ground nut oil purchased as the significance level was 0.591 which was greater at 1 percent level. There was no significant difference between family size and quantity of coconut oil purchased as the significance level was 0.501 which was greater at 1 percent level. There was no significant difference between family size and quantity of rice bran oil purchased as the significance level was 0.226 which was greater at 1 percent level. Hence, the null hypothesis (H0) was accepted in the case of sesame oil, palm oil, vanaspathi, olive oil, ground nut oil, coconut oil and rice bran oil and the alternative hypothesis was rejected.

There was a significant difference between family size and the quantity of sunflower oil purchased as the significance level was 0.026 which was less at 5 percent level. Hence the null hypothesis (H0) was rejected in the case of sunflower oil and the alternative hypothesis was accepted.

Ho: There was no significant difference between type of family and Qty   of oil purchased

H1: There was a significant difference between type of family and Qty of oil purchased

Table 4.33: ANOVA

		Sum of Squares	d.f	Mean Square	F	Sig.
Sunflower oil Qty. purchase	Between Groups	.114	1	.114	.229	.032
	Within Groups	357.215	717	.498		
	Total	357.330	718			
Sesame oil Qty. purchase	Between Groups	.671	1	.671	2.143	.144
	Within Groups	224.628	717	.313		
	Total	225.299	718			
Palm oil Qty. purchase	Between Groups	1.600	1	1.600	4.565	.035
	Within Groups	43.817	125	.351		
	Total	45.417	126			
Vanaspathi Qty. purchase	Between Groups	.142	1	.142	.352	.555
	Within Groups	26.157	65	.402		
	Total	26.299	66			
Olive oil Qty.pruchase	Between Groups	.294	1	.294	.541	.464
	Within Groups	50.506	93	.543		
	Total	50.800	94			
Ground Nut oil Qty.pruchase	Between Groups	.138	1	.138	.245	.022
	Within Groups	46.686	83	.562		
	Total	46.824	84			
Coconut oil Qty. Purchase	Between Groups	.212	1	.212	.463	.499
	Within Groups	31.159	68	.458		
	Total	31.371	69			
Rice bran oil Qty. Purchase	Between Groups	.848	1	.848	2.289	.158
	Within Groups	4.075	11	.370		
	Total	4.923	12			

From ANOVA Table 4.33 it was inferred, that there was no significant difference between type of family and quantity of vanaspathi purchased as the significance level was 0.555 which was greater at 1 percent level. There was no significant difference between type of family and quantity of olive oil purchased as the significance level was 0.464 which was greater at 1 percent level. There was no significant difference between type of family and quantity of coconut oil purchased as the significance level was 0.499 which was greater at 1 percent level. There was no significant difference between type of family and quantity of rice bran oil purchased as the significance level was 0.158 which was greater at 1 percent level. Hence, the null hypothesis (H0) was accepted in the case of vanaspathi, olive oil, coconut oil and rice bran oil and alternative hypothesis (H1) was rejected.

There was a significant difference between type of family and the quantity of sunflower oil purchased as the significance level was 0.032 which was less at 5 percent level. There was a significant difference between type of family and the quantity of sesame oil purchased as the significance level was 0.144 which was less at 5 percent level. There was a significant difference between type of family and the quantity of palm oil purchased as the significance level was 0.035 which was less at 1 percent level. There was a significant difference between type of family and the quantity of ground nut oil purchased as the significance level was 0.022 which was less at 1 percent level. Hence, the null hypothesis (H0) was rejected in the case of sunflower oil, sesame oil, palm oil and ground nut oil and alternative hypothesis (H1) was accepted.

Table 4.34: Brand of Sunflower Oil Purchased by the Respondents

Brand name	Rural (N=68)	Urban (N=117)	Total (N=185)
Gold winner	20 (29.41)	61 (52.14)	81 (43.78)
Fortune	22 (32.35)	24 (20.51)	46 (24.87)
Ganapathy	20 (29.41)	22 (18.80)	42 (22.70)
Dhara	05 (7.36)	01 (0.85)	06 (3.24)
Sundrop	01 (1.47)	09 (7.70)	10 (5.41)

Table 4.34 illustrates brand of sunflower oil purchased by the respondents. It could be inferred from the table, that, among the sunflower oil purchasing respondents, 43.78 percent were purchasing gold winner brand, 24.87 percent were purchasing fortune brand, 22.70 percent were purchasing ganapathy brand, 5.41 percent purchasing sundrop brand and 3.24 percent purchasing dhara brand. Among the rural sunflower oil purchasing respondents, 32.35 percent were purchasing fortune, 29.41 percent were purchasing gold winner brand and ganapathy brand, 7.36 percent were purchasing dhara brand and the remaining 1.47 percent was purchasing sundrop brand respectively. Among the urban sunflower oil purchasing respondents, 52.14 percent were purchasing gold winner brand, 20.51 percent were purchasing fortune brand, 18.80 percent were purchasing ganapathy brand, 7.70 percent were purchasing sundrop brand and the remaining 0.85 percent were purchasing dhara brand respectively.

The following chart 4.15 will statistically explain the brand of sunflower oil preferred by the respondents.

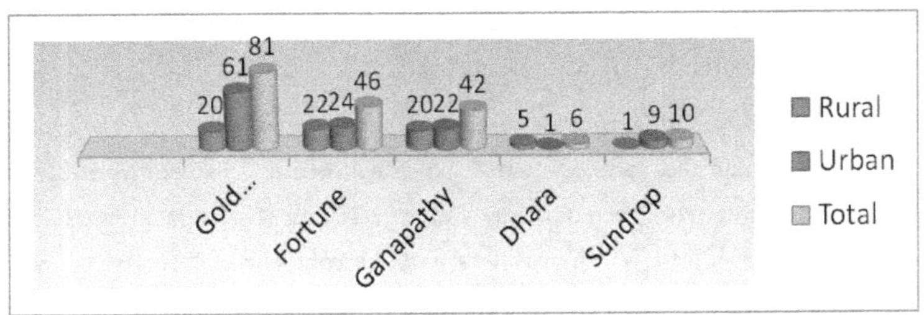

Chart 4.15: Brand of Sunflower Oil Preferred by the Respondents

Table 4.35: Brand of Sesame Oil Purchased by the Respondents

Brand name	Rural (N=42)	Urban (N=30)	Total (N=72)
Idhyam	21 (50)	20 (66.67)	41(56.94)
VVS	4 (9.52)	8 (26.67)	12 (16.67)
Anjali	5 (11.90)	2 (6.66)	7 (9.72)
Sangamam	12 (28.58)	0	12 (16.67)

Table 4.35 explains brand of sesame oil purchased by the respondents. It was understood from the table, that, among the sesame oil purchasing respondents, 56.94 percent were purchasing idhayam brand, 16.67 percent were purchasing VVS brand and sangamam brand and the remaining 9.72 percent were purchasing anjali brand. Among the rural sesame oil purchasing respondents, 50 percent were purchasing idhyam brand, 28.58 percent were purchasing sangamam brand, 11.90 percent were purchasing anjali brand and the remaining 9.52 percent were purchasing VVS brand. Among the urban sesame oil purchasing respondents, 66.67 percent were purchasing idhyam brand, 26.67 percent were purchasing VVS brand and the remaining 6.66 percent were purchasing anjali brand.

The following chart 4.16 will statistically explain the brand of sesame oil preferred by the respondents.

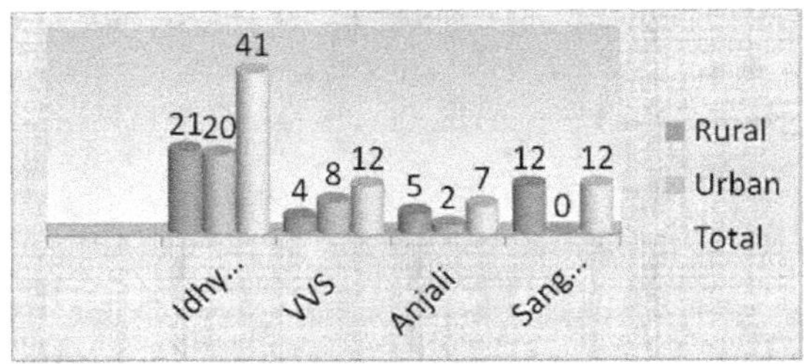

Chart 4.16: Brand of Sesame Oil Preferred by the Respondents

Table 4.36: Brand of Ground Nut Oil Purchased by the Respondents

Brand name	Rural (N=25)	Urban (N=60)	Total (N=85)
Idhyam Mantra	15 (60)	40 (66.67)	55 (64.71)
Ganapathy	8 (32)	15 (25)	23 (27.06)
Maharaja	2 (8)	5 (8.33)	7 (8.23)

Table 4.36 explains brand of ground nut oil purchased by the respondents. It was understood from the table, that, among the ground nut oil purchasing respondents, 64.71 percent were purchasing idhayam mantra brand, 27.06 percent were purchasing ganapathy brand and the remaining 8.23 percent were purchasing maharaja brand. Among the rural ground nut oil purchasing respondents, 60 percent were purchasing idhyam mantra brand, 32 percent were purchasing ganapathy brand and the remaining 8 percent were purchasing maharaja brand. Among the urban ground nut oil purchasing respondents, 66.67 percent were purchasing idhyam mantra brand, 25 percent were purchasing ganapathy brand and the remaining 8.33 percent were purchasing maharaja brand.

The following chart 4.17 will statistically explain the brand of ground nut oil preferred by the respondents.

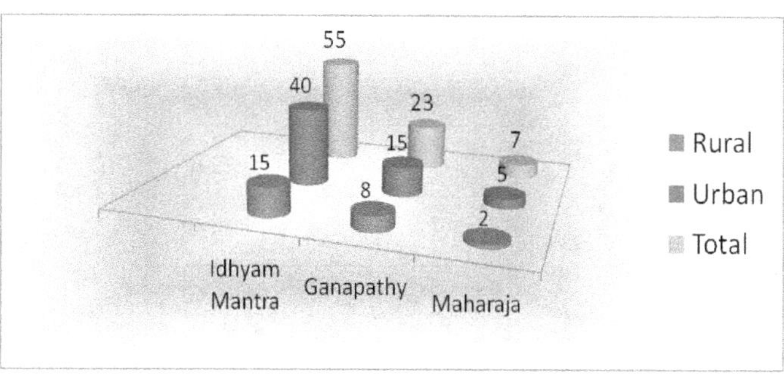

Chart 4.17: Brand of Ground Nut Oil Preferred by the Respondents

Table 4.37: Brand of Vanaspathi Oil Purchased by the Respondents

Brand name	Rural (N=25)	Urban (N=42)	Total (N=67)
Sunflower	08 (32)	10 (23.81)	18 (26.87)
Dalda	14 (56)	30 (71.43)	44 (65.67)
Others (no brand)	3 (12)	02 (4.76)	05 (7.46)

Table 4.37 reveals the brand of vanaspathi oil purchased by the respondents. It was inferred from the table, that, 65.67 percent of vanaspathi oil purchasing respondents were purchasing dalda brand, 26.87 percent were purchasing sunflower brand and the remaining 7.46 percent were purchasing oil without brand name. Among the rural vanaspathi oil purchasing respondents, 56 percent were purchasing dalda brand, 32 percent were purchasing sunflower brand and 12 percent were purchasing vanaspathi oil without brand. Among the urban vanaspathi oil purchasing respondents, 71.43 percent were purchasing dalda brand, 23.81 percent were purchasing sunflower brand and 4.76 percent were purchasing vanaspathi oil without brand. The following chart 4.18 will statistically explain the brand of vanaspathi oil preferred by the respondents.

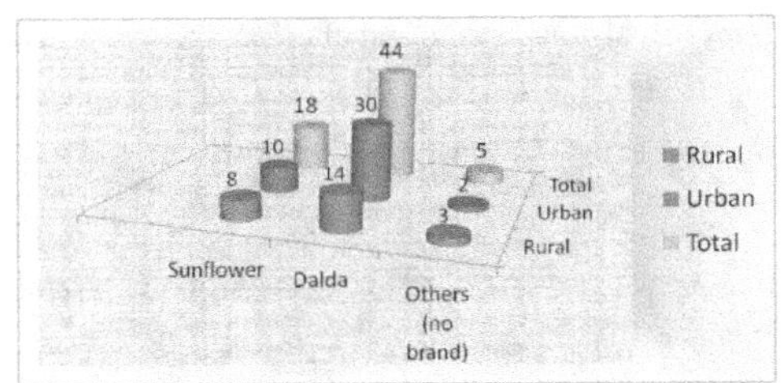

Chart 4.18: Brand of Vanaspathi Oil Preferred by the Respondents

Table 4.38: Brand of Olive Oil Purchased by the Respondents

Brand name	Rural (N=57)	Urban (N=38)	Total (N=95)
Cardio olive oil	50 (87.72)	30 (78.95)	80 (84.21)
Leonardo olive oil	07 (12.28)	08 (21.05)	15 (15.79)

Table 4.38 portrays the brand of olive oil purchased by the respondents. From the table, it was clear that 84.21percent of olive oil purchasing respondents were purchasing cardio brand and the remaining 15.79 percent of olive oil purchasing respondents were purchasing Leonardo brand. Among the rural olive oil purchasing respondents, 87.72 percent were purchasing cardio brand and the remaining 12.28 percent were purchasing Leonardo brand. Among the urban olive oil purchasing respondents, 78.95 percent were purchasing cardio brand and the remaining 21.05 percent were purchasing Leonardo brand.

The following chart 4.19 will statistically explain the brand of olive oil preferred by the respondents.

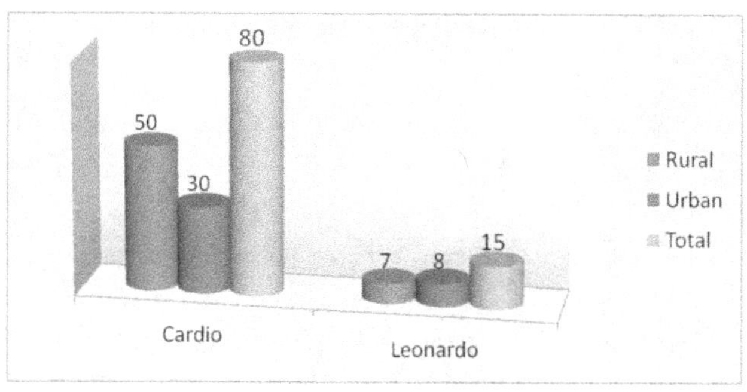

Chart 4.19: Brand of Olive Oil Preferred by the Respondents

Table 4.39: Brand of Palm Oil Purchased by the Respondents

Brand name	Rural (N=104)	Urban (N=23)	Total (N=127)
Supreme	60 (57.69)	10 (43.48)	70 (55.12)
RBD	44 (42.31)	13 (56.52)	57 (44.88)

Table 4.39 presents the brand of palm oil purchased by the respondents. From the table, it was clear that 55.12 percent of palm oil purchasing respondents were purchasing supreme brand and the remaining 44.88 percent of palm oil purchasing respondents were purchasing RBD brand. Among the rural palm oil purchasing respondents, 57.69 percent were purchasing supreme brand and the remaining 42.31 percent were purchasing RBD brand. Among the urban palm oil purchasing respondents, 56.52 percent were purchasing RBD brand and the remaining 43.48 percent were purchasing supreme brand.

The following chart 4.20 will statistically explain the brand of palm oil preferred by the respondents.

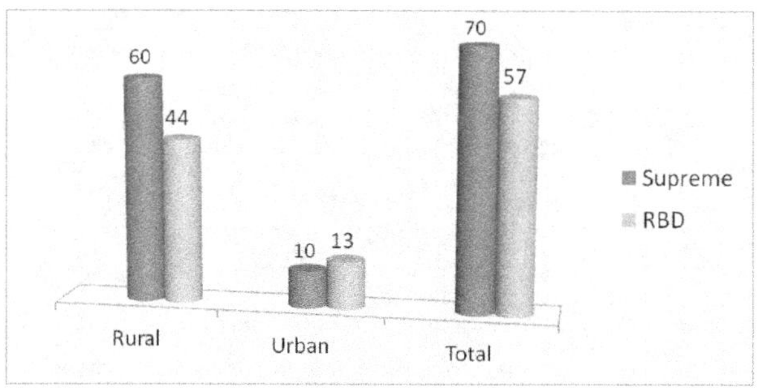

Chart 4.20: Brand of Palm Oil Preferred by the Respondents

Table 4.40: Brand of Coconut Oil Purchased by the Respondents

Brand name	Rural (N=28)	Urban (N=42)	Total (N=70)
VVD gold	10 (35.71)	30 (71.43)	40 (57.14)
Coconut parachute	14 (50)	11 (26.19)	25 (35.71)
Ganapathy	4 (14.29)	1 (2.38)	05 (7.15)

Table 4.40 explains brand of coconut oil purchased by the respondents. It was understood from the table, that, among the coconut oil purchasing respondents, 57.14 percent were purchasing VVD gold brand, 35.71 percent were purchasing coconut parachute brand and the remaining 7.15 percent were purchasing ganapathy brand. Among the rural coconut oil purchasing respondents, 50 percent were purchasing coconut parachute brand, 35.71 percent were purchasing VVD gold brand and the remaining 14.29 percent were purchasing ganapathy brand. Among the urban coconut oil purchasing respondents, 71.43 percent were purchasing VVD gold brand, 26.19 percent were purchasing coconut parachute brand and the remaining 2.38 percent were purchasing ganapathy brand.

The following chart 4.21 will statistically explain the brand of coconut oil preferred by the respondents.

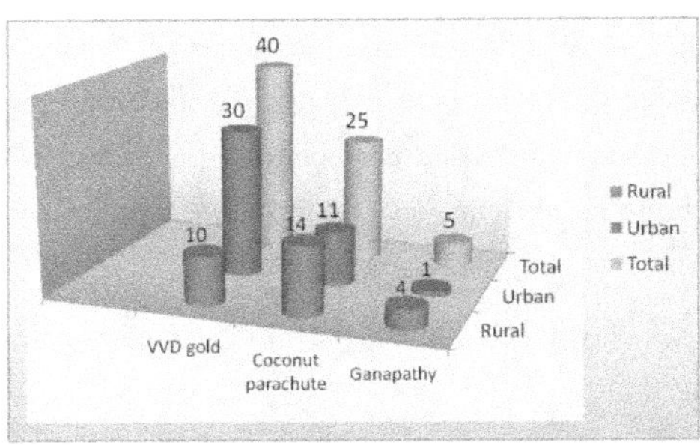

Chart 4.21: Brand of Coconut Oil Preferred by the Respondents

Table 4.41: Brand of Rice Bran Oil Purchased by the Respondents

Brand name	Rural (N=6)	Urban (N=7)	Total (N=13)
Diet	2 (33.33)	6 (85.71)	08 (61.54)
Good day	4 (66.67)	1 (14.29)	05 (38.46)

Table 4.41 presents the brand of rice bran oil purchased by the respondents. From the table, it was clear that 61.54 percent of rice bran oil purchasing respondents were purchasing diet brand and the remaining 38.46 percent of rice bran oil purchasing respondents were

purchasing good day brand. Among the rural rice bran oil purchasing respondents, 66.67 percent were purchasing good day brand and the remaining 33.33 percent were purchasing diet brand. Among the urban rice bran oil purchasing respondents, 85.71 percent were purchasing diet brand and the remaining 14.29 percent were purchasing good day brand.

The following chart 4.22 will statistically explain the brand of rice bran oil preferred by the respondents.

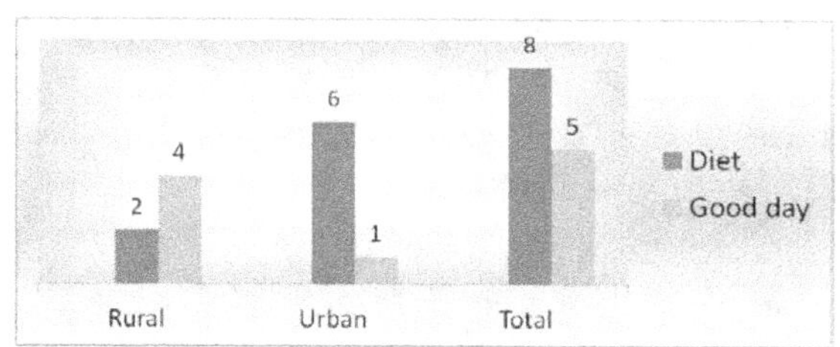

Chart 4.22: Brand of Rice Bran Oil Preferred by the Respondents

Table 4.42: Duration of Usage of Branded Oil Currently Purchased by the Rural Respondents

Type of oil	> 1 month	1-6 months	6months-1year	1-3 years	More than 3 years	Total
Sunflower oil	0	0	0	04 (5.88)	64 (94.12)	68(100)
Sesame oil	0	0	0	14 (33.33)	28 (66.67)	42(100)
Palm oil	0	0	0	30 (28.85)	74 (71.15)	104(100)
Vanaspathi	07(31.82)	03 (13.64)	0	7 (31.82)	5 (22.72)	22 (100)
Olive oil	56 (98.25)	01 (1.75)	0	0	0	57 (100)
Ground nut oil	0	0	0	0	25 (100)	25 (100)
Coconut oil	0	0	04(14.29)	04 (14.29)	20 (71.42)	28 (100)
Rice bran oil	05 (83.33)	01 (16.67)	0	0	0	6 (100)
Other oils	01(20)	0	02 (40)	0	02(40)	5 (100)
Total	69(19.33)	05 (1.40)	06 (1.68)	59 (16.53)	218(61.06)	357(100)

*All the respondents were purchasing only the branded cooking oil **except 3respondents** purchasing unbranded vanaspathi.*

Table 4.42 presents the duration of usage of cooking oil currently purchased by the rural respondents. From the table, it was evident that majority (61.06 percent) of the rural respondents were using the cooking oil purchased by them for more than three years, followed by 19.33 percent using for less than a month. 16.53 percent of the rural respondents were using the cooking oil purchased by them for one to three years. 1.68 percent and 1.40 percent of rural respondents were using the branded cooking oil purchased by them for six months to one year and one to six months respectively. 94.12 percent of branded sunflower oil purchasing rural respondents were using it for more than three years and 5.88 percent of respondents were using it for one to three years. 66.67 percent of branded sesame oil purchasing rural respondents were using it for more than three years and 33.33 percent of rural respondents were using it for one to three years. 100 percent of ground nut oil purchasing rural respondents were using it for more than three years.

71.15 percent of palm oil purchasing rural respondents were using it for more than three years and 28.85 percent of rural respondents were using it for one to three years. 31.82 percent of vanaspathi oil purchasing rural respondents were using it for less than a month and one to three years respectively. 22.72 percent of vanaspathi oil purchasing rural respondents were using it for more than three years and the remaining 13.64 percent were using it for one to six months.

98.25 percent and 1.75 percent of olive oil purchasing rural respondents were using it for less than a month and one to six months respectively. Among the coconut oil purchasing rural respondents, 71.42 percent were using it for more than three years and 14.29 percent were using it for six months to one year and one year to three years respectively.

83.33 percent and 16.67 percent of rice bran oil purchasing rural respondents were using it for less than a month and one to six months respectively. Among the other oil purchasing rural respondents 40 percent were using it for more than three years and another 40 percent were using it for six months to one year. The remaining 20 percent of other oil purchasing rural respondents were using it for less than a month.

Table 4.43: Duration of Usage of Branded Oil Currently Purchased by the Urban Respondents

Type of oil	> 1 month	1-6 months	6months -1year	1-3 years	More than 3 years	Total
Sunflower oil	02 (1.71)	06 (5.13)	05(4.27)	04 (3.42)	100(85.47)	117(100)
Sesame oil	0	0	0	02 (6.67)	28 (93.33)	30(100)
Palm oil	0	0	0	0	23 (100)	23 (100)
Vanaspathi	30 (75)	03 (7.5)	0	5 (12.5)	2 (5)	40(100)
Olive oil	05 (13.16)	33 (86.84)	0	0	0	38 (100)
Ground nut oil	0	0	0	0	60 (100)	60 (100)
Coconut oil	0	0	0	02 (4.76)	40 (95.24)	42 (100)
Rice bran oil	05 (71.43)	02 (28.57)	0	0	0	7 (100)
Other oils	0	0	1 (100)	0	0	1(100)
Total	42 (11.73)	44 (12.29)	06 (1.68)	13(3.63)	253 (70.67)	358 (100)

All the respondents were purchasing only the branded cooking oil except 2 respondents purchasing unbranded vanaspathi

Table 4.43 presents the duration of usage of branded cooking oil currently purchased by the urban respondents.

From the table, it was evident that majority (70.67 percent) of the urban respondents were using the cooking oil purchased by them for more than three years, followed by 12.29 percent using for one to six months.11.73 percent of the urban respondents were using the cooking oil purchased by them for less than a month.

3.63 percent and 1.68 percent of urban respondents were using the cooking oil purchased by them for one to three years and six months to one year respectively.

85.47 percent of sunflower oil purchasing urban respondents were using it for more than three years and 5.13 percent of urban respondents were using it for one to six months. 4.27 percent of sunflower oil purchasing urban respondents were using it for six months to one year and 3.42 percent of urban respondents were using it for one to three years. Only 1.71 percent of sunflower oil purchasing urban respondents were using it for less than a month.

93.33 percent and 6.67 percent of sesame oil purchasing urban respondents were using it for more than three years and one to three years respectively.

100 percent of palm oil purchasing urban respondents were using it for more than three years. 75 percent of vanaspathi purchasing urban respondents were using it for less than a month and 12.5 percent vanaspathi purchasing urban respondents were using it for one to three years. 7.5 percent of vanaspathi purchasing urban respondents were using it for one to six months and 5 percent vanaspathi purchasing urban respondents were using it for more than three years.

86.84 percent of olive oil purchasing urban respondents were using it for one to six months and 13.16 percent of urban respondents were using it for less than a month.

100 percent of ground nut oil purchasing urban respondents were using it for more than three years. 95.24 percent of coconut oil purchasing urban respondents were using it for more than three years and 4.76 percent of urban respondents were using it for one to three years.

71.43 percent of rice bran oil purchasing urban respondents were using it for less than a month and 28.57 percent of urban respondents were using it for one to six months. 100 percent of other oil purchasing urban respondents were using it for six months to one year.

Table 4.44: Duration of Usage of Branded Oil Currently Purchased by the Respondents

Type of oil	> 1 month	1-6 months	6months-1year	1-3 years	More than 3 years	Total
Sunflower oil	2(1.08)	6(3.24)	5(2.70)	8(4.33)	164(88.65)	185(100)
Sesame oil	0	0	0	16(22.22)	56(77.78)	72(100)
Palm oil	0	0	0	30(23.62)	97(76.38)	127(100)
Vanaspathi	37(59.68)	6(9.68)	0	12(19.35)	7(11.29)	62(100)
Olive oil	61(64.21)	34(35.79)	0	0	0	95(100)
Ground nut oil	0	0	0	0	85(100)	85(100)
Coconut oil	0	0	4(5.71)	6(8.57)	60(85.72)	70(100)
Rice bran oil	10(76.92)	3(23.08)	0	0	0	13 (100)
Other oils	1(16.67)	0	3 (50)	0	2(33.33)	6 (100)
Total	111(15.52)	49(6.85)	12(1.68)	72(10.07)	471(65.88)	715(100)

All the respondents were purchasing only the branded cooking oil (except 5 out of 720)

Table 4.44 presents the duration of usage of branded cooking oil currently purchased by the respondents. From the table, it was evident that majority (65.88 percent) of the respondents were using the branded cooking oil purchased by them for more than three years, followed by 15.52 percent using for less than a month.10.07 percent of the respondents were using the branded cooking oil purchased by them for one to three years. 6.85 percent and 1.68 percent of respondents were using the branded cooking oil purchased by them for one to six months years and six months to one year respectively.

88.65 percent of sunflower oil purchasing respondents were using it for more than three years and 4.33 percent of respondents were using it for one to three years. 3.24 percent of sunflower oil purchasing respondents were using it for one to six months and 2.70 percent of respondents were using it for six months to one year. Only 1.08 percent of sunflower oil purchasing respondents were using it for less than a month.77.78 percent of sesame oil purchasing respondents were using it for more than three years and the remaining 22.22 percent were using it for one to three years.

76.38 percent of palm oil purchasing respondents were using it for more than three years and the remaining 23.62 percent were using it for one to three years. 59.68 percent of vanaspathi purchasing respondents were using it for less than a month and 19.35 percent were using it for one to three years. 11.29 percent of vanaspathi purchasing respondents were using it for more than three years and 9.68 percent were using it for one to six months.

64.21 percent of olive oil purchasing respondents were using it for less than a month and the remaining 35.79 percent were using it for one to six months.100 percent of ground nut oil purchasing respondents were using it for more than three years.

85.72 percent of coconut oil purchasing respondents were using it for more than three years and 8.57 percent were using it for one to three years. Only 5.71 percent of coconut oil purchasing respondents were using it for six months to one year.

76.92 percent of rice bran oil purchasing respondents were using it for less than a month and the remaining 23.08 percent were using it for one to six months. 50 percent of other oil purchasing respondents were using it for six months to one year and 33.33 percent were using it for more than three years.16.67 percent of other oil purchasing respondents were using it for less than a month.

Table 4.45: Result of LMR Analysis Effects of Brand Preference on Rural Cooking Oil Customers

Model Summary									
Model	R	R Square	Adjusted R Square	Std. Error of the Estimate	Change Statistics				
					R Square Change	F Change	df1	df2	Sig. F Change
1	.681a	.079	.050	1.83610	.079	2.707	11	348	.002

ANOVAb

	Model	Sum of Squares	d.f	Mean Square	F	Sig.
1	Regression	100.396	11	9.127	2.707	.002a
	Residual	1173.204	348	3.371		
	Total	1273.600	359			

Coefficientsa								
Model		Un standardized Coefficients		Standardized Coefficients	t	Sig.	Co linearity Statistics	
		B	Std. Error	Beta			Tolerance	VIF
1	(Constant)	21.223	.953	.976	22.262	.000		
	Age	-.346	.144	-.130	-2.401	.017	.910	1.099
	Gender of the respondents	.603	.211	.154	2.859	0.05	.906	1.103
	Educational level	.086	.061	.074	1.400	.162	.946	1.057
	Marital status	.303	.234	.068	1.295	.196	.962	1.039
	Family Size	.140	.145	.051	.962	.337	.959	1.043
	Type of family	-.260	.239	-.059	-1.090	.276	.911	1.098
	Community	-.234	.125	-.102	-1.880	.061	.901	1.109
	Occupation	-.015	.089	-.009	-.170	.865	.867	1.153
	Income	.063	.114	.028	.548	.584	.988	1.012
	Expenditure	.081	.095	.046	.850	.396	.918	1.089

In order, to understand the effect of independent variable on the dependent variable namely brand preference among the rural customers Linear Multiple Regression model was employed. Ten independent variables namely age, gender, education level, marital status, family size, type of family, community, occupation, income and expenditure were statistically related to brand preference of rural customer as dependent variable.

As shown in the table 4.45, the model was significant and the r^2 value was 68 percent (i.e.) the effect on the dependent variable has been explained at 68 percent level. The results show that the demographic variables such as age (0.017), gender (0.05) and community (0.061) had significance effect on brand preference of the rural cooking oil consumers. Further the results show that among the ten dependent variables, education level (0.162), marital status (0.196), occupation (0.865), income (0.584) and expenditure (0.396) did not had any significant effect on brand preference among the rural cooking oil consumers.

However among the significant variables, age (0.017), gender (0.05) and community (0.061) were found to be prominent variable affecting significantly to a greater extent for high realisation of demographic contributors for brand preference of rural cooking oil consumers (i.e.) the standardised co-efficient β value was 0.976 which was greater than the other significant variable. Further the study reveals that higher age group of rural consumers have more relied on brand.

Table 4.46: Result of LMR Analysis effects of Brand preference on Urban cooking Oil Customers

Model Summary									
Model	R	R Square	Adjusted R Square	Std. Error of the Estimate	Change Statistics				
					R Square Change	F Change	df1	df2	Sig. F Change
1	.587[a]	.150	.123	1.94850	.150	5.580	11	349	.000

ANOVA[b]						
	Model	Sum of Squares	d.f	Mean Square	F	Sig.
1	Regression	233.056	11	21.187	5.580	.000[a]
	Residual	1325.038	349	3.797		
	Total	1558.094	360			

Co efficients[a]								
Model		Un-standardized Coefficients		Standardized Coefficients	t	Sig.	Co linearity Statistics	
		B	Std. Error	Beta			Tolerance	VIF
1	(Constant)	18.165	1.018	.931	17.836	.000		
	Age	.198	.137	.073	1.447	.049	.961	1.041
	Gender of the respondents	.778	.266	.154	2.927	.004	.880	1.136
	Educational level	.309	.073	.218	4.262	.000	.930	1.076
	Marital status	.300	.228	.068	1.319	.188	.917	1.090
	Family Size	.280	.177	.080	1.587	.113	.964	1.038
	Type of family	.530	.214	.126	2.472	.014	.946	1.058
	Community	.088	.143	.031	.617	.538	.963	1.039
	Occupation	-.206	.089	-.120	-2.309	.022	.904	1.106
	Income	.125	.121	.051	1.028	0.05	.976	1.024
	Expenditure	-.113	.107	-.054	-1.055	.292	.935	1.069

In order to have a further probe on the effect of demographic and economic indicators in particular on the perception of brand preference among the urban respondents, LMR analysis was carried out in details.

As shown in the table 4.46, the model was significant and the r^2 value was 0.587 percent i.e. the effect on the dependent variable has been exposed at 58.7 percent level. The demographic variable namely age, gender, family size, type of family, community and marital status and economic indicators such as educational qualification, income, occupation and expenditure had been analysed.

The results revealed that among variables age (0.049), gender (0.004), educational qualification (0.000), type of family(0.014), occupation (0.022) and income (0.05) categories have high influencing effect on brand preference among the urban consumers, whereas, the marital status (0.188), family size (0.113), community (0.538) and expenditure (0.292) did not have any effect on brand preference of urban cooking oil consumers.

However, among the significant variables educational qualification was found to be prominent variable affecting significantly to a greater extent for high realisation of brand preference among urban cooking oil consumers i.e. the standardised co-efficient β value was 0.931 which was greater than the other variables. We can conclude that there was increase in brand preference among the urban consumers and urban consumers can remain on brand preference only when the economic variable was appreciable and form significant proportion to brand preference.

Table 4.47: Result of LMR Analysis Effects of Brand Preference on Cooking Oil Customers

Model Summary									
M	R	R Square	Adjusted R Square	Std. Error of the Estimate	Change Statistics				
					R Square Change	F Change	df1	df2	Sig. F Change
1	.648ᵃ	.087	.073	1.91598	.087	6.157	11	708	.000

ANOVAᵇ						
Model		Sum of Squares	d.f	Mean Square	F	Sig.
1	Regression	248.625	11	22.602	6.157	.000ᵃ
	Residual	2599.040	708	3.671		
	Total	2847.665	719			

Coefficients[a]							
Model	Un-standardized Coefficients		Standardized Coefficients	t	Sig.	Col linearity Statistics	
	B	Std. Error	Beta			Tolerance	VIF
1 (Constant)	19.546	.689	.865	28.349	.000		
Age	-.064	.098	-.024	-.649	.516	.981	1.019
Gender of the respondents	.751	.164	.172	4.578	.000	.916	1.091
Educational level	.197	.047	.154	4.190	.000	.957	1.045
Marital status	.291	.162	.066	1.796	.073	.964	1.037
Family Size	.199	.112	.064	1.772	.077	.983	1.017
Type of family	.257	.156	.061	1.649	.099	.955	1.047
Community	-.137	.094	-.054	-1.466	.143	.961	1.040
Occupation	-.083	.062	-.050	-1.336	.082	.939	1.065
Income	.023	.084	.053	1.464	.044	.991	1.009
Expenditure	-.018	.071	-.009	-.257	.797	.954	1.049

The LMR model was worked in detail to know the effect of demographic and economic indicators in particular on the perception of brand preference among the respondents (rural and urban together).

As shown in the table-4.47, the model was significant and the r^2 value was 0.648 percent i.e. the effect on the dependent variable has been exposed at 64.8 percent level. The demographic variable namely age, gender, family size, type of family, community and marital status and economic indicators such as educational qualification, income, occupation and expenditure had been analysed.

The results revealed that among variables gender (0.000), educational qualification (0.000), type of family (0.099), occupation (0.082), marital status (0.073), family size (0.077) and income (0.044) categories have influencing effect on brand preference among the cooking oil consumers, whereas, the age (0.516), community (0.143) and expenditure (0.797) did not have any effect on brand preference of cooking oil consumers.

However, among the significant variables gender and educational qualification were found to be prominent variable affecting significantly to a greater extent for high realisation of brand preference among urban cooking oil consumers i.e. the standardised co-efficient β value was 0.865 which was greater than the other variables.

Table 4.48: Frequency of Purchase Made by the Respondents

Frequency	Weekly	Monthly	Total
Rural	60 (16.67)	300 (83.33)	360 (100)
Urban	20 (5.55)	340 (94.45)	360 (100)
Total	80 (11.11)	640 (88.89)	720 (100)

Figures in brackets are percents to row total

Source: Computed from primary data

Table 4.48 illustrates the frequency of purchase by the rural and urban respondents. From the table, it was clear that 88.89 percent of the respondents were making monthly purchase of cooking oil and 11.11 percent of the respondents were making weekly purchase of cooking oil. Among the rural respondents 83.33 percent were making monthly purchase of cooking oil and the remaining 16.67 percent were making weekly purchase of cooking oil. Among the urban respondents 94.45 percent were making monthly purchase of cooking oil and the remaining 5.55 percent were making weekly purchase of cooking oil.

Table 4.49: Preference to Change the Current Cooking Oil by the Respondents

Category	No. of. Respondents		Total
Level	Rural	Urban	
Yes	109 (30.28)	17 (4.72)	126 (17.5)
No	251 (69.72)	343 (95.28)	594 (82.5)
Total	360 (100)	360 (100)	720 (100)
Mean average	1.8250		

Figures in brackets are percents to column total

Source: Computed from primary data

Table 4.49 illustrates preference of the respondents to change the cooking oil which was currently purchased by them. It was inferred from the table, that, majority (82.5 percent) of the respondents doesn't want to change the current cooking oil purchased by them. Only 17.5 percent of the respondents expressed their opinion to change the current cooking oil purchased by them. Among the rural respondents, 69.72 percent doesn't want to change the current cooking oil purchased by them and the remaining, 30.28 percent expressed their opinion to change the current cooking oil purchased by them. Among the urban respondents, 95.28 percent doesn't want to change the current cooking oil purchased by them and the remaining, 4.72 percent expressed their opinion to change the current cooking oil purchased by them.

Table 4.50: Oil Preferred for Change by the Respondents

| Category | No. of. Respondents | | Total |
Oil	Rural	Urban	
Sunflower oil	60 (55.05)	09 (52.94)	69 (54.76)
Sesame oil	24 (22.02)	02 (11.77)	26 (20.63)
Groundnut oil	15 (13.76)	01 (5.88)	16 (12.70)
Olive oil	10 (9.17)	05 (29.41)	15 (11.91)
Total	109 (100)	17 (100)	126 (100)

Figures in brackets are percentage to column total

Source: Computed from primary data

Respondents wanted to shift from palm oil

Table 4.50 illustrates the type of oil the respondents wanted to shift from currently used oil. From the table, it was evident that majority of respondents (54.76 percent) wanted to shift to sunflower oil. 20.63 percent of the respondents wanted to shift to sesame oil. 12.70 percent of the respondents wanted to shift to groundnut oil. 11.91 percent of the respondents wanted to shift to olive oil. Among the rural respondents, 55.05 percent wanted to shift to sunflower oil, 22.02 percent wanted to shift to sesame oil, 13.76 percent wanted to shift to groundnut oil and 9.17 percent wanted to shift to olive oil. Among the urban respondents, 52.94 percent wanted to shift to sunflower oil, 29.41 percent wanted to shift to olive oil, 11.77 percent wanted to shift to sesame oil and 5.88 percent wanted to shift to groundnut oil.

Table 4.51: Frequency Time for Change by the Respondents

| Category | No. of. Respondents | | Total |
Frequency	Rural	Urban	
Often	10 (2.78)	149 (41.39)	159 (22.08)
Occasionally	199 (55.28)	183 (50.83)	382 (53.05)
Never	151 (41.94)	28 (7.78)	179 (24.87)
Total	360 (100)	360 (100)	720 (100)

Figures in brackets are percentages to column total

Source: Computed from primary data

Table 4.51 explains the time taken by the respondents to change the type of cooking oil. From the table, it was understood that, 53.05 percent of respondents were occasionally changing their type of cooking oil and 24.87 percents of respondents were never changed the type of cooking oil purchased by them. Only 22.08 percents of respondents were changing the type of cooking oil very quickly. Among the respondents who were changing the type of cooking oil occasionally, 55.28 percent belong to the rural area and 50.83 percent belong to the urban area. Among the respondents who were never changing the type of cooking oil, 41.94

percent belong to the rural area and 7.78 percent belong to the urban area. Among the respondents who were changing the type of cooking oil very quickly, 41.39 percent belongs to the urban area and 2.78 percent belongs to the rural area.

Table 4.52: Persons Influencing the Respondents to Change the Cooking Oil

Category	No. of. Respondents		Total
Persons	Rural	Urban	
Family	150 (71.77)	100 (30.12)	250 (46.21)
Friends	45 (21.53)	212 (63.86)	257 (47.51)
Neighbours	14 (6.70)	18 (5.42)	32 (5.91)
Others	0	02 (0.60)	02 (0.37)
Total	209 (100)	332 (100)	541 (100)

Figures in brackets are percentage to column total

Source: Computed from primary data

Table 4.52 explains the persons influencing the respondents to change the cooking oil. From the table it was clear that, 47.51 percent of the respondents were influenced by their friends and 46.21 percent of the respondents were influenced by their family members in changing the type and brand of cooking oil. 5.91 percent and 0.37 percent of the respondents were influenced by neighbours and others in changing the type and brand of cooking oil. Among the rural respondents, 71.77 percent were influenced by the family members and 21.53 percent were influenced by friends in changing the type and brand of cooking oil. Only 6.70 percent of rural respondents were influenced by the neighbours in changing the type and brand of cooking oil. Among the urban respondents, 63.86 percent were influenced by the friends and 30.12 percent were influenced by family members in changing the type and brand of cooking oil. 5.42 percent and 0.60 percent of urban respondents were influenced by neighbours and others respectively in changing the type and brand of cooking oil purchased.

Table 4.53: Level of Satisfaction with the Cooking Oil

Category	No. of. Respondents		Total
Level	Rural	Urban	
Low level	27 (7.5)	36 (10)	63 (8.75)
Moderate	73 (20.28)	41 (11.39)	114 (15.83)
High	260 (72.22)	283 (78.61)	543 (75.42)
Total	360 (100)	360 (100)	720 (100)

Figures in brackets are percentage to column total

* Source: computed from primary data*

Chi-square value between level of satisfaction with the cooking oil and of the respondents 11.242 which is significant at 00.01level

Table 4.53 explains the satisfaction level of the rural and urban respondents with the cooking oil they are currently using. From the above table it was evident that majority (75.42 percent) of the respondents were having high level of satisfaction with the oil they are using currently. 15.83 percent of respondents were having moderate satisfaction with the current oil and only 8.75 percent of respondents were having low satisfaction with the current oil purchased by them.

Among the rural respondents majority (72.22 percent) were having high level of satisfaction with the oil they are using currently. 20.28 percent of rural respondents were having moderate satisfaction with the current oil and only 7.5 percent of rural respondents were having low satisfaction with the current oil purchased by them. Among the urban respondents majority (78.61 percent) were having high level of satisfaction with the oil they are using currently. 11.39 percent of urban respondents were having moderate satisfaction with the current oil and only 10 percent of urban respondents were having low satisfaction with the current oil purchased by them.

Ho: There was no significant difference between rural and urban respondents with the level of satisfaction of cooking oil currently purchased by them.

H1: There was a significant difference between rural and urban respondents with the level of satisfaction of cooking oil currently purchased by them.

Table 4.54

ANOVA					
Overall satisfaction					
	Sum of Squares	d.f	Mean Square	F	Sig.
Between Groups	.272	1	.272	.684	.408
Within Groups	285.728	718	.398		
Total	286.000	719			

ANOVA table 4.54 illustrates the significance level of satisfaction between rural and urban respondents. From the above table, we can conclude that there was no significant difference between rural and urban respondents in the level of satisfaction with the cooking oil they are currently using as the significance level was 0.408 which was greater at 1 percent level.

Table 4.55: Opinion of the Respondents about the Price of the Oil Currently Used by Them

Category Price of the oil	No. of. Respondents		Total
	Rural	Urban	
Very low	104 (28.89)	23 (6.39)	127 (17.64)
Low	25 (6.94)	60 (16.67)	85 (11.81)
Reasonable	144 (40)	188 (52.22)	332 (46.11)
High	30 (8.33)	51 (14.17)	81 (11.25)
Very high	57 (15.84)	38 (10.55)	95 (13.19)
Total	360 (100)	360 (100)	720 (100)

Figures in brackets are percentage to column total

* Source: Computed from primary data*

Table 4.55 presents the opinion of the respondents about the price of the oil purchased by them. From the table, it was inferred that majority (46.11 percent) of the respondents opined that the price of the oil purchased by them was reasonable. 17.64 percent of the respondents felt that the price of the oil purchased by them was very low. 13.19 percent of the respondents felt that the price of the oil purchased by them was very high. 11.81 percent of the respondents felt that the price of the oil purchased by them was low. 11.25 percent of the respondents felt that the price of the oil purchased by them was high. Among the rural respondents, 40 percent felt that the price of the oil purchased by them was reasonable, 28.89 percent felt that the price of the oil purchased by them was very low, 15.84 percent felt that the price of the oil purchased by them was very high, 8.33 percent felt that the price of the oil purchased by them was high and the remaining 6.94 percent felts that the price of the oil purchased by them was low.

Among the urban respondents, 52.22 percent felt that the price of the oil purchased by them was reasonable, 16.67 percent felt that the price of the oil purchased by them was low, 14.17 percent felt that the price of the oil purchased by them was high, 10.55 percent felt that the price of the oil purchased by them was very high and the remaining 6.39 percent felts that the price of the oil purchased by them was very low.

CHAPTER V

PREFERENCE FOR SALES PROMOTIONAL ACTIVITIES–AN ANALYSIS

This chapter analyses the sales promotion activity preferred by the rural and urban cooking oil consumers, their opinion about various short -term sales promotion and the impact created on rural and urban cooking oil consumers by the sales promotion activity carried on by cooking oil manufacturers.

Table 5.1: Preference for Sales Promotional Activities by the Rural Respondents

S.No	Preference	Total score	Mean	Rank
1.	Cash Discount	2240	22.22	I
2.	Trade Discount	1637	16.24	IV
3.	Coupons	792	7.86	VI
4.	Contests	638	6.33	VII
5.	Freebies	1259	12.49	V
6.	Free offer	1704	16.91	III
7.	Extra quantity	1810	17.95	II
	Total	10080		

Table 5.1 presents the details of the preference of sales promotional activities preferred by rural customers. Variable cash discount was the most preferred sales promotion by the rural customers as it occupied the first rank with a total score of 2240, followed by extra quantity which occupied the second rank with a total score of 1810. The third and fourth ranked were assigned to the variables free offer and trade discount with a total score of 1704 and 1637 respectively. The fifth rank was assigned to the variable free bies with a total score of 1259, sixth rank was assigned to the variable coupons with a total score of 792. The seventh and last rank was secured by the variable contests with a total score of 638.

Table 5.2: Preference for Sales Promotional Activities by the Urban Respondents

S.No	Preference	Total score	Mean	Rank
1.	Cash Discount	2319	23.00	I
2.	Trade Discount	1310	13.00	IV
3.	Coupons	1053	10.45	VI
4.	Contests	982	9.74	VII
5.	Freebies	1133	11.24	V
6.	Free offer	1514	15.02	III
7.	Extra quantity	1769	17.55	II
	Total	10080		

Table 5.2 presents the details of the preference of sales promotional activities preferred by urban customers. Variable cash discount was the most preferred sales promotion by the rural customers as it occupied the first rank with a total score of 2319, followed by extra quantity which occupied the second rank with a total score of 1769. The third and fourth ranked were assigned to the variables free offer and trade discount with a total score of 1514 and 1310 respectively. The fifth rank was assigned to the variable free bies with a total score of 1133, sixth rank was assigned to the variable coupons with a total score of 1053. The seventh and last rank was secured by the variable contests with a total score of 982.

Table 5.3: (Rural+Urban) Preference for Sales Promotional Activities by the Respondents

S.No	Preference	Total score	Mean	Rank
1.	Cash Discount	4559	22.61	I
2.	Trade Discount	2947	14.62	IV
3.	Coupons	1845	9.15	VI
4.	Contests	1620	8.04	VII
5.	Freebies	2392	11.87	V
6.	Free offer	3218	15.96	III
7.	Extra quantity	3579	17.75	II
	Total	20160		

Table 5.3 presents the details of the preference of sales promotional activities preferred by rural and urban customers taken together. Variable cash discount was the most preferred sales promotion by the respondents as it occupied the first rank with a total score of 4559, followed by extra quantity which occupied the second rank with a total score of 3579. The third and fourth ranked were assigned to the variables free offer and trade discount with a total score of 3218 and 2947 respectively. The fifth rank was assigned to the variable free bies with a total score of 2392, sixth rank was assigned to the variable coupons with a total score of 1845. The seventh and last rank was secured by the variable contests with a total score of 1620.From the table-5.1, 5.2, and 5.3 we can conclude that there was no difference of opinion about various sales promotion among the rural and urban respondents as the rank assigned by them was exactly equal for all seven short-term sales promotion such as cash discount (Rank-I), extra quantity (Rank-II), free offer (Rank-III), trade discount (Rank-IV), free bies (Rank-V), coupons (Rank-VI) and contests (Rank-VII).

Table 5.4: Sales Promotion Availed by the Sunflower Oil Purchasing Respondents (Multiple Reply)

| Category | No. of. Respondents | | Total | Rank |
Sale Promotion	Rural (N=68)	Urban (N=117)	(N=185)	
Free Sample	39	40	79	VI
Coupon	38	62	100	IV
Trading or Bonus stamp	44	70	114	II
Price contests	26	59	85	V
Freebies	56	47	103	III
Cash Discount	58	110	168	I
Extra quantity	12	18	30	VII
Premium	01	07	08	VIII

Table 5.4 presents the details about the sales promotion availed by the sunflower oil purchasing respondents. The simple rank was assigned to various sales promotion activity based on the responses received. From the table, it was understood that, majority of the respondents availed cash discount during the purchase of sunflower oil as it ranked first with a total score of one hundred and sixty eight. The second rank was secured by trading or bonus stamp, third rank was secured by free bies and fourth rank was secured by coupons, fifth rank was secured by price contests, sixth rank was secured by free samples, seventh rank was secured by extra quantity and the last and eighth rank was secured by premium with a total scores of hundred and fourteen, hundred and three, hundred, eighty five, seventy nine, thirty and eight respectively.

Tabl 5.5: Sales Promotion Availed by the Sesame Oil Purchasing Respondents(Multiple Reply)

Sale Promotion	Rural (N=42)	Urban (N=30)	Total (N=72)	Rank
Free Sample	12	30	42	III
Coupon	19	27	46	II
Trading or Bonus stamp	11	19	30	V
Price contests	09	11	20	VI
Freebies	17	21	38	IV
Cash Discount	29	30	59	I
Extra quantity	05	10	15	VII
Premium	04	03	07	VIII

Table 5.5 presents the details about the sales promotion availed by the sesame oil purchasing respondents. The simple rank was assigned to various sales promotion activity

based on the responses received. From the table, it was clear that, majority of the respondent's availed cash discount during the purchase of sesame oil as it ranked first with a total score of fifty nine. The second rank was secured by coupons, third rank was secured by free samples and fourth rank was secured by freebies, fifth rank was secured by trading or bonus stamp, sixth rank was secured by price contests, seventh rank was secured by extra quantity and the last and eighth rank was secured by premium with a total scores of forty six, forty two, thirty eight, thirty, twenty, fifteen and seven respectively.

Table 5.6: Sales Promotion Availed by the Palm Oil Purchasing Respondents (Multiple Reply)

Sales promotion	Rural (N=104)	Urban (N=23)	Total (N=127)	Rank
Free Sample	62	12	74	III
Coupon	27	19	46	V
Trading or Bonus stamp	60	10	70	IV
Price contests	60	15	75	II
Freebies	29	17	46	VI
Cash Discount	87	17	104	I
Extra quantity	09	10	19	VII
Premium	02	07	09	VIII

Table 5.6 presents the details about the sales promotion availed by the palm oil purchasing respondents. The simple rank was assigned to various sales promotion activity based on the responses received. From the table, it was evident that, majority of the respondents availed cash discount during the purchase of palm oil as it ranked first with a total score of hundred and four. The second rank was secured by price contests, third rank was secured by free samples and fourth rank was secured by trading or bonus stamp, fifth rank was secured by coupon, sixth rank was secured by free bies, seventh rank was secured by extra quantity and the last and eighth rank was secured by premium with a total scores of seventy five, seventy four, seventy, forty six, forty six, nineteen and nine respectively.

Table 5.7: Sales Promotion Availed by the Vanaspathi Oil Purchasing Respondents (Multiple Reply)

Sales promotion	Rural (N=25)	Urban (N=42)	Total (N=67)	Rank
Free Sample	12	37	49	II
Coupon	03	23	26	IV
Trading or Bonus stamp	10	14	24	V
Price contests	20	16	36	III
Freebies	12	03	15	VI
Cash Discount	21	31	52	I
Extra quantity	02	01	03	VII
Premium	00	00	00	VIII

Table 5.7 presents the details about the sales promotion availed by the vanaspathi purchasing respondents. The simple rank was assigned to various sales promotion activity based on the responses received. From the table, it was under stood that, majority of the respondents availed cash discount during the purchase of vanaspathi as it ranked first with a total score of fifty two. The second rank was secured by free sample, third rank was secured by price contests and fourth rank was secured by coupons, fifth rank was secured by trading or bonus stamp, sixth rank was secured by free bies, seventh rank was secured by extra quantity and the last and eighth rank was secured by premium with a total scores of forty nine, thirty six, twenty six, twenty four, fifteen, three and zero respectively.

Table 5.8: Sales Promotion Availed by the Olive Oil Purchasing Respondents (Multiple Reply)

Sales promotion	Rural (N=57)	Urban (N=38)	Total (N=95)	Rank
Free Sample	11	25	36	IV
Coupon	07	13	20	VI
Trading or Bonus stamp	18	29	47	III
Price contests	11	06	17	VII
Freebies	24	34	58	II
Cash Discount	54	36	90	I
Extra quantity	09	17	26	V
Premium	00	00	0	VIII

Table 5.8 presents the details about the sales promotion availed by the olive oil purchasing respondents. The simple rank was assigned to various sales promotion activity based on the responses received. From the table, it was under stood that, majority of the respondent's availed cash discount during the purchase of olive oil as it ranked first with a total score of ninety. The second rank was secured by free bies, third rank was secured by trading or bonus stamp and fourth rank was secured by free samples, fifth rank was secured by extra quantity, sixth rank was secured by coupons, seventh rank was secured by price contests and the last and eighth rank was secured by premium with a total scores of fifty eight, forty seven, thirty six, twenty six, twenty, seventeen and zero respectively.

Table 5.9: Sales Promotion Availed by the Ground Nut Oil Purchasing Respondents (Multiple Reply)

Sales promotion	Rural (N=25)	Urban (N=60)	Total (N=85)	Rank
Free Sample	09	11	20	VI
Coupon	15	27	42	V
Trading or Bonus stamp	12	37	49	IV
Price contests	17	42	59	III
Freebies	21	49	70	II
Cash Discount	24	54	78	I
Extra quantity	03	07	10	VII
Premium	00	00	00	VIII

Table 5.9 presents the details about the sales promotion availed by the ground nut oil purchasing respondents. The simple rank was assigned to various sales promotion activity based on the responses received. From the table, it was under stood that, majority of the respondent's availed cash discount during the purchase of ground nut oil as it ranked first with a total score of seventy eight. The second rank was secured by free bies, third rank was secured by price contests and fourth rank was secured by trading or bonus stamps, fifth rank was secured by coupons, sixth rank was secured by free samples, seventh rank was secured by extra quantity and the last and eighth rank was secured by premium with a total scores of seventy, fifty nine, forty nine, forty two, twenty, ten and zero respectively.

Table 5.10: Sales Promotion Availed by the Coconut Oil Purchasing Respondents (Multiple Reply)

Sales promotion	Rural (N=28)	Urban (N=42)	Total (N=70)	Rank
Free Sample	07	12	19	VI
Coupon	10	24	34	V
Trading or Bonus stamp	10	25	35	IV
Price contests	17	32	49	II
Freebies	21	24	45	III
Cash Discount	19	31	50	I
Extra quantity	04	07	11	VII
Premium	00	00	0	VIII

Table 5.10 presents the details about the sales promotion availed by the coconut oil purchasing respondents. The simple rank was assigned to various sales promotion activity based on the responses received. From the table, it was under stood that, majority of the respondent's availed cash discount during the purchase of coconut oil as it ranked first with a total score of fifty. The second rank was secured by price contests, third rank was secured by free bies and fourth rank was secured by trading or bonus stamp, fifth rank was secured by coupons, sixth rank was secured by free samples, seventh rank was secured by extra quantity and the last and eighth rank was secured by premium with a total scores of forty nine, forty five, thirty five, thirty four, nineteen, eleven and zero respectively.

Table 5.11: Sales Promotion Availed by the Rice Bran Oil Purchasing Respondents (Multiple Reply)

Sales promotion	Rural (N=06)	Urban (N=7)	Total (N=13)	Rank
Free Sample	00	04	04	VI
Coupon	02	06	08	II
Trading or Bonus stamp	01	05	06	IV
Price contests	00	03	03	VII
Freebies	04	06	10	I
Cash Discount	01	05	06	III
Extra quantity	01	03	04	V
Premium	0	0	0	VIII

Table 5.11 presents the details about the sales promotion availed by the rice bran oil purchasing respondents. The simple rank was assigned to various sales promotion activity based on the responses received. From the table, it was under stood that, majority of the respondent's availed free bies during the purchase of rice bran oil as it ranked first with a total score of ten. The second rank was secured by coupon, third rank was secured by cash discount and fourth rank was secured by trading or bonus stamp, fifth rank was secured by extra quantity, sixth rank was secured by free samples, seventh rank was secured by price contests and the last and eighth rank was secured by premium with a total scores of eight, six, six, four, four, three and zero respectively.

5.1. Comparison of Rank between Sales Promotion Availed and Preferred

The Comparison of rank between sales promotion availed and preferred was made with a view to know whether the manufacturers met the requirements of the cooking oil consumers with regard to the types of consumer sales promotion.

Table 5.12: Comparative Table Comparison of Rank between Sales Promotion Availed and
Preferred by Cooking Oil Purchasing Rural Respondents

Sales promotion	Total of availed sales promotion	Availed rank	Preferred rank
Free Sample	152	V	III
Coupon	121	VI	VI
Trading or Bonus stamp	166	III	IV
Price contests	160	IV	VII
Freebies	184	II	V
Cash Discount	293	I	I
Extra quantity	45	VII	II
Premium	07	VIII	---

Table 5.12 analyses the similarities and differences between short-term sales promotion availed by the rural respondents and the short-term sales promotion preferred by the rural respondents. From the table it was clear, that there was similarity in cash discount as it ranked first in availed as well as preferred. Also the similarity existing between coupons as it ranked sixth in availed as well as preferred. The differences were existing between other short-term sales promotions such as free sample, trading or bonus stamp, price contests, free bies and extra quantity. But, there was significant difference for extra quantity and free bies, as extra quantity ranked seventh in availed and second in preferred and free bies ranked second in availed and fifth in preferred.

Table 5.13: Comparative Table Comparison of Rank between Sales Promotion Availed and
Preferred by Cooking Oil Purchasing Urban Respondents

Sales promotion	Total of availed sales promotion	Availed rank	Preferred rank
Free Sample	171	VI	III
Coupon	201	III	VI
Trading or Bonus stamp	209	II	IV
Price contests	184	V	VII
Freebies	201	IV	V
Cash Discount	314	I	I
Extra quantity	73	VII	II
Premium	17	VIII	---

** Source: Computed from primary data*

Table 5.13 analyses the similarities and differences between short-term sales promotion availed by the urban respondents and the short-term sales promotion preferred by the urban respondents. From the table it was clear, that there was similarity in cash discount as it ranked first in availed as well as preferred. The differences were existing between other short-term sales promotions such as free sample, coupon, trading or bonus stamp, price contests, free bies and extra quantity. But there was significant difference for extra quantity, free sample and coupon as extra quantity ranked seventh in availed and second in preferred, free sample ranked sixth in availed and third in preferred and coupon ranked third in availed and sixth in preferred.

Table 5.14: Comparative Table Comparison of Rank between Sales Promotion Availed and Preferred by Cooking Oil Purchasing Respondents (Rural+ Urban)

Sales promotion	Total of availed sales promotion	Preferred rank	Availed rank
Free Sample	323	III	V
Coupon	322	VI	VI
Trading or Bonus stamp	375	IV	III
Price contests	344	VII	IV
Freebies	385	V	II
Cash Discount	607	I	I
Extra quantity	118	II	VII
Premium	24	---	VIII

** Source: Computed from primary data*

Table 5.14 analyses the similarities and differences between short-term sales promotion availed by the respondents and the short-term sales promotion preferred by the respondents. From the table it was clear, that there was similarity in cash discount as it ranked first in availed as well as preferred. Also there was similarity in coupon as it ranked sixth in availed as well as preferred. The differences were existing between other short-term sales promotions such as free sample, trading or bonus stamp, price contests, free bies and extra quantity. But there was significant difference for extra quantity, free sample and coupon as extra quantity ranked seventh in availed and second in preferred, price contests ranked fourth in availed and seventh in preferred and free bies ranked second in availed and fifth in preferred.

5.2. Opinion

Opinion is a belief, judgment, or way of thinking about something; what someone thinks about a particular thing. The opinion of the respondents about the sales promotion was collected.

Table 5.15: Opinion about free samples by the respondents

Category Opinion	No. of. Respondents		Total
	Rural	Urban	
Illusory	39 (10.83)	14 (3.88)	53(7.36)
Satisfactory	38 (10.56)	38 (10.56)	76 (10.56)
Good	244 (67.78)	213 (59.17)	457 (63.47)
Very good	0	57 (15.83)	57 (7.92)
Excellent	39 (10.83)	38 (10.56)	77 (10.69)
Total	360 (100)	360 (100)	720 (100)

Figures in brackets are percentages to column total, Source: Computed from primary data.

Table 5.15 presents the opinion of rural and urban respondents about the free sample. From the table it was evident that, majority (63.47 percent) of the respondents felt good about the free sample, followed by the opinion of excellent (10.69 percent), satisfactory (10.56 percent), very good (7.92 percent) and illusory (7.36 percent). Among the rural respondents, majority (67.78 percent) felt good about the free sample followed by the opinion of excellent (10.83 percent), illusory (10.83 percent) and satisfactory (10.56 percent). Among the urban respondents, majority (59.17 percent) felt good about the free sample followed by the opinion of very good (15.83 percent), excellent (10.56 percent), satisfactory (10.56 percent) and illusory (3.88 percent).

Table 5.16: Opinion about Coupons by the Respondents

Category	No. of. Respondents		Total
Opinion	Rural	Urban	
Illusory	25(6.94)	33 (9.17)	58 (8.06)
Satisfactory	335(93.06)	327 (90.83)	662 (91.94)
Total	360 (100)	360 (100)	720 (100)

Figures in brackets are percentages to column total, Source: Computed from primary data

Table 5.16 presents the opinion of rural and urban respondents about the coupons. From the table it was evident that, majority (91.94 percent) of the respondents had satisfaction with coupons and the remaining 8.06 percent felt illusory about the coupon. Among the rural respondents, 93.06 percent were satisfied and the remaining 6.94 percent felt illusory about the coupon. Among the urban respondents, 90.83 percent had satisfaction with coupons and the remaining 9.17 percent felt illusory about the coupon.

Table 5.17: Opinion about Trading or Bonus Stamp by the Respondents

Category	No. of. Respondents		
Opinion	Rural	Urban	Total
Illusory	38 (10.56)	19 (5.28)	57 (7.92)
Satisfactory	0	0	0
Good	91 (25.28)	93 (25.83)	184 (25.55)
Very good	174 (48.33)	148 (41.11)	322 (44.72)
Excellent	57 (15.83)	100 (27.78)	157 (21.81)
Total	360 (100)	360 (100)	720 (100)

Figures in brackets are percentages to column total, Source: Computed from primary data

Table 5.17 presents the opinion of rural and urban respondents about the trading or bonus stamp. From the table it was evident that, majority (44.72 percent) of the respondents felt very good about the trading or bonus stamp, followed by the opinion of good (25.55 percent), excellent (21.81 percent), and illusory (7.92 percent). Among the rural respondents, majority (48.33 percent) felt very good about the trading or bonus stamp, followed by the opinion of good (25.28 percent), excellent (15.83 percent) and illusory (10.56 percent). Among the urban respondents, majority (41.11 percent) felt very good about the trading or bonus stamp, followed by the opinion of excellent (27.78 percent), good (25.83 percent) and illusory (5.28 percent).

Table 5.18: Opinion about Price Contests by the Respondents

| Category | No. of. Respondents | | |
| | Rural(360) | Urban (360) | Total (720) |
Opinion			
Illusory	16 (4.45)	15 (4.17)	31 (4.31)
Satisfactory	12 (3.33)	7 (1.94)	19 (2.64)
Good	328 (91.11)	335 (93.06)	663 (92.08)
Very good	0	0	0
Excellent	4 (1.11)	3 (0.83)	7 (0.97)

Figures in brackets are percentages to column total, Source: Computed from primary data

Table-5.18 presents the opinion of rural and urban respondents about the price contests. From the table it was evident that, majority (92.08 percent) of the respondents felt good about the price contests, followed by the opinion of illusory (4.31 percent), satisfactory (2.64 percent) and excellent (0.97 percent). Among the rural respondents, majority (91.11 percent) felt good about the price contests followed by the opinion of illusory (4.45 percent), satisfactory (3.33 percent) and excellent (1.11 percent). Among the urban respondents, majority (93.06 percent) felt good about the price contests, followed by the opinion of illusory (4.17 percent), satisfactory (1.94 percent) and excellent (0.83 percent).

Table-5.19 Opinion about free bies by the respondents

| Category | No. of. Respondents | | |
| | Rural | Urban | Total |
Opinion			
Illusory	15 (4.17)	11 (3.05)	26 (3.61)
Satisfactory	19 (5.28)	19 (5.28)	38 (5.28)
Good	322 (89.44)	312 (86.67)	634 (88.06)
Very good	3 (0.83)	2 (0.56)	5 (0.69)
Excellent	1 (0.28)	16 (4.44)	17 (2.36)
Total	360 (100)	360 (100)	720 (100)

Figures in brackets are percentages to column total, Source: Computed from primary data

Table 5.19 presents the opinion of rural and urban respondents about the free bies. From the table it was evident that, majority (88.06 percent) of the respondents felt good about the free bies, followed by the opinion of satisfactory (5.28 percent), illusory (3.61 percent), excellent (2.36 percent) and very good (0.69 percent). Among the rural respondents, majority (89.44 percent) felt good about the free bies, followed by the opinion of satisfactory (5.28 percent), illusory (4.17 percent), very good (0.83 percent) and excellent (0.28 percent). Among the urban respondents, majority (86.67 percent) felt good about the free bies, followed by the opinion of satisfactory (5.28 percent), excellent (4.44 percent), illusory (3.05 percent) and very good (0.56 percent).

Table 5.20: Opinion about Cash Discount by the Respondents

Category	No. of. Respondents		
Opinion	Rural	Urban	Total
Illusory	4 (1.11)	0	4 (0.55)
Satisfactory	291 (80.83)	303 (84.17)	594 (82.5)
Good	64 (17.78)	57 (15.83)	121 (16.81)
Very good	1 (0.28)	0	1 (0.14)
Total	360 (100)	360 (100)	720 (100)

Figures in brackets are percentages to column total, Source: Computed from primary data

Table 5.20 presents the opinion of rural and urban respondents about the cash discount. From the table it was evident that, majority (82.50 percent) of the respondents were satisfied about the cash discount, followed by the opinion of good (16.81 percent), illusory (0.55 percent) and very good (0.14 percent). Among the rural respondents, majority (80.83 percent) were satisfied about the cash discount, followed by the opinion of good (17.78 percent), illusory (1.11 percent) and very good (0.28 percent). Among the urban respondents, 84.17 percent were satisfied with cash discount and the remaining 15.83 percent respondents felt good about cash discount.

Table 5.21: Opinion about Extra Quantity by the Respondents

Category	No. of. Respondents		
Opinion	Rural	Urban	Total
Good	352 (97.78)	359 (99.72)	711 (98.75)
Very good	8 (2.22)	1 (0.28)	9 (1.25)
Total	360 (100)	360 (100)	720 (100)

Figures in brackets are percentages to column total, Source: Computed from primary data

Table 5.21 presents the opinion of rural and urban respondents about the extra quantity. From the table it was evident that, majority (98.75 percent) of the respondents felt good about the extra quantity and the remaining 1.25 percent of the respondents felt very good about the extra quantity. Among the rural respondents, 97.78 percent of respondents felt good about the extra quantity and the remaining 2.22 percent of the respondents felt very good about the extra quantity. Among the urban respondents, 99.72 percent of respondents felt good about the extra quantity and the remaining 0.28 percent of the respondents felt very good about the extra quantity.

Table 5.22: Opinion about Premium by the Respondents

Category	No. of. Respondents		
Opinion	Rural	Urban	Total
Illusory	346 (96.11)	349 (96.95)	695 (96.53)
Satisfactory	10 (2.78)	08 (2.22)	18 (2.5)
Good	04 (1.11)	03 (0.83)	07 (0.97)
Total	360 (100)	360 (100)	720 (100)

Figures in brackets are percentages to column total, Source: Computed from primary data

Table 5.22 presents the opinion of rural and urban respondents about the premium. From the table it was evident that, majority (96.53 percent) of the respondents opinioned that premium was illusory, followed by the opinion of satisfactory (2.50 percent) and good (0.97 percent). Among the rural respondents, 96.11 percent opined that premium was illusory, followed by opinion of satisfactory (2.78 percent) and good (1.11 percent). Among the urban respondents, 96.95 percent opinioned that premium was illusory, followed by opinion of satisfactory (2.22 percent) and good (0.83 percent).

Table 5.23: Opinion Rank Obtained by Various Sales Promotion Activities

Sales promotion	Rural rank	Urban rank	Total rank
Free Sample	IV (1042)	II (1147)	II (2189)
Coupon	VII (695)	VII (687)	VII (1382)
Trading or Bonus stamp	I (1292)	I (1390)	I (2682)
Price contests	III (1044)	V (1049)	V (2093)
Freebies	V (1036)	IV (1073)	IV (2109)
Cash Discount	VI (782)	VI (777)	VI (1559)
Extra quantity	II (1088)	III (1081)	III (2169)
Premium	VIII (378)	VIII (374)	VIII (752)

Figures in brackets are total scores obtained,   Source: Computed from primary data

Table 5.23 presents the opinion rank obtained by eight types of sales promotion namely free sample, coupon and trading or bonus stamp, price contests, free bies, cash discount, extra quantity and premium. The weighted rank was calculated by assigning top score to excellent (five) and the least score to illusory (one). From the table it was clear that, the first rank was obtained by trading or bonus stamp with a total score of two thousand six hundred and eighty two. The second rank was obtained by free sample with a total score of two thousand and one hundred and eighty nine. The third rank was obtained by extra quantity with a total score of two thousand and one hundred and sixty nine. The fourth rank was obtained by free bies with a total score of two thousand and one hundred and nine. The fifth rank was obtained by price contests with a total score of two thousand and ninety three. The sixth rank was obtained by cash discount with a total score of thousand five hundred and fifty nine. The seventh rank was obtained by coupon with a total score of one thousand and three hundred and eighty two. The eighth rank was obtained by premium with a total score of seven hundred and fifty two.

As per the opinion of the rural respondents, trading or bonus stamp ranked first with a total score of one thousand and two hundred and ninety two, extra quantity ranked second with a total score of one thousand and eighty eight, price contests ranked third with a total score of one thousand and forty four, free sample ranked fourth with a total score of one thousand and forty two, free bies ranked fifth with a total score of one thousand and thirty six, cash discount ranked sixth with a total score of seven hundred and eighty two, coupon ranked seventh with a total score of six hundred and ninety five and premium ranked last(eighth) with a total score of three hundred and seventy eight.

As per the opinion of the urban respondents, trading or bonus stamp ranked first with a total score of one thousand and three hundred and ninety, free sample ranked second with a total score of one thousand and one hundred and forty seven, extra quantity ranked third with a total score of one thousand and eighty one, free bies ranked fourth with a total score of one thousand and seventy three, price contests ranked fifth with a total score of one thousand and forty nine, cash discount ranked sixth with a total score of seven hundred and seventy seven, coupon ranked seventh with a total score of six hundred and eighty seven and premium ranked last(eighth) with a total score of three hundred and seventy four.

5.3. Judgment

Judgment is the evaluation of evidence to make a decision. The judgment of the respondents about the sales promotion was collected to know the effectiveness of the sales promotion schemes.

Table 5.24: Judgment of the Respondents about the Sales Promotion

Category / Opinion	No. of. Respondents		Total (N=720)
	Rural (N=360)	Urban (N=360)	
1.Price Discount			
Not Influential	13 (3.61)	9 (2.5)	22 (3.06)
Least Influential	26 (7.22)	10 (2.78)	36 (5)
Neutral	8 (2.22)	15 (4.16)	23 (3.19)
Influential	86 (23.89)	118 (32.78)	204 (28.33)
Most Influential	227 (63.06)	208 (57.78)	435 (60.42)
2.Contests			
Not Influential	293 (81.39)	230 (63.90)	523 (72.64)
Least Influential	20 (5.56)	7 (1.94)	27 (3.75)
Neutral	1 (0.28)	7 (1.94)	8 (1.11)
Influential	35 (9.72)	99 (27.5)	134 (18.61)
Most Influential	11(3.05)	17 (4.72)	28 (3.89)
3.Free gift			
Not Influential	23 (6.39)	12 (3.33)	35 (4.86)
Least Influential	41 (11.39)	0	41 (5.69)
Neutral	6 (1.67)	7 (1.94)	13 (1.81)
Influential	72 (20)	159 (44.17)	231 (32.08)
Most Influential	218 (60.55)	182 (50.56)	400 (55.56)
4.Loyalty rewards program			
Not Influential	28 (7.78)	3 (0.83)	31 (4.30)
Least Influential	46 (12.78)	3 (0.83)	49 (6.81)
Neutral	13 (3.61)	6 (1.67)	19 (2.64)
Influential	73 (20.28)	77 (21.39)	150 (20.83)
Most Influential	200 (55.55)	271 (75.28)	471 (65.42)
5.Extra quantity			
Not Influential	19 (5.28)	18 (5)	37 (5.14)
Least Influential	26 (7.22)	5 (1.39)	31 (4.31)
Neutral	12 (3.33)	13 (3.61)	25 (3.47)
Influential	83 (23.06)	173 (48.06)	256 (35.55)
Most Influential	220 (61.11)	151 (41.94)	371 (51.53)
6.Free Sample			
Not Influential	0	0	0
Least Influential	0	0	0
Neutral	11 (3.06)	17 (4.72)	28 (3.89)
Influential	44 (12.22)	25 (6.95)	69 (9.58)
Most Influential	305 (84.72)	318 (88.33)	623 (86.53)
7.Price pack deal			
Not Influential	18 (5)	15 (4.17)	33 (4.58)
Least Influential	3 (0.83)	1 (0.28)	4 (0.56)
Neutral	4 (1.11)	2 (0.55)	6 (0.83)
Influential	39 (10.84)	23 (6.39)	62 (8.61)
Most Influential	296 (82.22)	319 (88.61)	615 (85.42)
8.Trade Discount			
Not Influential	10 (2.78)	10 (2.78)	20 (2.78)
Least Influential	23 (6.39)	27 (7.5)	50 (6.94)
Neutral	12 (3.33)	11 (3.05)	23 (3.19)
Influential	134 (37.22)	72 (20)	206 (28.62)
Most Influential	181 (50.28)	240 (66.67)	421 (58.47)

Figures in brackets are percentages to column total, Source: computed from primary data

Table 5.24 presents the five judgments in making their purchase such as not influential, least influential, neutral, influential and most influential of the respondents about the sales promotion such as price discount, contests, free gift, loyalty rewards program, extra quantity, free sample, price pack deal and trade discount. The overall judgment of the respondents about the price discount was in the order of most influential (60.42%), influential (28.33%), least influential (5%), neutral (3.19%) and not influential (3.06%). The overall judgment of the respondents about the contests was in the order of not influential (72.64%), influential (18.61%), most influential (3.89%), least influential (3.75%) and neutral (1.11%). The overall judgment of the respondents about the free gift was in the order of most influential (55.56%), influential (32.08%), least influential (5.69%), not influential (4.86%) and neutral (1.81%). The overall judgment of the respondents about the loyalty rewards program was in the order of most influential (65.42%), influential (20.83%), least influential (6.81%), not influential (4.30%) and neutral (2.64%). The overall judgment of the respondents about the extra quantity was in the order of most influential (51.53%), influential (35.55%), not influential (5.14%), least influential (4.31%) and neutral (3.47%). The overall judgment of the respondents about the free sample was in the order of most influential (86.53%), influential (9.58%), and neutral (3.89%). The overall judgment of the respondents about the price pack deal was in the order of most influential (85.42%), influential (8.61%), not influential (4.58%), neutral (0.83%) and least influential (0.56%). The overall judgment of the respondents about the trade discount was in the order of most influential (58.47%), influential (28.62%), least influential (6.94%), neutral (3.19%) and not influential (2.78%).

The judgment of the rural respondents about the price discount was in the order of most influential (63.06%), influential (23.89%), least influential (7.22%), not influential (3.61%) and neutral (2.22%). The judgment of the rural respondents about the contests was in the order of not influential (81.39%), influential (9.72%), least influential (5.56%), most influential (3.05%) and neutral (0.28%). The judgment of the rural respondents about the free gift was in the order of most influential (60.55%), influential (20%), least influential (11.39%), not influential (6.39%) and neutral (1.67%). The judgment of the rural respondents about the loyalty rewards program was in the order of most influential (55.55%), influential (20.28%), least influential (12.78%), not influential (7.78%) and neutral (3.61%). The judgment of the rural respondents about the extra quantity was in the order of most influential (61.11%), influential (23.06%), least influential (7.22%), not influential (5.28%) and neutral (3.33%). The judgment of the rural respondents about the free sample was in the order of most influential (84.72%), influential (12.22%) and neutral (3.06%). The judgment of the rural respondents about the price pack deal was in the order of most influential (82.22%), influential (10.84%), not influential (5%), neutral (1.11%) and least influential (0.83%). The judgment of the rural respondents about the trade discount was in the order of most influential (50.28%), influential (37.22%), least influential (6.39%), neutral (3.33%) and not influential (2.78%).

The judgment of the urban respondents about the price discount was in the order of most influential (57.78%), influential (32.78%), neutral (4.16%), least influential (2.78%) and not influential (2.5%). The judgment of the urban respondents about the contests was in the order of not influential (63.90%), influential (27.5%), most influential (4.72%), least influential (1.94%) and neutral (1.94%). The judgment of the urban respondents about the free gift was in the order of most influential (50.56%), influential (44.17%), not influential (3.33%) and neutral (1.94%). The judgment of the urban respondents about the loyalty rewards program was in the order of most influential (75.28%), influential (21.39%), neutral (1.67%) least influential (0.83%) and not influential (0.83%). The judgment of the urban respondents about the extra quantity was in the order of influential (48.06%), most influential (41.94%), not influential (5%), neutral (3.61%) and least influential (1.39%). The judgment of the urban respondents about the free sample was in the order of most influential (88.33%), influential (6.95%) and neutral (4.72%). The judgment of the urban respondents about the price pack deal was in the order of most influential (88.61%), influential (6.39%), not influential (4.17%), neutral (0.55%) and least influential (0.28%). The judgment of the urban respondents about the trade discount was in the order of most influential (66.67%), influential (20%), least influential (7.5%), neutral (3.05%) and not influential (2.78%).

Table 5.25: Purchase Made by the Respondents Induced by Sales Promotion

Category	No. of. Respondents		
Sale Promotion	Rural(N=360)	Urban(N=360)	Total (N=720)
Yes	336 (93.33)	306 (85)	642 (89.17)
No	24 (6.67)	54 15)	78 (10.83)

Figures in brackets are percentages to column total, Source: computed from primary data

Table 5.25 presents the purchase made by the respondents motivated by sales promotion. From the above table, it was evident that majority (89.17%) of the respondents were induced by sales promotion in making their purchase and the remaining 10.83 percent were not induced by sales promotion in making their purchase. Among the rural respondents 93.33 percent were induced by sales promotion in making their purchase and the remaining 6.67 percent were not induced by sales promotion in making their purchase. Among the urban respondents 85 percent were induced by sales promotion in making their purchase and the remaining 15 percent were not induced by sales promotion in making their purchase.

Table 5.26: Overall Opinion about the Sale Promotion by the Respondents

| Category | No. of. Respondents | | Total |
Level	Rural	Urban	
4- 16 (Low level)	111 (30.83)	106 (29.44)	217 (30.14)
16 -32 (Moderate)	224 (62.23)	191 (53.06)	415 (57.64)
32-48 (High)	25 (6.94)	63 (17.5)	88 (12.22)
Total	360 (100)	360 (100)	720(100)

Figures in brackets are percentages to column total

Source: computed from primary data

Chi-square value between opinion sale promotion and of the respondents 19.148 which is significant at 0.001 level

Table 5.26 illustrates the overall opinion of the respondents about the sales promotion activity carried on by the cooking oil manufacturers. 57.64 percent of the respondents had moderate opinion about the sales promotion. 30.14 percent of the respondents had low level opinion and 12.22 percent of the respondents had high opinion about the sales promotion. Among the rural respondents 62.23 percent had moderate opinion, 30.83 percent had low level opinion and the remaining 6.94 percent had high opinion about the sales promotion. Among the urban respondents 53.06 percent had moderate opinion, 29.44 percent had low level opinion and the remaining 17.5 percent had high opinion about the sales promotion.

Ho: There was no significant difference between the overall opinion of the rural and urban respondents about the sales promotion.

H1: There was a significant difference between the overall opinion of the rural and urban respondents about the sales promotion.

Table 5.27

ANOVA					
	Sum of Squares	d.f	Mean Square	F	Sig.
Between Groups	2.568	1	2.568	6.601	.010
Within Groups	279.319	718	.389		
Total	281.888	719			

From the above table 5.27 it was inferred that in one way ANOVA, the total variation was partitioned into two components, between groups represents variation of the group means around the overall mean and within groups represents variation of the individual scores around their respective group means. Significance indicated the significance level of the F-test. Small significance value (<.05) indicated the group difference. In the above table, the significance level (0.010) was observed to be less than .05. Hence, null hypothesis (H0) was rejected and we can conclude that there was significant difference observed between the overall opinion of the rural and urban groups about the sales promotion.

Table 5.28: Perception on Sales Promotion Activities by the Respondents

Sales Promotional Activities	Rural			Urban		
	A	DA	NADA	A	DA	NADA
I do not consider sales promotion schemes while purchasing the cooking oil.	43	269	48	93	242	25
I purchase the cooking oil with sales promotion schemes.	276	51	33	296	39	25
I enjoy trying cooking oil with sales promotion schemes.	298	22	40	306	22	32
I think little about sales promotion schemes.	140	199	21	203	141	16
I usually aware about the sales promotion schemes of the cooking oil I purchase.	301	24	35	315	19	26
I don't usually bother to aware about sales promotion schemes.	10	350	--	--	328	32
I believe it is important to know the sales promotion schemes.	72	265	23	159	189	12
I have found that knowing about sales promotion schemes don't make difference in purchase.	13	316	31	9	334	17
I am not really curious about sales promotion schemes.	2	335	23	--	348	12
Generally, People are aware about sales promotion schemes of the popular cooking oils.	246	87	27	182	152	26
Cooking oils with sales promotion schemes are good.	350	10	--	328	18	14
Company provides sales promotion schemes when it is not able to sell.	93	246	21	161	189	10
If I see people purchasing products with sales promotion schemes, I think they are rational.	205	155	--	202	158	--
I have often found that sales promotion schemes are available on not so good cooking oils.	27	283	50	21	316	23
Sales promotion schemes are designed considering customers need.	253	69	38	232	80	48
I think customer should not pay attention to sales promotion schemes while purchasing the cooking oils.	118	222	20	163	191	6
Sales promotion schemes are beneficial to me.	236	--	124	166	--	194
Sales promotion schemes mislead customers from purchasing the good cooking oils.	267	40	53	277	26	57
Sales promotion schemes make the cooking oil favorite.	27	308	25	45	288	27
I usually see cooking oil are personalities without considering sales promotion schemes.	289	21	50	289	16	55
Good cooking oil has more frequent sales promotions.	281	27	52	273	36	51
I think sales promotion schemes create the image of the cooking oil.	30	304	26	54	270	36
I think cash discount is the good option as a sales promotion scheme.	333	11	16	317	15	28
I enjoy to avail cash discount on purchase	318	24	18	277	46	37
I believe cash discount is not a good option of sales promotion.	13	318	29	16	324	20
I love to receive free gift compare to cash discount.	11	333	16	10	24	26
Free gift provided with purchase doesn't have good quality.	307	24	29	285	44	31
There is no use of Free gift provided with purchase.	325	11	24	328	18	14
I value free gift the most.	12	286	59	9	195	149
I prefer to wait to take the advantage of the schemes.	303	---	57	215	----	145
I normally buy a brand which is on deal.	5	293	62	45	167	148

Source: computed from primary data

Table 5.29: LMR Model for Opinion about the Sales Promotions (Rural)

Model Summary									
Model	R	R Square	Adjusted R Square	Std. Error of the Estimate	Change Statistics				
					R Square Change	F Change	df1	df2	Sig. F Change
1	0.342a	0.062	0.032	.91200	0.049	1.795	10	543	0.060

ANOVAb						
Model		Sum of Squares	d.f	Mean Square	F	Sig.
1	Regression	11.501	10	1.150	1.795	0.072a
	Residual	301.931	349	0.641		
	Total	313.432	359			

Coefficientsa						
Model		Un-standardized Coefficients		Standardized Coefficients	t	Sig.
		B	Std. Error	Beta		
1	(Constant)	4.033	0.404		9.971	0.00
	Age	0.174	0.063	0.152	2.775	0.06
	Gender of the respondents	0.013	0.095	0.008	0.135	0.761
	Educational level	-0.006	0.026	-0.012	-0.236	0.659
	Marital status	-0.005	0.102	-.003	-0.049	0.874
	Family Size	0.005	0.063	0.004	0.081	0.759
	Type of family	0.122	0.103	0.064	1.179	0.239
	Community	-0.048	0.054	-0.049	-0.889	0.375
	Occupation	0.003	0.039	0.005	0.088	0.930
	Income	-0.043	.031	-0.076	-1.368	0.264
	Expenditure	0.088	.042	0.117	2.132	0.034

Y=4.033=(0.174)X1+(0.013)X2+(-0.006)X3+(-0.005)X4+(0.005)X5+(0.122)X6+(-0.048)X7+(0.003)X8+(-0.043)X9+(0.088)X10.

Multiple R= 0.342, F value= 1.795, P-value<0.01, R square= 0.062

The Linear multiple regression model indicates the rural respondent's opinion about the overall sales promotional tools adopted by cooking oil manufacturers and shows the effect of overall sales promotion on cooking oil purchasing rural consumers. In order to understand the effect of independent variables on the dependent variable namely opinion on overall sales promotion activities among the rural respondents linear multiple regression model was employed. Ten independent variables were statistically related to overall perception on sales promotional activities.

The result of 't' test reveals that the calculated significant of the partial regression co-efficient (0.174), (-0.006), (-0.005), (-0.048), (-0.043) are varied at 1 percent level respectively. The multiple 'R' found to be 0.342 which reveals that there was a relationship of 34 percent between the independent variable and the group of variable. The results of the multiple regression analysis show that variables age, gender, family size, type of family, occupation and expenditure have positive and significant effect on the overall sales promotional activities in rural consumers. The variables education level, marital status, community and income level have negative and less significant effect on the overall sales promotional activities.

Table 5.30: LMR Model for Opinion about the Sales Promotions (Urban)

Model Summary

Model	R	R Square	Adjusted R Square	Std. Error of the Estimate	Change Statistics				
					R Square Change	F Change	df1	df2	Sig. F Change
1	0.194[a]	0.038	0.010	1.02534	0.038	1.372	10	349	0.192

ANOVAb

Model		Sum of Squares	d.f	Mean Square	F	Sig.
1	Regression	14.421	10	1.442	1.372	0.192[a]
	Residual	366.910	349	1.051		
	Total	381.331	359			

Coefficients[a]

Model		Un-standardized Coefficients		Standardized Coefficients	t	Sig.
		B	Std. Error	Beta		
1	(Constant)	4.095	0.502		8.159	0.000
	Age	-0.062	0.072	-0.046	-0.862	0.231
	Gender of the respondents	0.089	0.144	0.036	0.617	0.637
	Educational level	-0.002	0.038	-0.003	-0.046	0.042
	Marital status	-0.285	0.120	-0.130	-2.375	0.018
	Family Size	0.079	0.093	0.045	0.849	0.097
	Type of family	0.197	0.113	0.094	1.746	0.082
	Community	-.020	0.075	-0.014	-0.266	0.790
	Occupation	0.102	0.047	0.120	2.168	0.031
	income1	-.041	0.045	-0.052	-0.894	0.372
	Expenditure	.024	0.058	0.023	0.415	0.580

$Y=4.095=(-0.062)X1+(0.089)X2+(-0.002)X3+(-0.285)X4+(0.079)X5+(0.197)X6+(-.020)X7+(0.102)X8+(-0.041)X9+(0.024)X10$

The Linear multiple regression model indicates the urban respondent's opinion about the overall sales promotional tools adopted by cooking oil manufacturers and shows the effect of overall sales promotion on cooking oil purchasing urban consumers. In order to understand the effect of independent variables on the dependent variable namely opinion on overall sales promotion activities among the urban respondents linear multiple regression model was employed. Ten independent variables were statistically related to overall perception on sales promotional activities.

The result of 't' test reveals that the calculated significant of the partial regression co-efficient (-0.062), (-0.002), (-0.285), (0.197), (-.020), (0.102),

(-0.041) are varied at 1percent level respectively. The multiple R found to be 0.194 which reveals that there was a relationship of 19 percent between the independent variable and the group of variable. The results of the multiple regression analysis show that variables gender, family size and expenditure had positive and significant effect on the overall sales promotional activities in urban consumers. The variables age, education level, marital status, type of family, community, occupation and income had negative and less significant effect on the overall sales promotional activities. From the above two analysis, we can conclude that there was significant difference between rural and urban consumers about the opinion of sales promotional activities.

5.4. Factor Analysis

In order to check the appropriateness of factor analysis, Kaiser-Meyer- Ogling (KMO) and Bartlett's test were used. The results are shown in the table (5.31) below. The opinion about the sales promotional activities were examined with the help of factor analysis. The rating on the importance of variables influences the customer opinion about the sales promotional activities have been taken for analysis. Initially, the KMO measures the sampling adequacy and Bartlett's test of sphericity have been conducted to test the validity of data for factor analysis.

Table 5.31: Factor Analysis

KMO and Bartlett's Test		
Kaiser-Meyer-Olkin Measure of Sampling Adequacy.		.602
Bartlett's Test of Sphericity	Approx. Chi-Square	8.521E2
	d.f	582
	Sig.	.000

Factor analysis was used for data reduction. The result revealed a chi-square value of 8.521E2 with 582 as degrees of freedom with level of significance at 0.000. KMO measures of sampling adequacy value were 0.602 revealing its validity of factor analysis.

Communalities

	Initial	Extraction
I do not consider sales promotion schemes while purchasing the cooking oil.	1.000	.962
I purchase the cooking oil with sales promotion schemes.	1.000	.842
I enjoy trying cooking oil with sales promotion schemes.	1.000	.776
I think little about sales promotion schemes.	1.000	.465
I usually aware about the sales promotion schemes of the cooking oil I purchase.	1.000	.571
I don't usually bother to aware about sales promotion schemes.	1.000	.968
I believe it is important to know the sales promotion schemes.	1.000	.743
I have found that knowing about sales promotion schemes don't make difference in purchase.	1.000	.963
I am not really curious about sales promotion schemes.	1.000	.872
Generally, People are aware about sales promotion schemes of the popular cooking oils.	1.000	.739
Cooking oils with sales promotion schemes are good.	1.000	.926
Company provides sales promotion schemes when it is not able to sell.	1.000	.658
If I see people purchasing products with sales promotion schemes, I think they are rational.	1.000	.655
I have often found that sales promotion schemes are available on not so good cooking oils.	1.000	.481
Sales promotion schemes are designed considering customers need.	1.000	.649
I think customer should not pay attention to sales promotion schemes while purchasing the cooking oils.	1.000	.706
Sales promotion schemes are beneficial to me.	1.000	.673
Sales promotion schemes mislead customers from purchasing the good cooking oils.	1.000	.461
Sales promotion schemes make the cooking oil favorite.	1.000	.909
I usually see cooking oil are personalities without considering sales promotion schemes.	1.000	.541
Good cooking oil has more frequent sales promotions.	1.000	.675
I think sales promotion schemes create the image of the cooking oil.	1.000	.567
I think cash discount is the good option as a sales promotion scheme.	1.000	.554
I enjoy to avail cash discount on purchase	1.000	.840
I believe cash discount is not a good option of sales promotion.	1.000	.652
I love to receive free gift compare to cash discount.	1.000	.873
Free gift provided with purchase doesn't have good quality.	1.000	.938
There is no use of Free gift provided with purchase.	1.000	.663
I value free gift the most.	1.000	.837
I prefer to wait to take the advantage of the schemes.	1.000	.824
I normally buy a brand which is on deal.	1.000	.728

5.5. Communalities

Communalities represent the proportion of variance that was explained by the underlying components. The communality of a variable in this case is the variance of given variable share with all the other variables and the value of which ranged between 0 and 1. The communalities are all one in the initial value column, since principal component analysis uses the initial assumption that all variance was common. After extraction some of the information is lost and the communalities in the extraction column show the amount of variance in every variable that the retained components explain. If the communalities after the extraction exceed 0.25, the variable can be considered as a part of principal component. With the help of principal component method and through normalisation the communalities of the variables were extracted from it. The result of the principal component analysis was shown in the following table.

The initial Eigen values of the variables and its percent of variance for all the cases were sequenced in descending order. The extraction is made with the help of Eigen values obtained by the variables. The variables that scored the Eigen value of more than one was extracted and the percent variance and its cumulative percentages were estimated.

Total Variance Explained									
Component	Initial Eigenvalues			Extraction Sums of Squared Loadings			Rotation Sums of Squared Loadings		
	Total	% of Variance	Cumulative %	Total	% of Variance	Cumulative %	Total	% of Variance	Cumulative %
1	3.939	12.706	12.706	3.939	12.706	12.706	2.840	9.161	9.161
2	3.004	9.689	22.395	3.004	9.689	22.395	2.742	8.844	18.005
3	2.457	7.925	30.320	2.457	7.925	30.320	2.352	7.586	25.591
4	2.301	7.422	37.742	2.301	7.422	37.742	2.246	7.245	32.836
5	1.739	5.609	43.351	1.739	5.609	43.351	1.801	5.809	38.646
6	1.615	5.209	48.561	1.615	5.209	48.561	1.791	5.777	44.423
7	1.431	4.617	53.177	1.431	4.617	53.177	1.751	5.647	50.070
8	1.363	4.397	57.574	1.363	4.397	57.574	1.737	5.605	55.675
9	1.323	4.269	61.843	1.323	4.269	61.843	1.719	4.681	60.356
10	1.107	3.570	65.413	1.107	3.570	65.413	1.179	2.921	63.277
11	1.046	3.373	68.786	1.046	3.373	68.786	1.167	6.560	69.837
12	.999	3.224	72.010						
13	.956	3.083	75.093						
14	.798	2.573	77.666						
15	.767	2.474	80.139						
16	.709	2.286	82.425						
17	.648	2.091	84.516						
18	.632	2.037	86.553						
19	.590	1.902	88.456						
20	.574	1.851	90.307						
21	.458	1.476	91.783						
22	.440	1.418	93.201						
23	.408	1.315	94.516						
24	.379	1.224	95.740						
25	.317	1.024	96.765						
26	.299	.964	97.728						
27	.234	.754	98.482						
28	.185	.596	99.078						
29	.150	.485	99.563						
30	.093	.300	99.863						
31	.042	.137	100.000						

It was observed from the above table that the principal component method has been grouped in the total variable under study in to eleven components with the help of Eigen values that are greater than one. The components were sequenced in a way that the factor with maximum Eigen value was extracted first and the factor with the next maximum value placed second likewise the entire components were extracted. The components is extracted with the maximum Eigen value of 3.939 as first factor and the minimum Eigen value of 1.046 as the last factor. Further, extraction of variables comes under each components was made with principal component method and by using matrix rotation and Kaiser normalization. All the thirty one variables were grouped in to eleven components and were shown in the following table.

Rotated Component Matrix[a]											
	Component										
	1	2	3	4	5	6	7	8	9	10	11
Sales promotion schemes make the cooking oil favorite.	.933										
I enjoy to avail cash discount on purchase	.905										
I value free gift the most.		.901									
I prefer to wait to take the advantage of the schemes.		.879									
I normally buy a brand which is on deal.		.844									
Sales promotion schemes are designed considering customers need.		.413									
There is no use of Free gift provided with purchase.			.802								
I believe cash discount is not a good option of sales promotion.			.785								
I usually see cooking oil are personalities without considering sales promotion schemes.			.694								
Generally, People are aware about sales promotion schemes of the popular cooking oils.			.537								
Cooking oils with sales promotion schemes are good.				.928							
Sales promotion schemes are beneficial to me.				.847							
I usually aware about the sales promotion schemes of the cooking oil I purchase.				.493							
Free gift provided with purchase doesn't have good quality.					.736						
I think customer should not pay attention to sales promotion schemes while purchasing the cooking oils.					-.710						
I am not really curious about sales promotion schemes.						.872					
I believe it is important to know the sales promotion schemes.						.685					
I think little about sales promotion schemes.						.479					
I love to receive free gift compare to cash discount.							.746				
I think cash discount is the good option as a sales promotion scheme.							.712				
Sales promotion schemes mislead customers from purchasing the good cooking oils.							.491				
Company provides sales promotion schemes when it is not able to sell.								-.791			
If I see people purchasing products with sales promotion schemes, I think they are rational.								.607			
I have often found that sales promotion schemes are available on not so good cooking oils.								.506			
I purchase the cooking oil with sales promotion schemes.									.118		
Good cooking oil has more frequent sales promotions.									.108		
I have found that knowing about sales promotion schemes don't make difference in purchase.										.431	
I think sales promotion schemes create the image of the cooking oil.										.112	
I don't usually bother to aware about sales promotion schemes.										.234	
I do not consider sales promotion schemes while purchasing the cooking oil.											.540
I enjoy trying cooking oil with sales promotion schemes.											.432

	1	2	3	4	5	6	7	8	9	10	11
Eigen values	3.939	3.004	2.457	2.301	1.739	1.615	1.431	1.363	1.323	1.107	1.046
Percentage of variance	9.161	8.844	7.586	7.245	5.809	5.777	5.647	5.605	4.681	2.921	6.560
Cumulative variance	9.161	18.005	25.591	32.836	38.646	44.423	50.070	55.675	60.356	63.277	69.837

Based on the factor analysis reduction method, factors were classified in to eleven components. They are as follows:

Two components were loaded on the factor first. It has been labelled as sales promotion schemes make the cooking oil favourite; I enjoy availing cash discount on purchase; related to the opinions on sales promotion. The first factor consists of two variables with an Eigen value of 3.939 explains 9.161 percent of variance. Among the two variables, first one was with a maximum load of 0.933, and the second component with a least load of 0.905 points.

In the second step, four components were loaded on the factor. It has been labeled as I value free gift the most; I prefer to wait to take the advantage of the schemes; I normally buy a brand which is on deal; Sales promotion schemes were designed considering customers need; related to the opinions on sales promotion. The second factor consists of four variables with an Eigen value of 3.004 explains 8.844 percent of variance. Among the four variables, first one was with a maximum load of 0.901, followed by second component with a load of 0.879, third component with a load of 0.844 and the last component with a least load of 0.413 points.

In the third step, another four components were loaded on the factor labelled as there was no use of free gift provided with purchase; I believe cash discount is not a good option of sales promotion; I usually see cooking oil are personalities without considering sales promotion schemes; Generally, People were aware about sales promotion schemes of the popular cooking oils; related to the opinions on sales promotion. The third factor consists of four variables with an Eigen value of 2.457 explains 7.586 percent of variance. Among the four variables, first one was with a maximum load of 0.802, followed by second component with a load of 0.785, third component with a load of 0.694 and the last component with a least load of 0.537 points.

In the fourth step, three components were loaded on the factor labelled as cooking oils with sales promotion schemes are good; Sales promotion schemes are beneficial to me; I usually aware about the sales promotion schemes of the cooking oil I purchase; related to the opinions on sales promotion. The fourth factor consists of three variables with an Eigen value of 2.301 explains 7.245 percent of variance. Among the three variables, first one was with a maximum load of 0.928, followed by second component with a load of 0.847 and the last component with a least load of 0.493 points.

In the fifth step, two components were loaded on the factor labelled as free gift provided with purchase doesn't have good quality; I think customer should not pay attention to sales promotion schemes while purchasing the cooking oils; related to the opinions on sales promotion. The fifth factor consists of two variables with an Eigen value of 1.739 explains

5.809 percent of variance. Among the two variables, first one was with a maximum load of 0.736 and the second component with a negative load of -0.710 points.

In the sixth step, three components were loaded on the factor labeled as I am not really curious about sales promotion schemes; I believe it is important to know the sales promotion schemes; I think little about sales promotion schemes; related to the opinions on sales promotion. The sixth factor consists of three variables with an Eigen value of 1.615 explains 5.777 percent of variance. Among the three variables, first one was with a maximum load of 0.872, followed by second component with a load of 0.685 and the last component with a least load of 0.479 points.

In the seventh step, three components were loaded on the factor labeled as I love to receive free gift compare to cash discount; I think cash discount is the good option as a sales promotion scheme; Sales promotion schemes mislead customers from purchasing the good cooking oils; related to the opinions on sales promotion. The seventh factor consists of three variables with an Eigen value of 1.431 explains 5.647 percent of variance. Among the three variables, first one was with a maximum load of 0.746, followed by second component with a load of 0.712 and the last component with a least load of 0.491 points.

In the eighth step, another three components were loaded on the factor labelled as company provides sales promotion schemes when it is not able to sell; If I see people purchasing products with sales promotion schemes, I think they are rational; I have often found that sales promotion schemes are available on not so good cooking oils; related to the opinions on sales promotion. The eighth factor consists of three variables with an Eigen value of 1.363 explains 5.605 percent of variance. Among the three variables, second one was with a maximum load of 0.607, followed by third component with a load of 0.506 and the first component with a negative load of -0.791 points.

In the nineth step, two components were loaded labelled as I purchase the cooking oil with sales promotion schemes; Good cooking oil has more frequent sales promotions; related to the opinions on sales promotion. The nineth factor consists of two variables with an Eigen value of 1.323 explains 4.681 percent of variance. Among the two variables, first one was with a maximum load of 0.118 and the last component with a least load of 0.108 points.

In the tenth step, three components were loaded labelled as I have found that knowing about sales promotion schemes don't make difference in purchase; I think sales promotion schemes create the image of the cooking oil; I don't usually bother to aware about sales promotion schemes; related to the opinion on sales promotion. The tenth factor consists of three variables with an Eigen value of 1.107 explains 2.921 percent of variance. Among the three variables, first one was with a maximum load of 0.431, followed by third component with a load of 0.234 and the second component with a least load of 0.112 points.

In the eleventh step, two components were loaded labelled as I do not consider sales promotion schemes while purchasing the cooking oil; I enjoy trying cooking oil with sales promotion schemes; related to the opinion on sales promotion. The eleventh factor consists of two variables with an Eigen value of 1.046 explains 6.560 percent of variance. Among the two variables, first one was with a maximum load of 0.540 and the last component with a least load of 0.432 points.

The cumulative percentage of this entire factor was estimated at 69.837 which show that the present study identified the maximum possible factors that influence the opinion about the sales promotion on cooking oils.

Table 5.32: Media Preferred by the Respondents to Know about the Sales Promotion Scheme

Category Media	No. of. Respondents				Total Mean score (N=720)	Rank
	Rural Mean score (N=360)	Rank	Urban Mean score (N=360)	Rank		
Television	17.35	I	14.83	II	16.09	I
Newspaper	8.36	VII	15.93	I	12.15	IV
Point of purchase display	5.76	VIII	13.24	III	9.5	VII
Hoardings	15.02	II	9.32	VII	12.17	III
Banners	13.73	IV	7.11	VIII	10.42	VI
Pamphlet	12.43	V	3.70	IX	8.06	IX
Wall painting	9.70	VI	11.26	VI	10.48	V
Internet	3.73	XI	12.75	IV	8.24	VIII
Radio	13.92	III	11.86	V	12.89	II

Table 5.32 presents the media preferred by the respondents in knowing the sales promotions offered by cooking oil manufacturers. Television was preferred by majority of the respondents as it occupied the first rank with a mean score of 16.09, followed by radio which occupied second rank with a mean score of 12.89. The third and fourth ranked were assigned to the hoardings and news paper with a mean score of 12.17 and 12.15 respectively. The fifth rank was assigned to wall painting with the mean score of 10.48, sixth rank was assigned to banners with the mean score of 10.42 and the seventh and eighth rank were secured by point of purchase display and internet with the mean score of 9.5 and 8.24 respectively. The last rank (9th) was secured by the pamphlets with the mean score of 8.06.

The media preferred by the rural respondents in knowing sales promotion offered by the cooking oil manufacturers was in the order of television (First rank), hoardings (second rank), radio (third rank), banners (fourth rank), pamphlet (fifth rank), wall painting (sixth rank), newspaper (seventh rank), point of purchase display (eighth rank) and internet (nineth rank) with the mean score of 17.35, 15.02, 13.92, 13.73, 12.43, 9.70, 8.36, 5.76 and 3.73 respectively.

The media preferred by the urban respondents in knowing sales promotion offered by the cooking oil manufacturers was in the order of newspaper (First rank), television (second rank), point of purchase display (third rank), internet (fourth rank), radio (fifth rank), wall painting (sixth rank), hoardings (seventh rank), banners (eighth rank) and pamphlet (nineth rank) with the mean score of 15.93, 14.83, 13.24, 12.75, 11.86, 11.26, 9.32, 7.11 and 3.70 respectively.

Ho: There was no significant difference between the media preferred by the rural and urban respondents in knowing the sales promotion scheme.

H1: There was a significant difference between the media preferred by the rural and urban respondents in knowing the sales promotion scheme.

Table 5.33

ANOVA					
Opinion media					
	Sum of Squares	d.f	Mean Square	F	Sig.
Between Groups	15.022	1	15.022	12.472	.000
Within Groups	864.839	718	1.205		
Total	879.861	719			

From the ANOVA Table-5.33 it was inferred that, there was significant difference between the media preferred by the rural and urban respondents in knowing the sales promotion scheme, as the significance was 0.000 which was less at 1 percent level. Hence the hypothesis Ho was rejected and H1 was accepted.

Table 5.34: Reasons given by the Respondents for Purchase of this Particular Brand or Non Brand of Cooking Oil

Category	No. of. Respondents		Total
Reason	Rural (N=360)	Urban (N=360)	(N=720)
Quality	12 (3.33)	187 (51.94)	199 (27.64)
Price	128 (35.56)	59 (16.39)	187 (25.97)
Advertising	10 (2.78)	23 (6.39)	33 (4.58)
Sales Promotion	70 (19.44)	21 (5.83)	91 (12.64)
Point of purchase display	15 (4.17)	68 (18.89)	83 (11.53)
Word of mouth	125 (34.72)	02 (0.56)	127 (17.64)

Table 5.34 presents the reasons for purchase of the particular brand or non brand of cooking oil by the respondents. Majority (27.64%) of the respondents were purchasing this particular brand of cooking oil for their quality, followed by price (25.97%), word of mouth (17.64%), sales promotion (12.64%), point of purchase display (11.53%) and advertising (4.58%). Majority (35.56%) of the rural respondents were purchasing this particular brand of cooking oil for their price, followed by word of mouth (34.72%), sales promotion (19.44%), point of purchase display (4.17%), quality (3.33%) and advertising (2.78%). Majority (51.94%) of the urban respondents were purchasing this particular brand of cooking oil for their quality, followed by point of purchase display (18.89%), price (16.39%), advertising (6.39%), sales promotion (5.83%) and word of mouth (0.56%).

Ho: There was no significant difference between the reasons for the purchase of particular brand of cooking oil by the rural and urban respondents.

H1: There was a significant difference between the reasons for the purchase of particular brand of cooking oil by the rural and urban respondents.

Table 5.35

ANOVA					
	Sum of Squares	d.f	Mean Square	F	Sig.
Between Groups	25.312	1	25.312	10.902	.001
Within Groups	1667.075	718	2.322		
Total	1692.388	719			

From the ANOVA Table-5.35 it was clear that, there was significant difference between the reasons mentioned by the rural and urban respondents for the purchase of particular brand of cooking oil, as the significance was 0.001 which was less at 1 percent level. Hence the hypothesis Ho was rejected and H1 was accepted.

Table 5.36: Factors Consider by the Respondents in Selecting the Oil Used by Them

Category	No. of. Respondents				Total mean score	Rank
Factors	R.mean score (N=360)	Rank	U. mean score (N=360)	Rank	(N=720)	
Taste	14.30	I	14.31	IV	14.30	II
Quality	13.38	II	14.5	III	13.94	III
Cost	12.80	III	8.14	VII	10.47	VI
Familiarity	12.27	IV	9.08	VI	10.68	V
Health	12.06	V	19.29	I	15.68	I
Brand name	11.92	VI	14.81	II	13.36	IV
Sales promotion offer	11.65	VII	12.40	V	12.02	VII
Pride	7.88	VIII	5.05	VIII	6.47	VIII
Advertising	3.74	IX	2.42	IX	3.08	IX

Table 5.36 explains the factors considered by the respondents in selecting the oil used by them. Health was the most influencing factor for the respondents in selecting the oil used by

them as it occupied the first rank with a mean score of 15.68. The other factors influencing the respondents in selecting the cooking oil used by them were in the order of taste (II rank), quality (III rank), brand name (IV rank), familiarity (V rank), cost (VI rank), sales promotion offer (VII rank), pride (VIII rank) and advertising (IX rank) with a mean score of 14.30, 13.94, 13.36, 10.68, 10.47, 12.02, 6.47 and 3.08 respectively. Taste was the most influencing factor for the rural respondents in selecting the oil used by them as it occupied first rank with a mean score of 14.30. The other factors influencing the rural respondents in selecting the cooking oil used by them were in the order of quality (II rank), cost (III rank), familiarity (IV rank), health (V rank), brand name (VI rank), sales promotion offer (VII rank), pride (VIII rank) and advertising (IX rank) with a mean score of 13.38, 12.80, 12.27, 12.06, 11.92, 11.65, 7.88 and 3.74 respectively. Health was the most influencing factor for the urban respondents in selecting the oil used by them as it occupied first rank with a mean score of 19.29. The other factors influencing the urban respondents in selecting the cooking oil used by them were in the order of brand name (II rank), quality (III rank), taste (IV rank), sales promotion offer (V rank), familiarity (VI rank), cost (VII rank), pride (VIII rank) and advertising (IX rank) with a mean score of 14.81, 14.5, 14.31, 12.40, 9.08, 8.14, 5.05 and 2.42 respectively.

CHAPTER VI

SUMMARY OF MAJOR FINDINGS, SUGGESTIONS AND CONCLUSIONS

In the present era of liberalisation and globalisation, there are numerous manufactures for cooking oil throughout the world. All of them wanted to attract the consumers. Increase in literacy, income and health consciousness among the Indian consumers made a drastic change in the purchase of type of cooking oil. The favourable demographics of India attracted the multinational companies to enter the Indian market. In this backdrop the researcher would like to underline the significance of the concept "Consumer behaviour" and "Sales promotion" at to the disposal of various cooking oil manufacturing companies in the field. This study will help the companies in the field to analyse the consumers and their response to the sales promotional efforts made by them. There were countless studies made on the consumer behaviour and sales promotion about the various products throughout the world. But no study was made on consumer behaviour and sales promotion about cooking oil in Tamilnadu till date. Thus to fill this research gap the researcher decided to make a study on the topic *"A study on Consumer behaviour towards the sales promotional tools adopted by cooking oil manufacturers with special reference to the Coimbatore city"*

6.1. Major Findings of the Study

6.1.1. Gender of the Respondents

Majority of the women were decision maker in the purchase of cooking oil both in rural and urban areas. In rural areas more than 63 percent of the women and in urban areas more than 78 percent of the women were decision makers in the purchase of cooking oil.

6.1.2. Age of the Respondents

Majority (51.11%) of the respondents were in the age group of 41-50years. In rural areas 56.94 percent and in urban areas 45.28 percent of the respondents were in the age group of 41-50 years.

6.1.3. Education Level of the Respondents

Majority (41.25%) of the respondents were graduates or post graduates. 52.78 percent of the urban respondents and 29.72 percent of the rural respondents were graduates or post graduates.

6.1.4. Community of the Respondents

Majority (47.36%) of the respondents belongs to the backward class based on their community. 48.89 percent of the urban respondents and 45.83 percent of the rural respondents belongs to backward class.

6.1.5. Religion of the Respondents

Majority (51.80%) of the respondents belongs to Hindu religion. 51.94 percent of the urban respondents and 51.67 percent of the rural respondents belong to Hindu religion.

6.1.6. Marital Status of the Respondents

Majority (71.94%) of the respondents was married. 76.94 percent of the rural respondents and 66.94 percent of the urban respondents were married.

6.1.7. Family Size of the Respondents

Majority (49.31%) of the respondents were having the small family size of only two to three members. 53.06 percent of the urban respondents and 45.55 percent of the rural respondents were having the small family size of only two to three members.

6.1.8. Type of Family of the Respondents

Majority (67.5%) of the respondents belong to the nuclear family. In rural areas, 76.39 percent and in urban areas 58.61 percent belong to the nuclear family.

6.1.9. Occupation Status of the Respondents

Majority (52.5%) of the respondents were working in the private concern. 54.72 percent of the rural respondents and 50.28 percent of the urban respondents were working in private concern.

6.1.10. Family Annual Income of the Respondents

Majority (52.22%) of the respondent's family annual income was in the range from two lakhs to four lakhs. 57.78 percent of the urban respondents and 46.67 percent of the rural respondents family annual income was in between two to four lakhs.

6.2. Place of Purchase of Cooking Oil by the Respondents

Majority (50%) of the respondents were purchasing cooking oil in departmental stores. 50.56 percent of the urban respondents and 49.44 percent of the rural respondents were purchasing cooking oil in the departmental stores. The result of ANOVA shows that there was a significant difference between rural and urban groups with that of place of purchase of cooking oil as the significance level (0.000) was observed to be less than 0.05.

6.2.1. Type of Oil Purchased by the Respondents

Majority (25.69%) of the respondents were purchasing sunflower oil for their cooking. In urban areas 32.5 percent were purchasing sunflower oil for cooking whereas in rural areas only 18.89 percent were purchasing sunflower oil for their cooking. Further, majority (28.89%) of the rural respondents were purchasing palm oil for their cooking. The result of ANOVA shows that there was significant difference between the variables gender (0.002), education (0.004), marital status (0.001) and family size (0.010), type of family (0.000), community (0.01), occupation (0.000), age (0.52) and income (0.004) with the type of oil purchased for cooking as the significance level was less at 1 percent level. Further, there was a significant difference between the rural and urban respondents with the type of oil purchased as the significance level was 0.000 which was less at 1 percent level.

6.3. Quantity of Oil Purchased by the Respondents

Majority (60.14%) of the respondents were purchasing below two liters of cooking oil per month. 61.11 percent of the rural respondents and 59.17 percent of the urban respondents were purchasing below two liters of cooking oil per month.

6.3.1. Quantity of Sunflower Oil Purchased by the Respondents

Majority (63.78%) of the sunflower oil purchasing respondents were purchasing below two liters of sunflower oil per month. 65.81 percent of the urban respondents and 60.29 percent of the rural respondents were purchasing below two liters of sunflower oil per month. The result of ANOVA shows that there was a significant difference between marital status (0.028), educational qualification (0.098), income (0.050), family size (0.026), type of family (0.032) and quantity of sunflower oil purchased as the significance level was less at 5 percent significance level.

6.3.2. Quantity of Sesame Oil Purchased by the Respondents

Majority (47.22%) of the sesame oil purchasing respondents were purchasing below two liters of sesame oil per month. 80 percent of the urban respondents and 23.80 percent of the rural respondents were purchasing below two liters of sesame oil per month. 52.40 percent of the rural respondents were purchasing two to three liters of sesame oil per month. The result of ANOVA shows that there was significant difference between age (0.165), educational qualification (0.081), income (0.238), type of family (0.144) and quantity of sesame oil purchased as the significance level was less at 5 percent significance level.

6.3.3. *Quantity of Palm Oil Purchased by the Respondents*

Majority (50.39%) of the palm oil purchasing respondents were purchasing below two liters of palm oil per month. 60.58 percent of the rural respondents and 4.35 percent of the urban respondents were purchasing below two liters of palm oil per month. 69.56 percent of the urban respondents were purchasing two to three liters of palm oil per month. The result of ANOVA shows that there was a significant difference between age (0.025), gender (0.027), type of family (0.035) and quantity of palm oil purchased as the significance level was less at 1 percent significance level.

6.3.4. *Quantity of Vanaspathi Purchased by the Respondents*

Majority (56.72%) of the vanaspathi purchasing respondents were purchasing below two liters of vanaspathi per month. 80 percent of the rural respondents and 42.86 percent of the urban respondents were purchasing below two liters of vanaspathi per month. 47.62 percent of the urban respondents were purchasing two to three liters of vanaspathi per month.

6.3.5. *Quantity of Olive Oil Purchased by the Respondents*

Majority (76.84%) of the olive oil purchasing respondents were purchasing below two liters of olive oil per month. 86.84 percent of the urban respondents and 70.18 percent of the rural respondents were purchasing below two liters of olive oil per month. The result of ANOVA shows that there was a significant difference between age (0.024), income (0.002) and quantity of olive oil purchased as the significance level was less at 1 percent level.

6.3.6. *Quantity of Ground Nut Oil Purchased by the Respondents*

Majority (43.53%) of the ground nut oil purchasing respondents were purchasing two to three liters of ground nut oil per month. 50 percent of the urban respondents and 28 percent of the rural respondents were purchasing two to three liters of ground nut oil per month. 60 percent of the rural respondents were purchasing below two liters of ground nut oil per month. There was a significant difference between type of family and the quantity of ground nut oil purchased as the significance level was 0.022 which was less at 1 percent level.

6.3.7. *Quantity of Coconut Oil Purchased by the Respondents*

Majority (81.43%) of the coconut oil purchasing respondents were purchasing below two liters of coconut oil per month. 85.71 percent of the rural respondents and 78.57 percent of the urban respondents were purchasing below two liters of coconut oil per month. There was a significant difference between marital status and quantity of coconut oil purchased as the significance level was 0.012 which was less at 1 percent level.

6.3.8. *Quantity of Rice Bran Oil Purchased by the Respondents*

Majority (92.31%) of the rice bran oil purchasing respondents were purchasing below two liters of rice bran oil per month. 100 percent of the rural respondents and 85.71 percent of the urban respondents were purchasing below two liters of rice bran oil per month.

6.3.9. *Quantity of Other Oil Purchased by the Respondents*

Majority (50%) of the other oils purchasing respondents were purchasing two to three liters of other oils per month. 60 percent of the rural respondents were purchasing two to three liters of other oils per month. 100 percent of the urban respondents were purchasing below two liters of other oils per month.

6.4. Brand of Cooking Oil Purchased by the Respondents

Almost all the respondents were purchasing the branded cooking oil except the few purchasing vanaspathi and other type of oils.

6.4.1. *Brand of Sunflower Oil Purchased by the Respondents*

Majority (43.78%) of the respondents were purchasing gold winner brand of sunflower oil. 52.14 percent of the urban respondents and 29.41 percent of the rural respondents were purchasing gold winner brand of sunflower oil. Majority (32.35%) of the rural respondents were purchasing fortune brand of sunflower oil.

6.4.2. *Brand of Sesame Oil Purchased by the Respondents*

Majority (56.94%) of the respondents were purchasing idhyam brand of sesame oil. 66.67 percent of the urban respondents and 50 percent of the rural respondents were purchasing idhyam brand of sesame oil.

6.4.3. *Brand of Ground Nut Oil Purchased by the Respondents*

Majority (64.71%) of the respondents were purchasing idhyam mantra brand of ground nut oil. 66.67 percent of the urban respondents and 60 percent of the rural respondents were purchasing idhyam mantra brand of ground nut oil.

6.4.4. *Brand of Vanaspathi Purchased by the Respondents*

Majority (65.67%) of the respondents were purchasing dalda brand of vanaspathi. 71.43 percent of the urban respondents and 56 percent of the rural respondents were purchasing dalda brand of vanaspathi.

6.4.5. *Brand of Olive Oil Purchased by the Respondents*

Majority (84.21%) of the respondents were purchasing cardio brand of olive oil. 87.72 percent of the rural respondents and 78.95 percent of the urban respondents were purchasing cardio brand of olive oil.

6.4.6. *Brand of Palm Oil Purchased by the Respondents*

Majority (55.12%) of the respondents were purchasing supreme brand of palm oil. 57.69 percent of the rural respondents and 43.48 percent of the urban respondents were purchasing supreme brand of palm oil. Majority (56.52%) of the urban respondents were purchasing RBD brand of palm oil.

6.4.7. *Brand of Coconut Oil Purchased by the Respondents*

Majority (57.14%) of the respondents were purchasing VVD gold brand of coconut oil. 71.43 percent of the urban respondents and 35.71 percent of the rural respondents were purchasing VVD gold brand of coconut oil. Majority (50%) of the rural respondents were purchasing coconut parachute brand of coconut oil.

6.4.8. *Brand of Rice Bran Oil Purchased by the Respondents*

Majority (61.54%) of the respondents were purchasing diet brand of rice bran oil. 85.71 percent of the urban respondents and 33.33 percent of the rural respondents were purchasing diet brand of rice bran oil. Majority (66.67%) of the rural respondents were purchasing good day brand of rice bran oil.

6.5. Duration of Usage of Branded Oil Currently Purchased by the Respondents

Majority (65.88%) of the respondents were using the branded oil currently purchased by them for more than three years. 70.67 percent of the urban respondents and 61.06 percent of the rural respondents were using the branded oil currently purchased by them for more than three years.

6.5.1. *Duration of Usage of Branded Sunflower Oil Currently Purchased by the Respondents*

Majority (88.65%) of the branded sunflower oil purchasing respondents were using it for more than three years. 94.12 percent of the rural respondents and 85.47 percent of the urban respondents were using the branded sunflower oil currently purchased by them for more than three years.

6.5.2. Duration of Usage of Branded Sesame Oil Currently Purchased by the Respondents

Majority (77.78%) of the branded sesame oil purchasing respondents were using it for more than three years. 93.33 percent of the urban respondents and 66.67 percent of the rural respondents were using the branded sesame oil currently purchased by them for more than three years.

6.5.3. Duration of Usage of Branded Palm oil Currently Purchased by the Respondents

Majority (76.38%) of the branded palm oil purchasing respondents were using it for more than three years. 100 percent of the urban respondents and 71.15 percent of the rural respondents were using the branded palm oil currently purchased by them for more than three years.

6.5.4. Duration of Usage of Branded Vanaspathi Currently Purchased by the Respondents

Majority (59.68%) of the branded vanaspathi purchasing respondents were using it for less than a month. 75 percent of the urban respondents and 31.82 percent of the rural respondents were using the branded vanaspathi currently purchased by them for less than a month.

6.5.5. Duration of Usage of Branded Olive Oil Currently Purchased by the Respondents

Majority (64.21%) of the branded olive oil purchasing respondents were using it for less than a month. 98.25 percent of the rural respondents and 13.16 percent of the urban respondents were using the branded olive oil currently purchased by them for less than a month. Majority (86.84%) of the urban respondents were using the branded olive oil currently purchased by them for one to six months.

6.5.6. Duration of Usage of Branded Ground Nut Oil Currently Purchased by the Respondents

All (100%) branded sesame oil purchasing respondents were using it for more than three years.

6.5.7. Duration of Usage of Branded Coconut Oil Currently Purchased by the Respondents

Majority (85.72%) of the branded coconut oil purchasing respondents were using it for more than three years. 95.24 percent of the urban respondents and 71.42 percent of the rural respondents were using the branded coconut oil currently purchased by them for more than three years.

6.5.8. *Duration of Usage of Branded Rice Bran Oil Currently Purchased by the Respondents*

Majority (76.92%) of the branded rice bran oil purchasing respondents were using it for less than a month. 83.33 percent of the rural respondents and 71.43 percent of the urban respondents were using the branded rice bran oil currently purchased by them for less than a month.

6.6. Effect of Brand Preference on Cooking Oil Customers

The Linear Multiple Regression model was worked in detail to know the effect of demographic and economic indicators in particular on the perception of brand preference among the respondents (rural and urban).

The overall results revealed that variables gender (0.000), educational qualification (0.000), type of family (0.099), occupation (0.082), marital status (0.073), family size (0.077) and income (0.044) categories have influencing effect on brand preference. (i.e.) the standardised coefficient β value is 0.865 which was greater than the other variables.

6.6.1 *Effect of Brand Preference on Rural Cooking Oil Customers*

The results revealed that variables age (0.017), gender (0.005) and community (0.061) categories have high influencing effect on brand preference among rural consumers. (i.e.) the standardised coefficient β value was 0.976 which was greater than the other significant variables.

6.6.2 *Effect of Brand Preference on Urban Cooking Oil Customers*

The results revealed that variables age (0.049), gender (0.004), educational qualification (0.000), type of family (0.014), occupation (0.022) and income (0.005) categories have high influencing effect on brand preference among urban consumers. (i.e.) the standardised coefficient β value is 0.931 which was greater than the other significant variables.

6.7. Frequency of Purchase Made by the Respondents

Majority (88.89%) of the respondents were making monthly purchase of cooking oil. 94.45 percent of the urban respondents and 83.33 percent of the rural respondents were making the monthly purchase of cooking oil.

6.8. Preference to Change the Current Cooking Oil by the Respondents

Majority (82.5%) of the respondents does not want to change the current cooking oil purchased by them. 95.28 percent of the urban respondents and 69.72 percent of the rural respondents does not want to change the current cooking oil purchased by them.

6.8.1 Oil Preferred for Change by the Respondents

Majority (54.76%) of the respondents wanted to shift to sunflower oil. 55.05 percent of the rural respondents and 52.94 percent of the urban respondents wanted to shift to sunflower oil. All the respondents who desire to shift are currently using the palm oil.

6.8.2 Frequency Time for Change by the Respondents

Majority (53.05%) of the respondents were occasionally changing their type of cooking oil. 55.28 percent of the rural respondents and 50.83 percent of the urban respondents were occasionally changing their type of cooking oil.

6.8.3 Persons Influencing the Respondents to Change the Cooking Oil

Majority (47.51%) of the respondents were influenced by their friends in changing the type of cooking oil. 63.86 percent of the urban respondents and 21.53 percent of the rural respondents were influenced by their friends in changing the type of cooking oil. Majority (71.77%) of the rural respondents were influenced by their family members in changing the type of cooking oil.

6.8.4 Level of Satisfaction with the Cooking Oil

Majority (75.42%) of the respondents were highly satisfied with the cooking oil currently used by them. 78.61 percent of the urban respondents and 72.22 percent of the rural respondents were highly satisfied with the cooking oil currently used by them.

6.8.5 Opinion of the Respondents About the Price of the Cooking Oil

Majority (46.11%) of the respondents felt that the price of the cooking oil currently used by them was reasonable. 52.22 percent of the urban respondents and 40 percent of the rural respondents felt that the price of the cooking oil currently used by them was reasonable.

6.9. Preference for Sales Promotional Activities by the Respondents

Majority of the respondents preferred cash discount as it ranked first according to the opinion of the respondents with the mean score of 22.61. Majority of the urban respondents preferred cash discount as it ranked first according to the opinion of the urban respondents with the mean score of 23. Majority of the rural respondents preferred cash discount as it ranked first according to the opinion of the rural respondents with the mean score of 22.22. There was no difference of opinion about various sales promotion among the rural and urban respondents as the rank assigned by them was exactly equal for all seven short-term sales promotion such as cash discount (Rank-I), extra quantity (Rank-II), free offer (Rank-III), trade discount (Rank-IV), free bies (Rank-V), coupons (Rank-VI) and contests (Rank-VII).

6.9.1 *Sales Promotion Availed by the Respondents*

Majority of the respondents availed cash discount while purchasing the sunflower oil, sesame oil, palm oil, vanaspathi, olive oil, ground nut oil and coconut oil as cash discount ranked first with a score of one hundred and sixty eight, fifty nine, one hundred and four, fifty two, ninety, seventy eight and fifty respectively. Majority of the respondents availed free bies while purchasing the rice bran oil as it ranked first with a score of ten.

6.9.2 *Similarities and Differences between Sales Promotions Availed and Preferred by the Respondents*

There was similarity in cash discount as it ranked first in availed as well as preferred. Also there was similarity in coupon as it ranks sixth in availed as well as preferred. The differences were existing between other short-term sales promotions such as free sample, trading or bonus stamp, price contests, free bies and extra quantity. But there was significant difference for extra quantity, free sample and coupon as extra quantity ranked seventh in availed and second in preferred, price contests ranked fourth in availed and seventh in preferred and free bies ranks second in availed and fifth in preferred.

6.9.3 *Similarities and Differences between Sales Promotions Availed and Preferred by the Rural Respondents*

There was similarity in cash discount as it ranked first in availed as well as preferred. Also the similarity existing between coupons as it ranked sixth in availed as well as preferred. The differences were existing between other short-term sales promotions such as free sample, trading or bonus stamp, price contests, free bies and extra quantity. But there was significant difference for extra quantity and free bies, as extra quantity ranked seventh in availed and second in preferred and free bies ranked second in availed and fifth in preferred.

6.10. Similarities and Differences between Sales Promotions Availed and Preferred by the Urban Respondents

There was similarity in cash discount as it ranked first in availed as well as preferred. The differences were existing between other short-term sales promotions such as free sample, coupon, trading or bonus stamp, price contests, free bies and extra quantity. But there was significant difference for extra quantity, free sample and coupon as extra quantity ranked seventh in availed and second in preferred, free sample ranked sixth in availed and third in preferred and coupon ranked third in availed and sixth in preferred.

6.11. Opinion of the Respondents about the Free Samples

Majority (63.47%) of the respondents felt good about the free sample. 67.78 percent of the rural respondents and 59.17 percent of the rural respondents felt good about the free samples.

6.11.1 Opinion of the Respondents About the Coupons

Majority (91.94%) of the respondents felt satisfactory about the coupons. 93.06 percent of the rural respondents and 90.83 percent of the urban respondents felt satisfactory about the coupons.

6.11.2 Opinion of the Respondents About the Trading or Bonus Stamp

Majority (44.72%) of the respondents felt very good about the trading or bonus stamp. 48.33 percent of the rural respondents and 41.11 percent of the urban respondents felt very well about the trading or bonus stamp.

6.11.3 Opinion of the Respondents About the Price Contests

Majority (92.08%) of the respondents felt good about the price contests. 93.06 percent of the urban respondents and 91.11 percent of the rural respondents felt good about the price contests.

6.11.4 Opinion of the Respondents About the Free Bies

Majority (88.06%) of the respondents felt good about the free bies. 89.44 percent of the rural respondents and 86.67 percent of the urban respondents felt good about the free bies.

6.11.5 Opinion of the Respondents About the Cash Discount

Majority (82.5%) of the respondents felt satisfactory about the cash discount. 84.17 percent of the urban respondents and 80.83 percent of the rural respondents felt satisfactory about the cash discount.

6.11.6 Opinion of the Respondents About the Extra Quantity

Majority (98.75%) of the respondents felt good about the extra quantity. 99.72 percent of the urban respondents and 97.78 percent of the rural respondents felt good about the extra quantity.

6.11.7 Opinion of the Respondents About the Premium

Majority (96.53%) of the respondents felt illusory about the premium. 96.95 percent of the urban respondents and 96.11 percent of the rural respondents felt illusory about the premium.

6.11.8 Opinion Rank Obtained by the Sales Promotion

Trading or bonus stamp occupied the first rank in the opinion of the respondents with the total score of two thousand and six hundred and eighty two. It also occupied first rank in the opinion of the urban respondents as well as the rural respondents with a total score of one thousand three hundred and ninety and one thousand two hundred and ninety two respectively.

6.12. Judgment of the Respondents about the Sales Promotion Activity

Majority (86.63%) of the respondents judged free sample as the most influential sales promotion activity. 88.33 percent of the urban respondents and 84.72 percent of the rural respondents judged free sample as the most influential sales promotion activity.

6.12.1 Purchase Made by the Respondents Induced by the Sales Promotion

Majority (89.17%) of the respondents were induced by the sales promotion in making the purchase of cooking oil. 93.33 percent of the rural respondents and 85 percent of the urban respondents were induced by the sales promotion in making the purchase of cooking oil.

6.12.2 Overall Opinion About the Sales Promotion by the Respondents

Majority (57.64%) of the respondents opined moderate about the sales promotion. 62.23 percent of the rural respondents and 53.06 percent of the urban respondent's opined moderate about the sales promotion. There was significant difference observed between the overall opinion of the rural and urban groups about the sales promotion as the significance value was 0.10 which was less at 1 percent level.

6.12.3 Result of LMR Analysis for Opinion on Overall Sales Promotion Activities

The results of the multiple regression analysis shows that viz. age, gender, family size, type of family, occupation and expenditure have positive and significant effect on the overall sales promotional activities in rural consumers. The results of the multiple regression analysis show that variables gender, family size and expenditure had positive and significant effect on the overall sales promotional activities in urban consumers. There was significant difference between rural and urban consumers about the opinion of sales promotional activities.

6.13. Media Preferred by the Respondents to know About the Sales Promotion Scheme

Majority of the respondents preferred television as a media to know the sales promotion scheme as it ranked first with a mean score of 16.09. Majority of the rural respondents preferred television as a media to know the sales promotion scheme as it ranked first with a mean score of 17.35 and the urban respondents preferred the television in the second place as it ranked second with a mean score of 14.83. Majority of the urban respondents preferred newspaper to know the sales promotion scheme as it ranked first with a mean score of 15.93. The result of ANOVA shows that, there was a significant difference between the media preferred by the rural and urban respondents in knowing the sales promotion scheme, as the significance was 0.000 which was less as 1 percent level.

6.14. Reasons Given by the Respondents for the Purchase of this Particular Brand of Cooking Oil

Majority (27.64%) of the respondents mentioned quality as the reason for purchasing this particular brand of cooking oil. Majority (51.94%) of the urban respondents mentioned quality as the reason for purchasing this particular brand of cooking oil. Majority (35.36%) of the rural respondents mentioned price as the reason for purchasing this particular brand of cooking oil.

The result of ANOVA shows that, there was a significant difference between the reasons mentioned by the rural and urban respondents for the purchase of particular brand of cooking oil, as the significance was 0.001 which was less at 1 percent level.

6.15. Reasons Given by the Respondents for the Purchase of This Particular Brand of Cooking Oil

Health was the most influencing factor for the majority of the respondents in selecting the oil used by them as it occupied first rank with a mean score of 15.68. Health was the most influencing factor for the majority of the urban respondents in selecting the oil used by them as it occupied first rank with a mean score of 19.29. Taste was the most influencing factor for the majority of the rural respondents in selecting the oil used by them as it occupied first rank with a mean score of 14.30.

6.16. Suggestions

The researcher has made personal contact with the respondents who have purchased the cooking oil. It was concluded that there was significant difference between the rural and urban consumers regarding the type of oil purchased. Most of the respondents have a moderate opinion about the sales promotion scheme, though there were so many problems to be improved by the manufacturers of the cooking oil. These suggestions are as follows:

- Although majority of the respondents prefer and avail cash discount, they have confusion in their mind about the cash discount whether it is real or illusory. So the manufacturers should take the necessary steps to remove the doubts of the consumers about cash discount by printing the previous price of the cooking oil without cash discount and current price with cash discount.

- Manufacturers of cooking oil has to design separate sales promotion scheme for rural and urban consumers as the same type of sales promotion except cash discount will not produce the same result.

- Health is the major factor considered by the urban respondents. Hence, the manufacturers of cooking oil have to stress on the health provided by their cooking oil to consumers through advertisement, medical camp, etc.

- Taste is the major factor considered by the rural respondents. Hence, the manufacturers of cooking oil must try to issue free samples of food liked by the rural consumers prepared out of their cooking oil. In this way, they can introduce new type of cooking oil to the rural consumers.

- Quality is the important factor for urban respondents in selecting the brand of cooking oil. So the manufacturers must try to maintain the same quality of their branded cooking oil.

- Price is an important factor for rural respondents in selecting the brand of cooking oil. The manufacturers of cooking oil may try low priced cooking oil for the rural consumers.

- Premium is considered illusory by both the rural and urban respondents. So the manufacturers of cooking oil has to avoid the premium and try for another type of sales promotion like surprise gift in any of the pack of cooking oil.

6.17. Area for Further Research

Consumer behaviour will different from one area to another area and one product to another product. Consumer behaviour will not remain constant even for the same area over a period of time. Hence, the research aspirants may try to study the consumer behaviour towards the sales promotion in other parts of the country on the same product as well as on the other fast moving consumer products.

6.18. Conclusions

In the past, consumer's choices were limited to three or four types of oil only. But in the present era of liberalisation and globalisation they have numerous type of cooking oil to make their selection. New types of sales promotion were also introduced by the manufacturers of cooking oil. The development in the education of the consumers made them to take the rational decision. So the manufactures must try to serve the needs of the consumers by understanding their behaviour better. They have also try to introduce new sales promotion schemes to attract the consumers. The Coimbatore city population consists of all types of people from different areas of the country as it provides enormous employment opportunity for all types of employees. It has many industries, estates, corporate hospitals and good number of engineering colleges. In future, the sales of cooking oil are bound to grow in a big way, given the growing youth and children's population.

Bibliography

Books

[1]   Bhattacharyya, "Research Methodology", 2nd Edition, 2006, Excel Books, New Delhi.

[2]   Blythe, Jim. "Essentials of Marketing (4th ed)", Pearson education, Pp. 148, 2008.

[3]   R.C. Donald and S.S. Pamela, "Business Research Methods", Tata McGraw Hill, 2007, New Delhi.

[4]   M. Fishbein, "Attitude and prediction of behaviour", In M. Fishbein (Ed.), Readings in attitude theory and measurement. New York: John Wiley, Pp. 477-492, 1967.

[5]   K.A. Coney, R.J. Best and D.I. Hawkins, "Consumer Behaviour: Building Marketing Strategy", Boston, Massachusetts: Irwin McGraw-Hill, Pp. 775, 2003.

[6]   J. Howard and J.N. Sheth, "Theory of Buyer Behavior", Wiley & Sons, New York, NY, 1968.

[7]   D. Hoyer Wayne and Deborah J. Macinnis, "Consumer Behavior", Fifth edition mason, ohio: south-western cengage Learning, Pp. 13-16, 2010.

[8]   Y. Jen, "Culture and self:perspectives of easterners and westerners", first edition, Taipei, Yuen-Liu Press Co., Ltd, translated from Massella, Anthony, 1990.

[9]   B. Kazmi, "Advertising & Sales Promotion", 1st Edition, 2007, Excel Books, New Delhi, Pp. 24.

[10]   C.R. Kothari, "Research Methodology: Methods & Techniques", 2nd Edition, New age, New Delhi, 2009.

[11]   P. Kotler, "Marketing management analysis planning and Control", 9th Ed prentice hall, Englewood cliffs, NJ, Pp. 122-175, 1967.

[12]   Krishnaswamy, Sivkumar and Mathirajan, "Management Research Methodology", 2nd Edition, Pearson Pub, New Delhi, 2008.

[13]   Kroeber-Riel and Werner, "Konsumentenverhalten", second Edition, Vahlen, München, Germany, 1980.

[14]   G.L. Lilien, K. Philip & M.K. Sridhar,"Marketing Models",New Jersey:Prentice Hall, 1992.

[15]   Mohan and Elangovan, "Research Methodology in Commerce", 1st Edition, Deep & Deep, New Delhi, 2007.

[16]   C.G. Morris, "Psychology: An Introduction", Upper Saddle River, New Jersey: Prentice Hall, 1996.

[17]   J.C. Mowen and M. Minor, "Consumer behaviour", 5th edition New Jersey : prentice hall, 1998.

[18]   A. Wilson, V.A. Zeithaml, M.J. Bitner and D.D. Gremler, "Service marketing:Integrating customer focus across the firm", Tata McGraw hill, New Delhi, 2008.

[19]   L.J. Schiffman and L.L. Kanuk, "Consumer behaviour", 7th edition page-144 New Jersey: prentice hall, 2000.

[20]   M. Solomon, "Consumer Behavior: Buying, Having and Being", 5th ed. Prentice Hall, Upper Saddle River, NJ, 2002.

[21]   E.B. Taylor, "Primitive culture", New York: Harper, 1958.

[22]   R.S. Winer, "Marketing Management", Prentice Hall, Upper Saddle River, NJ, 2000.

Journals

[23]   "4,000-year-old 'kitchen' unearthed in Indiana" Archaeo News, 2006.

[24]   D. Aaker, "Managing Brand Equity", New York: The Free Press, 1991.

[25]   Abraham, M. Magid and M. Leonard Lodish, "Getting the Most out of Advertising and Promotion", Harvard Business Review, Pp. 50-63, 1990.

[26]   P.J. Albanese, "The Paradox of Personality in Marketing: A New Approach to the Problem", In Bloom, P. et al. (Eds), Enhancing Knowledge Development in Marketing, American Marketing Association, Chicago, IL, Pp. 245-249, 1989.

[27]   B.A. Alvarez and R.V. Casielles, "Consumer evaluation of sales promotion: the effect on brand choice", European Journal of Marketing, Vol. 39, Pp. 54-70, 2005.

[28]   R.C. Anderson, D. Fell, R.L. Smith, E.N. Hansen and S. Gomon, "Current Consumer behaviour research in forest products", Journal of Forest Products, Vol. 55, No. 1, Pp. 21-27, 2005.

[29]   A. Hasslinger, S. Hodzic and C. Opazo, "Consumer behaviour in shopping, working paper number", Department of Business studies, Kristianstad university, Sweeden, Vol. 11, No. 26, Pp. 16-19, 2007.

[30]   Anonymous, "Handcuffs on the high street", The Economist, Vol. 355, No. 8170, 2000.

[31]   L. Joao Assuncao and Robert Meyer, "The rational effect of price promotions on sales and consumption", Management Sci., Vol. 39, Pp. 517–535, 1993.

[32]   R.P. Bagozzi, M. Gopinath and P.U. Nyer, "The role of emotions in marketing", Journal of the Academy of Marketing Science, Vol. 27, No. 2, Pp. 184-206, 1999.

[33]   K. Bawa and R.W. Shoemaker, "The effects of a direct mail coupon on brand choice behavior", Journal of Marketing Research, Vol. 24, Pp. 370-376, 1987.

[34]   A. Bhattacherjee, "Understanding information systems continuance: An expectation confirmation model", MIS Quarterly, Vol. 25, No. 3, Pp. 351-370, 2001.

[35]   R.C. Blatt Berg and S.A. Neslin, "Sales Promotion: Concepts, Methods, and Strategies", Engiewood Cliffs, NJ: Prentice Hall, 1990.

[36]   Robert Blattberg, Gary Eppen and Joshua Liebermann, "A Theoretical and Empirical Evaluation of Price Deals in Consumer Nondurables", Journal of Marketing, (winter), Vol. 45, Pp. 116-129, 1981.

[37]   Buzzell, Robert, John Quelch and Walter Salmon, "The Costly Bargain of Trade Promotion", Harvard Business Review, Pp. 141-49, 1990.

[38]   Chandon, Pierre and Brian Wansink, "When are stockpiled products consumed faster?", A convenience-salience framework of post purchase Consumption incidence and quantity. J. Marketing Res., Vol. 39, Pp. 321–335, 2002.

[39]   L.C. Chang, "The Study of Subculture and Consumer Behaviour: An Example of Taiwanese University Students' Consumption Culture", Journal of American Academy of Business, Cambridge. Hollywood, Vol. 7, No. 2, Pp. 258-265, 2005.

[40]   Corn Refiners Association. Corn Oil 5th Edition, 2006.

[41]   J. Cummins, "Sales Promotion: How to Create and Implement Campaigns that Really Work", 2nd ed., Kogan Page, London, 1998.

[42]   P.R. Das, "Semantic cues and buyer evaluation of promotional communication", In R.P. Leone and V. Kumar, (Eds), Enhancing Knowledge Development in Marketing, American Marketing Association, Chicago, IL, Pp. 12-17, 1992.

[43]   D. DelVecchio, D.H. Henard and T.H. Freling, "The effects of sales promotion on post-promotion brand preference: a meta-analysis", Journal of Retailing, Vol. 82 No. 3, Pp. 203-13, 2006.

[44]   Z.S. Demirdjian and T. Senguder, "Perspectives in Consumer Behaviour: Paradigm Shifts in Prospect", Journal of American Academy of Business, Cambridge, Hollywood, Vol. 4, No. ½, Pp. 348-356, 2004.

[45]   Derek D. Rucker and Richard E. Petty, "Emotion Specificity and Consumer behaviour: Anger, Sadness and preference for activity", Journal of Motivation and Emotion, Vol. 28, No. 1, Pp. 16-17, 2004.

[46]   S. Dhinesh Babu and P.S Venkateshwaran, "Review article titled "Marketing problems of edible oil industry in the state of Tamilnadu", Asian Journal of Management Research, Pp. 61-62, 2010.

[47]   Dilip Kumar Jha, "Vegetable oil consumption likely to hit record high", business standard dated, 2010.

[48]   Donald E. Vinson, Jerome E. Scott and Lawerence M. Lamont, "The roles of personal values in marketing and consumer behaviour", American Marketing association, Journal of Marketing, Vol. 41, No. 2, 1997.

[49]   J.F. Engel, D.T. Kollat and R.D. Blackwell, "Consumer Behavior", Holt, Rinehart and Winston, 1968.

[50]   V.S. Folkes, I.M. Martin and K. Gupta, "When to say when: Effects of supply on usage", J. Consumer Res., Vol. 20, Pp. 467–477, 1993.

[51]   E.R. Foxman, Patrtya S. Tansuhaj and John K. Wong, "Evaluating Cross- National Sales Promotion Strategy: An Audit Approach", International Marketing Review, Vol. 5, No. 4, Pp. 7-15, 1988.

[52]   Frain and John, "Customers and customer buying behaviour", Introduction to marketing (4th ed), Cengage Learning EMEA ISBN, 1999.

[53]   Sunil Gupta, "Impact of Sales Promotions on When, What, and How Much to Buy", Journal of Marketing Research, Vol. 25, Pp. 342-355, 1988.

[54]   D.J. Howard and R. Kerin, "Broadening the scope of reference price advertising research: a field study of consumer shopping involvement", Journal of Marketing, Vol. 70, Pp. 185-204, 2006.

[55]   L.A. Hudson and J.L. Ozanne, "Alternative Ways of seeking Knowledge in Consumer Research", Journal of Consumer Research, Vol. 14, No. 4, Pp. 508-521, 1988.

[56]   L.C. Huff and D.L. Alden, "An investigation of consumer response to sales promotions in developing markets: a three country analysis", Journal of Advertising Research, Vol. 38, No. 3, Pp. 47-56, 1998.

[57]   Oilseeds: World Market and Trade. FOP 1-09. USDA, Table 03: Major Vegetable Oils: World Supply and Distribution at Oilseeds: World Markets and Trade Monthly Circular, 2009.

[58]   D. Jobber and G. Lancaster, "Selling and sales management", 2006.

[59]   John M.C. Fall, "Priority Patterns and Consumer behaviour", Journal of Marketing, published by American marketing association, Vol. 33, No. 4, Pp. 55, 1969.

[60]   A.R. Johnson and D.W. Stewart, "A reappraisal of the role of emotion in consumer behaviour: traditional and contemporary approaches", In Malhotra, N.K. (Ed.), Review of Marketing Research, ME Sharpe, Armonk, NJ, Vol. 1, Pp. 3-33, 2005.

[61]   B.E. Kahn and L. McAlister, Grocery Revolution, The New Focus on the Consumer-Reading, Massachusetts: Addison-Wesley, 1997.

[62]   Kamran Kashani and John A. Quelch, "Can Sales Promotion Go Global?", Business Horizons, Vol. 33, No. 3, Pp. 37-43, 1990.

[63]   H.H. Kassarjian, "Some Recollections from a Quarter Century Ago", Advances in Consumer Research, Frank R. Kardes and Mita Sujan, editors, 1995.

[64]   Kendall and D. Stephanine, "Customer service from the customer's perspective", In Fogli, Lawerence. Customer service delivery: Research and best practices. J-B SIOP professional practice series 20, John willey & sons, 2007.

[65]   Kirshnan, V. Trichy & Ram C. Rao, "Double Couponing and Retail pricing in a Couponed Product Category", Journal of Marketing Research, Vol. 32, No. 4, Pp. 419-432, 1995.

[66]   A. Krishna, R. Briesch, D.R. Lehmann & H. Yuan, "A meta-analysis of the impact of price presentation on perceived savings", Journal of Retailing, Vol. 78, No. 2, Pp. 101-118, 2002.

[67]   Lan Xia and Kent B. Monroe, "The influence of pre-purchase goals on Consumers 'perceptions of price promotions", International Journal of Retail & Distribution Management, Vol. 37, No. 8, Pp. 680-694, 2009.

[68]   Leonard Lee and Dan Ariely, "Shopping goals, goal concreteness and conditional promotions", Journal of consumer research, Vol. 33, No. 1, Pp. 60-71, 2006.

[69]   P.S. Leeflang, and A. Boonstra, "Some Comments on the Development and Application of Linear Learning Models", Management Science, Pp. 1233-1246, 1982.

[70]   R.P. Leone and S.S. Srinivasan, "Coupon face value: its impact on coupon redemptions, brand sales, and brand profitability", Journal of Retailing, Vol. 73, No. 3, Pp. 273-89, 1996.

[71]   G.L. Lilien, "Application of a Modified Linear Learning Model of Buyer Behavior", Journal of Marketing Research, Pp. 279-285, 1974.

[72]   M. Foret and J. Padera, "Healthy Life style and buying behaviour in the Czech Republic", AGRIC.ECON-CZECH, supported by the ministry of education, Youth and Sports of the Czech Republic (grant no.MSM 6215648904). Vol. 54, No. 7, Pp. 307-313, 2007.

[73]   Mahavir Sherawet and C. Kundu Subhash, "Buying behaviour of Rural and Urban consumers in India: the impact of packaging", International Journal of consumer studies Vol. 31, No. 6, Pp. 630-638, 2007.

[74]   Marketing week.

[75]   McAlister and Leigh, "A Theory of Consumer Promotions: The Model", SSM Working Paper #1457-83, Massachusetts Institute of Technology, 1983.

[76]   C.F. Mela, S. Gupta and D.R. Lehmann, "The Long-Term Impact of Promotion and Advertising on Consumer Brand Choice", Journal of Marketing Research, Pp. 248-261, 1997.

[77]   Surabhi Mittal, "Demand- Supply Trends and Projections of Food in India", Indian Council for Research on International Economic Relations, Pp. 5-7, 2008.

[78]   R. Prema, "An Empirical study on Brand Preference towards edible oil in rural areas with special reference to Coimbatore district", Indian Journal of Applied Research, Vol. 3, No. 3, 2013.

[79]   R.L Oliver, "A cognitive model for the antecedents and consequences of satisfaction", Journal of Marketing Research, Vol. 17, Pp. 460-469, 1980.

[80]   J.S. Otts, "The organizational culture perspective", Chicago: Dorsey Press, 1989.

[81]   K. Pauwels, D.M. Hanssens and S. Siddarth, "The Long Term Effects of Price Promotions on Category Incidence, Brand Choice and Purchase Quantity", Journal of Marketing, Pp. 27-29, 2002.

[82]   M.T. Pham, J.B. Cohen, J.W. Pracejus and G.D. Hughes, "Affect monitoring and the primacy of feelings in judgment", Journal of Consumer Research, Pp. 167– 188, 2001.

[83]   Pierre Chandon and Brian Wansink, "A benefit congruency framework of sales promotion effectiveness", Journal of Marketing, 2000.

[84]   Promotion Marketing Association of America, Inc. Winning with Promotion Power: The Reggie Awards Winners. Ravenswood, IL: Dartnell Corporation, 1994.

[85]   P. Raghubir, "Free gift with purchase: promoting or discounting the brand?", Journal of Consumer Psychology, Vol. 14, No. 1/2, Pp. 181-186, 2004.

[86]   Reizenstein and C. Richard, "Customer encyclopedia of health care management", Sage, 2004.

[87]   Roberts and H. John, "A Review of International Research into Promotional Effectiveness and Its Implications for an Australian Research Agenda", Australasian Journal of Market Research, Vol. 3, No. 2, Pp. 25-38, 1995.

[88]   T.S. Robertson, "How to reduce market penetration cycle times", Sloan Management Review, Vol. 35, Pp. 87–96, 1993.

[89]   Robin Dand, "The International Cocoa Trade", Woodhead Publishing, Pp. 169, 1999.

[90]   M.L. Rothschild and W.C. Gaidis, "Behavioral learning theory: its relevance to marketing and promotions", Journal of Marketing, Pp. 70–78, 1981.

[91] Sadaomi Oshikawa "Can Cognitive Dissonance Theory Explain Consumer Behavior?", Journal of Marketing, Vol. 33, No. 4, 1969.

[92] Sandra Luxton, "Sales Promotion in the Australian Food Industry: A Review of Industry Practice and Its Implications", Journal of Food Products Marketing, Vol. 7, No. 4, Pp. 37-55, 2001.

[93] A.G. Sawyer, and P.R. Dickson, "Psychological Perspectives on Consumer Response to Sales Promotion", Research on Sales Promotion: Collected Papers, Pp. 84-104, 1984.

[94] E.H. Schein, "Organizational culture and leadership: A dynamic view", San Francisco, CA: Jossey-Bass, 1985.

[95] S. Shavitt, S. Swan, T.M. Lowrey and M. Wanke, "The interaction of endorser attractiveness and involvement in persuasion depends on the goal that guides message processing", Journal of Consumer Psychology, Vol. 3 No. 2, Pp. 137-62, 1994.

[96] I. Simonson, Z. Carmon and S. O'Curry, "Experimental evidence on the negative effect of product features and sales promotions on brand choice", Marketing Science, Vol. 13, No. 1, Pp. 23–40, 1994.

[97] I. Sinha and M.F. Smith, "Consumers perceptions of promotional framing of price", Psychology & Marketing, Vol. 17 No. 3, Pp. 257-275, 2000.

[98] I. Sinha, R. Chandran and S. Srinivasan, "Consumer evaluations of price and promotional restrictions–a public policy perspective", Journal of Public Policy & Marketing, Vol. 18, No. 1, Pp. 37-51, 1999.

[99] Stuart Mitchell, "Resale price maintenance and the character of resistance in the conservative party: 1949-64", Canadian Journal of History, Vol. 40, No. 2, Pp. 259-289, 2005.

[100] U. Sumarwan, "An Analysis of Perceived Popularity, Quality, Price, and their Relationship with the use of cooking oil brands", The Journal of Nutrition and family studies (Media Gizi dankeluarga), Pp. 41-47, 2000.

[101] R. Suprihatini, "Concept test for the red palm Cooking Oil", The journal of Plantation Agri Business study (Jurnal pengkajian agri bisnis perkebunan), Vol. 1, No. 2, Pp. 25-35, 1995b.

[102] Suprihatini, "Preferences of Fried-Food Home Industries on Cooking Oil Characteristics: A case study at Ten Indonesian Home Industries in Bandung", The journal of Plantation Agri Business study(Jurnal pengkajian agri bisnis perkebunan), Vol. 1, No. 3, Pp. 1-6, 1995a.

[103] R. Suri, R.V. Manchada and C.S. Kohli, "Brand evaluations: a comparison of fixed price and discounted price offers", The Journal of Product & Brand Management, Vol. 9, No. 3, Pp. 193-207, 2000.

[104] U. Ujang Sumarwan, "Factors Influencing Attitudes towards Claims of Cooking oil", Jurnal Manajemen don Agri bisnis, Vol. 2, No. 2, Pp. 81-91, 2004.

[105] E. Valenstein, V. Cox and J. Kakolewski, "Reexamination of the Role of the Hypothalamus in Motivation", Psychological Review, Vol. 77, Pp. 16-31, 1970.

[106] Wansink and Brian, "Does package size accelerate usage volume?", J. Marketing, 601–614, 1996.

[107] L. Watson and M.T. Spence, "Causes and consequences of emotions on consumer behaviour A review and integrative theory cognitive appraisal", European Journal of Marketing, Vol. 41, No. 5, Pp. 587-511, 2007.

[108] H.U. Wuyang and Kevin Chen, "Can Chinese consumers be persuaded?", Department of Rural Economics University of Alberta, Edmonton Ag Bioforum, Vol. 7, No. 3, Pp. 124-132, 2004.

[109] Y. Zhang, R.M. Proenca, M. Maffel, L.L Barone and J. Friedman, "Positional Cloning of the Mouse Obese Gene and Its Human Homologue", Nature, Vol. 372, Pp. 425-432, 1994.

[110] P. Zimbardo and R.J. Gerrig, "Psychology and Life", New York, N.Y.: Harper Collins College Publishers, 1996.

Websites

[1] "Dietary fats explained". Retrieved from internet, 2012. (7th ed.), Harlow: Pearson education. http://www.pearson education.com

[2] http://etheses. Saurashtra university repository @ sauna.ernet.in

[3] http://etheses. Saurashtra university.edu/id/eprint/578

[4] http://www.consumer psychologist.com/

[5] http://www.edms.matrade.gov.my/...nsf/.../ (October 2005: product market study)

[6] http://www.newagepublishers.com

[7] http://www.erim.eur.n1

[8] N. Rajaveni and Dr.M. Ramasamy, "A study on Consumer brand preference on the consumption of cooking oil of various income groups in Chennai", online article, Sathyabama University, Chennai, Pp. 6-10, 2012.

[9] http://www.jstor.org/stable/1248672

[10] Sandhusen and L. Richard, Marketing Cf. S. 218,219, 2011.

[11]   Source: http://etheses. Saurashtra university.edu/id/eprint/611

[12]   Source: http://ssrn.com/abstract=1894093

[13]   Stable URL: http://www.jstor.org/stable/1250633

[14]   Wright01381_1844 refer

[15]   www.responservice.com

[16]   www.superhaat.com

Government Records

[1]   20ll census data

[2]   R. Ferber, "Selected Aspects of Consumer Behaviour: A Summary from the Perspective of Different Disciplines", Washington: U.S. Government Printing Office, 1977.

News papers and Magazines

[1]   Economic and Political Weekly February 27, 1988 M-22, 25.

[2]   C. Shea, "Playing to Win", Promo Magazine, 1996.

[3]   The Indian Express news paper, 2009.

PhD Thesis

[1]   Achiruddin, "An Analysis of Consumer Segmentation of Cooking Oil Based on Demographic Characteristics", Unpublished Master's thesis, Master of Management in Agri Business graduate school, Bogor Agricultural University, Bogor-Indonesia, 1997.

[2]   Dhadhal and H. Chitralekha, "A study of Brand loyalty and its effect on buying behaviour in case of selected cosmetic products in the state of Gujarat", thesis PhD Saurashtra University, 2011.

[3]   Dr.W.K. Sarwade, PhD thesis on "Brand Preferences and Consumption Pattern of Edible Oils in Maharashtra State", International Conference on Economics and Finance Research IPEDR, Vol. 4, Pp, 332-333, 2011.

[4]   C.M.J.V. Klemann, "The effects of premium promotions on consumer's category incidence, brand choice and purchase quantity decisions", final PhD thesis, Universiteit Maastricht, Pp. 62-66, 2007.

[5]   Linda Harmina Teunter, "Analysis of sales promotion effects on the households purchase behaviour", Erasmus Research Institute of Management (ERIM). Erasmus university Rotterdam ERIM PhD series research in management, Vol. 16, Pp.195-204, 2002.

[6]   Paul Allen Smethers and Alaistair France, Deep business intelligence analysis project titled "Five myths of consumer behaviour: Create technology product consumers will love".

[7]   P.N. Sastri, "Consumer Behaviour Analysis of Cooking Oils and Its Implications of marketing strategy", Unpublished Master's thesis, Master of Management in Agri Business graduate school, Bogor Agricultural University, Bogor-Indonesia, 2003.

[8]   Sindhu and Asha, "Sales promotion strategy of selected companies of FMCG sector in Gujarat region", PhD thesis, Saurashtra university, Pp. 291-292, 2011.

[9]   Vaishnani and B. Haresh, "Effects of Sales promotions on Consumer preferences and brand equity perception", With special reference to FMCG products, PhD thesis Saurashtra university, Pp. 338-343, 2011.